BLIND TRUST

The True Story of Enid Greene and Joe Waldholtz

Other books by Lee Benson

And They Came To Pass

Trials & Triumphs (with Doug Robinson)

Athens to Atlanta

Chamonix to Lillehammer

LaVell: Airing It Out (with LaVell Edwards)

The Breakthrough Factor (with Henry Marsh)

The Glory & The Games

BLIND TRUST

The True Story of Enid Greene and Joe Waldholtz

By
Lee Benson

Blind Trust

First Printing: November 1997
10 9 8 7 6 5 4 3 2 1

Publisher's Cataloging-in-Publication
(Provided by Quality Books, Inc)

Benson, Lee 1948-
Blind trust : the true story of Enid Greene and Joe Waldholtz / Lee Benson, -- 1st ed.
p. cm.
LCCN: 97-076917
ISBN: 1-888106-97-2

1. Waldholtz, Enid Greene--Marriage. 2. Waldholtz, Joe. 3. Women legislators--United States--Biography. I. Title.

E748.W35B46 1997 328.73`092
QB197-41208

Front cover photography by Tom Smart, Deseret News.
Back cover top photography by Jeffery Allred, Deseret News.
Back cover bottom photography by Gary McKellar, Deseret News.
Family photographs provided by Jim Parkinson, Parkinson Family Album.
Chuck Roistacher photograph provided by Chuck Roistacher.
Cover design by John Barnhill.

Designed, printed and bound
in the
United States of America
by
Agreka Books
(800) 360-5284
www.agreka.com

"Intellect is invisible to the man who has none."

– From Schopenhauer's *Essays*, "Our Relations to Others"

For Forrest, who gave his heart

ACKNOWLEDGEMENTS

To Chuck Roistacher, for, among a lot of other things, flying to Santa Barbara during a monsoon; to Senator Orrin Hatch, for his assistance to a fellow author; to my brother Dee for a most judicious edit, and for "cutting down on the glib factor"; to Ron Peeleman for his unique and insightful edit; to Ladonna Lee, for all those calls from Montana and for understandin' country songs; to Eddie and everyone at the Eddie Mahe offices for the use of the "back room"; to Fred Miller, for doing something I thought not possible, bringing life to accounting; to Tom Smart, the finest photographer I know; to Greg Engeman and Dave Harmer, for telling it straight; to Mrs. Emily Cleckley and the late Dr. Hervey Cleckley, for permission to quote from his book; to the D.C. cab driver who found my tape recorder; to Isaac's mom for the Title; to Audrey Merkin, for crystal clear snapshots; to my son Eric, for letting me know they speak English in Nigeria; to my nephew Luke, for riding out all the waves; to Kate, Mike, Linda, Phil, Sean, Alison and the rest of Enid's summer staff of '96, for being gracious and letting me use "the cage"; to "17-second" Mel Berger and the William Morris Agency, for believing; to Agreka Books, for starting the presses; to the Greenes, all of them, for opening their home, and their lives; to Dennis Roddy, for great copy; to Dale and Corinne Bowen, for understanding; to Jolene, for all those nights at Norm's; to everyone who talked to me before hanging up; and, especially, to Jim Parkinson, a man with a drive exceeded only by his heart, and without whom this story would never have been told . . .

. . . thank you.

Table of Contents

AUTHOR'S INTRODUCTION

The groundwork for this book was laid in a T.G.I.Friday's restaurant in southern California. I was having lunch with my brother and an old law school buddy of his named Jim Parkinson, who I'd never heard referred to as anything other than "Parky." After ordering the soup of the day with an apologetic "I'm just one Butterfinger away from 250," Parky, a born story-teller, began talking of his recent adventures in Washington, D.C. with his wife's sister, the Congresswoman Enid Greene from Utah, and her former husband, the con man Joe Waldholtz from Pennsylvania.

An hour later he was still holding court. You knew it was good material when the kid pouring water kept coming by to check our glasses, even though none of us had taken a sip, and the waitress didn't hover near our table to ask us to leave, but to eavesdrop.

Good material, but also tragic. The story of "Enid & Joe" is the kind that no one in Hollywood would make up, nor, I suspect would mystery/suspense writers a la John le Carré, Frederick Forsyth, William Goldman (to name my all-time favorite) or even Stephen King. They wouldn't dare, because it's a story that fits only in the cracks, too far out to be believable and not far enough out to be unbelievable. A story that checks into the no-fly zone of human behavior: It better be true or they'll laugh you out of the screen writer's guild.

Left to the limits of my own imagination, I know I couldn't have invented a character as chilling as Joseph Phillip Waldholtz. None of his species lived at the end of my street, or, if they did, I was luckily spared the details.

Neither could I have conceived of a cast of characters that includes, among others, an ambitious, competent, intelligent, madly-in-love wife; her kindly, incredibly frugal multi-millionaire father; Joe's millionaire grandmother who is alive but descended into dementia; and an infant daughter whose birth underscores the ruthlessness of the ruse. Nor could I have imagined audacity enough to have this story reach into the highest corridors of power in the most powerful nation on earth, able to lead, at its height, not just the nightly network newscasts, but the Letterman and Leno monologues as well.

But most of all, I could not have conceived of a con without the usual objective of life on Easy Street–of one day sailing into the sunset to a desert island with a mistress, a yacht, and speed-dial access to a numbered Swiss bank account. In my wildest flights of fabrication, I could not have created a con that had no point other than instant gratification; that treated the future as if it did not exist; in essence, sky-diving without a chute. And wearing a Rolex.

Being true doesn't, of course, preclude disbelievers–as Enid Greene and her father, Dunford Forrest Greene, have especially found out. When it comes to the sympathy vote, being a politician doesn't help, and neither does being wealthy. Heaven help those who are both.

That's the part of Parky's story that most intrigued me the first time I heard it at T.G.I.Friday's. He knew–and they knew–that his sister-in-law and his father-in-law were innocent of any wrongdoing, but after losing four million dollars to Joe, they found themselves dropping another million and more just for self-defense–and even that wasn't enough. In the court of public opinion, they wound up getting a backlash from the same storm that swamped them in the first place.

The writer came out in me. "This ought to be a book," I said, and Parky agreed.

I didn't want to write a *Blood Sport*, the ponderous treatise on the Whitewater scandal that bogs down in minutiae and yet still manages to lack the most important testimony of all (Bill Clinton's); or a *Primary Colors*, where fiction hides behind nonfiction and all the names are changed (including Joe Klein's) to protect the guilty. While *BLIND TRUST* is, like both of those recent best-selling books, grounded in real-life politics, the object here is neither about minutiae or about insulating the guilty. Politics sets the stage, no question, but this story isn't about politics; it's about people, and about the cold consequences that result from their confluences once humanity leaves the equation. It's about nice guys and bad guys, about loyalty and betrayal, about open agendas and hidden agendas, about villains and victims, about good and evil.

The presentation in these pages isn't about taking a side. Although there has been much public conjecture about how a person as intelligent as Enid Greene could have been so bamboozled; that "she had to know," the facts suggest that being "bamboozled" is the only possible reason anyone with even a modicum of intelligence could give for going on this ride. As Chuck Roistacher, an attorney and former prosecutor with uncommon street smarts, put it once while driving through the streets of Washington, "She had to know what?"

"Know that her husband was a thief? Know that her political career was founded on a house of cards? Know that Joe was incapable of telling her or anyone else the truth?"

The Congresswoman had nothing to gain and everything to lose, including her congressional seat.

I have chosen to present the story the way it unfolded, which eliminates telling it through the thought processes of the sole beneficiary of the charade: Joseph Waldholtz. To anyone else involved, however peripherally, it was all as real as the sun coming up, and it is through their senses that the drama played out as I've scripted it. To everyone else, the *Trust*–and trust–always existed. To Joe and Joe alone, it was all merely a cold-blooded, four hundred million dollar, twenty-four-hour-a-day lie.

I talked to lawyers, consultants, politicians, accountants, family members, and to Enid, whom I had not met previously. As for Joe, he said he preferred to keep his version to himself; that he would "write my own book." In some cases I ran into dead ends and brick walls. Elsie Hillman, one of the wealthiest women in America, was one of them, refusing to expose her own victimization at the hands of Joe Waldholtz even after it became obvious that had she done so earlier she might have made it more difficult for him to move on to bigger prey.

Wherever there is dialogue, it is not a product of conjecture or hearsay, but a recollection of at least one, and most often both, of the parties involved. As for people's thoughts, usually presented in italics, they reflect a recollection communicated after the fact.

For the most part, I obeyed that old Watergate axiom: Follow the money. I followed it to a drawer in Georgetown filled with hundred dollar Hermés ties, and nobody left to wear them. Mute and incontrovertible testimony of a convict, a con artist, and a very bad man. This is a story about what Joe Waldholtz set out to do, what he did, and how he did it. What you are about to read is true. Unfortunately.

Lee Benson
Santa Barbara, California

PART I

BEFORE

CHAPTER I

Washington, D.C., November, 1996

The Congresswoman leaned back in her office chair and considered the reporter's question carefully. She decided it wasn't a trap. She had become a wary woman, and maybe just a little paranoid, but then she had her reasons.

The writer was from a newspaper back home, sent by an editor for a wrapup story on the Congresswoman's term. This wasn't a reporter from the investigative staff, the kind who would rummage through your desk if you turned your back, the kind she had drawn her line in the sand with months ago (*political questions only!*). Within two months the Honorable Enid Greene, R-Utah, would be gone from office. This was a feature writer, here to do an obit.

Despite the scandal, will there still be a lot about your days here in Washington you'll miss?

The question took the Congresswoman back to a time and place that seemed part of another lifetime, not a mere eighteen months ago . . . to a time when her last name was Waldholtz, not Greene, and she and her husband, Joe, climbed on a wave that appeared headed straight into the sunset.

They drove to work together. That's one thing she remembered. Every morning they would leave their townhouse–*the townhouse where Henry Kissinger once lived*–in Georgetown together. Joe, always a driver's seat kind of guy, would maneuver through the swarming Washington traffic, talking on the cellular as he one-handed the wheel, while Enid would check her calendar, sizing up another day of congressional business–and the thing was, *that drive never got old.*

Mrs. Waldholtz didn't just like being a member of the United States Congress, she *loved* being a member of the United States Congress. Growing up, her friends always wanted to go to the mall; Enid, she wanted to go to the *Mall.* Ever since she could remember she had been interested in government and policy and laws–odd interests, she'd come to find out, as far as the mainstream was concerned. It wasn't like being interested in modeling. It didn't exactly get you dates.

But then she met and married a man whose feelings for politics were *exactly* like hers, right down to the fundamentals of the Grand Old Party, and after her victory in 1994 that won her the congressional seat from Utah's second district, she and Joe had come together to this place of political nirvana where being interested in government and policy and laws *was* mainstream. Where they thought you were odd if those weren't your interests.

Nobody could say their timing wasn't perfect. Not only had Mrs. Waldholtz gone to Congress, but she joined on just as the Republicans were gaining Congressional majority for the first time in forty years. Newt Gingrich, the new majority leader, quickly commissioned Enid as one of his soldiers, naming her to the prestigious Rules Committee, the first freshman Republican on that panel in eighty years. She was, by all accounts, a genuine Republican Revolutionary: an integral part of the Contract With America and The Hundred Days–a time when the Republicans set out to overhaul Congress with the hours of a 7-Eleven. In her office she had an eight-by-ten framed photo that was not just signed, but personally sent, by Rush Limbaugh. The press called her "The Mormon Maggie Thatcher."

On top of all that good fortune, they'd gotten pregnant–right on schedule, just as she'd hoped–as soon as they'd arrived in Washington. Her congressional peers had given her a baby shower in Newt's office, with pink and blue balloons draped above the Tyrannosaurus Rex skeleton that sits in the Speaker's office. Elizabeth Greene Waldholtz, just the second baby in the history of the House to be born to a sitting member, was even considerate enough to arrive during August recess. *People* Magazine did a story on her.

As much as Enid loved the life, she loved it no more than Joe. Not only did he work daily right alongside her, he did it without either pay or resentment. He was glad she was the member of congress. He took great delight that she was the one who got to vote. He reveled in her office. He enjoyed being behind the scenes, his wife's Lee Atwater, as one magazine article put it, her backroom man. Even in the '90s, you had to look a while before you found a man like that.

Funny, the things you think about, thought Enid as she remembered back to those intense yet curiously carefree spring mornings when Joe would back their Mercury Cougar out of the townhouse's narrow garage and Enid, riding shotgun, would get in at the sidewalk. Then they were off, past the Francis Scott Key Park at the bottom of 34th Street, past the Watergate Hotel, past the Kennedy Center, the Lincoln Memorial, the Washington Monument–past all that history they were now a part of–and finally all the way up the Mall along Independence Avenue to the crest of Capitol Hill, where the Congresswoman's office sat on the top floor of the Cannon Building, kitty-corner from the Capitol itself.

Those days when she was sure she had the best morning commute in America . . . and the best husband . . . .

CHAPTER II

Newport Beach, California, November, 1990

The black stretch limo swung into the entrance of the Hyatt Newporter Hotel & Tennis Club stylishly late. Three people got out, led by a large man with a swagger, who tipped the driver with a flourish and made his way toward the hotel ballroom.

Inside the ballroom, Enid Greene did not look up as the big man arrived-even if she was talking about him.

"He's a trust fund *what*?" asked Enid as delegates to the 1990 Young Republican National Federation fall board meeting streamed noisily into the room.

"A trust fund baby," answered Audrey Merkin, Enid's friend, confidante, and source of all Young Republican gossip. "You know, a guy who lives off a family trust. He always shows up in a limo. It's a Joe Waldholtz trademark."

"You need to get to know him," Audrey added, her eyebrows arching the way they always did when she wanted to make a political point, which was most of the time. The part of politics Audrey absolutely loved was the behind-the-scenes part, the positioning, the maneuvering, the networking. The *politicking*. Briefing was her specialty; deep background was her long suit. If you were a YR and Audrey Merkin didn't know who you were, you had reason to worry.

Audrey and Enid had met a decade earlier, also in southern California, also at a Republican convention. They became fast

Young Republican compadres; and beyond that, good friends. They had their dissimilarities. You couldn't get much more dissimilar than Audrey being pro-choice and Enid being pro-life. But they had a lot more similarities, not the least of which was a passion for politics. In Audrey, who, at thirty-five, was two years older, Enid saw a woman whose political interests sometimes made hers, which were not inconsiderable, look almost pedestrian. Audrey liked all facets of the trade. To her, it was professional *and* personal. Far from a hobby, politics were her life. She didn't just remember birthdays of her YR friends, she remembered their kids' birthdays. The Young Republicans was family. They didn't call her "Mama Merkin" for nothing.

From 1987 through 1989, Audrey had been national co-chairman of the Young Republicans–a group that, as the name suggests, is made up of up-and-coming Republicans under the age of 40. The only person in the organization with more power was the chairman, Richard Jacobs. When Jacobs' term was over in 1989, Audrey had decided to take the next step and run for chairman. But the line forming on the hard-right turned out to be a long and hostile one–there is no conservative as staunch as a young conservative–and if the more liberal Audrey knew how to do anything, she knew how to tell which way the wind was blowing. But even if it was blowing defeat, she also knew that her rival for the chairmanship, Terry Campo from Illinois, didn't know that as well as she did. She reasoned–correctly as it turned out–that he would be willing to part with a nice consolation prize if she would agree to bow out of the running early. So she cut a deal: She wouldn't run for chairman if Campo would allow her to help select his co-chairman. Her choice was her good friend from Utah, Enid Greene.

So it was that in the summer of 1989, at the Young Republicans national convention in Nashville, that Audrey had passed on her co-chairmanship to Enid.

Now, a little more than a year later, it was time to line up game plans for the upcoming 1991 chairman elections that would take place the following summer. This time, Audrey and Enid decided, Enid should give it a try.

The well-connected Audrey Merkin would be her campaign manager.

Audrey, who lived in Orange County, and Enid, who lived in Salt Lake City, laid preliminary plans by telephone until they were able to finally get together personally in Newport Beach. The annual board meeting, attended by around two hundred of the most influential Young Republicans in the country, was traditionally the time to launch your chairmanship campaign. They both knew this, and they were ready to launch. Not only did they have a full-page ad in the board meeting's official program, Audrey had also managed to get Enid's hospitality suite listed in the official itinerary–the only prospective candidate to pull off such an early coup.

Audrey had driven from her home to the hotel earlier that afternoon, the opening day of the convention, and it wasn't so she could get a little more beach time or to meet men. She had a room to work. She had votes to line up. She had a candidate to point in all the right directions. It was Audrey, thrilled about the prospects of another race, who came up with their campaign slogan: "Run Enid Run!!!"–and it was Audrey who intended to make sure Enid did just that.

In her hotel room, Audrey selected a suit jacket–green, of course–and black slacks. She was plump, and she dressed as unobtrusively as possible. She added a strand of pearls, a la Barbara Bush, and a pair of pumps and went downstairs to the ballroom, where, she was reasonably sure, not much would get past her.

Especially not the man from Pittsburgh who had her by a good hundred pounds, and was now, after easing his not inconsiderable bulk out of the back seat of the black limo, making his grand entrance into the hotel.

Joe Waldholtz impressed Audrey Merkin. Behind the three hundred pounds, behind the glasses, behind the three chins, even behind the thousand dollar suits and the ever-present limo was this: He was a real politician. He didn't just go through the motions. He didn't come to the conventions to hit on women or drink cocktails or make business connections, like a lot of the delegates swarming the room right now. He came because he loved what

Audrey loved. He loved politics. Beyond that, he was good at the game. At just twenty-seven, he was already a legend in Young Republican circles. In Pennsylvania, where he was *the* Young Republicans, he had been at the front of a campaign that had unseated Doug Walgren from the United States Congress. *Unseated Doug Walgren, a seven-term incumbent!* Rick Santorum had been legal counsel for the Allegheny County Young Republicans and he had gone to Congress (and after that the United States Senate), sent there in large part by Joe and his band of never-say-die Pennsylvanians. Waldholtzes' Warriors had also gotten a young woman named Melissa Hart, just twenty-eight years old, elected to the Pennsylvania State Senate, which was considered a very big deal. If the national Young Republicans had had an all-star game in 1990, the Pennsylvanians would have been first team.

It was also well known that Joe had so impressed the Pittsburgh political socialite Elsie Hillman, a distant relative to George Bush (her cousin married his uncle) and the wife of billionaire industrialist Henry Hillman, that she hired him as her Chief of Staff. Ms. Hillman, a national committeewoman for the Republican Party, ran a non-profit political machine in Pittsburgh that shared offices with the charitable Hillman Foundation. As extroverted as her husband was introverted–"I regret I have but one wife to give to the Republican Party," Henry Hillman once said in a rare public appearance–Elsie furnished her support both to Pennsylvania Republicans locally as well as to her celebrated "cousin" in the White House. Joe was Elsie's righthand man, the person she personally chose to run her political shop.

All this news, and more, preceded the arrival of Joseph Phillip Waldholtz to the 1990 Young Republicans National Federation fall board meeting. The "more" included his financial situation, which everyone knew fell somewhere between "beyond adequate" and "just won the lottery." The word on the street was that Joe had "don't ask" money. He had enough "family money" that he could go bass fishing or play golf or drive sports cars the rest of his natural life. That was common knowledge among Young Republican soldiers like Audrey, who would watch in awe as this rich guy from Pittsburgh would bring the entire Pennsylvania delegation to meetings and conventions in limos and then rent penthouse suites for all of them; and when the bill came he would pay for it all. Here in California, he hired the limo and driver for the week, so they could see Rodeo Drive and the stars' homes and the beaches. None of them had been to California before. Their Newport Beach introduction wasn't bad for starters. Their hotel suite included separate bedrooms for everyone in the entourage, plus a private swimming pool.

The cool thing about Joe, Audrey thought (as did a considerable number of others in the YR family), the *most cool thing,* was that he didn't need to work and he still did. He didn't need to fight the good Republican fight. But he chose to anyway. For what appeared to be all the right reasons.

Enid Greene hadn't heard much about the Joe Waldholtz story before, but now, with the convention about to get underway, she was getting a rapid-fire earful from Audrey. A full-on audio assault. By nature, Enid was neither as easily impressed nor swayed as her more excitable close friend/campaign manager, who, at this moment, was starting to get on her nerves with this full-court press about "Joe Waldholtz from Pittsburgh" and how important it was for Enid to have his support if she wanted to be elected chairman.

"He can get you votes," said Audrey, playing her trump card.

"Go over and say something."

"Get over there!"

"Geez, give it a rest," answered Enid, as she cast a calculating look in the direction of the man who had arrived by limo.

"I'll talk to him . . . sometime."

Joe Waldholtz knew a little about Enid Greene too. As cochairman of the Young Republicans she was visible enough. He knew she was running for national chairman; he knew she would probably make it official this weekend after she'd gauged the depths of her support among the board members. That was no secret. He also knew the most important thing on earth to Audrey

Merkin that weekend was to have Enid Greene meet Joe Waldholtz, the Pennsylvania king-maker.

The first time they passed each other–on the evening of Nov. 16, 1990, in a hotel hallway–Joe and his small entourage, which included his best friend Guy Ciarocci, who Joe had helped get elected Pennsylvania Young Republican state chairman, and Guy's girlfriend (and future wife) Christine Czarnecki, had said a collective "hi" to Enid. She had said "hi" back and kept on walking. Joe, feigning hurt feelings, went straight to Audrey and told her he didn't know if the Pennsylvanians would support her friend Enid or not.

"She brushed us off," he said indignantly.

At a poolside reception later that day, as Audrey kept pushing Enid in his direction, Joe purposely kept moving away. Finally, with Guy and Chris in tow, he simply turned around and left.

Enid knew a brush-off when she felt one; she also knew when Audrey Merkin was being had. Politicians will be politicians. The game-playing had already begun.

It all ended happily on the next night's boat cruise around Balboa Island, when all of them–Audrey, Enid, Joe, Chris, Guy and a few other Pennsylvania delegates–sat down in the lounge. They continued to banter but to Audrey's relief, it was obvious this was *good* banter. The joke was on her. Nobody was honestly offended. Well, OK. As long as that's all it was.

For a good couple of hours, Enid and Joe, in conversation for the first time, fired verbal volleys back and forth. Enid would feign ignorance about who this Elsie Hillman was that Joe worked for. Joe would shoot back some comment about Utah applying for statehood. Back and forth their retorts went. Both were scrambling for the high ground. To Enid's surprise, Joe got there first.

Enid Greene, never easily (or quickly) impressed, sat across from the tall, heavyset, twenty-seven-year-old-going-on-fifty balding man wearing glasses and, in spite of herself, made several concessions. She was no dummy, she knew that, but she felt dumb around *him.* If she was quick, he was lightning. He could make a pun or a quip out of anything. You had to really pay attention to keep up. He liked to laugh. He enjoyed his friends. He obviously enjoyed his relationship with Audrey Merkin, and Audrey obviously adored him. He teased her. He was good at it. But, it seemed to Enid, he knew how to stop short of being malicious.

Plus, he worked for one of the richest women in America, a relative of the President, and, in sharp contrast to some YR clubs that just got together once a month to drink, he was part of a hard-working YR group that *got people elected!*

As the boat docked and Enid moved to her "Enid for Chairman" hospitality suite she found she had quickly acquired good feelings about the Pennsylvanians and about the rich guy who led them. She felt the admiration was mutual and thus felt confident she could count on their support in the next summer's chairman election. Beyond that, as she moved on to other hands to shake and votes to court, she didn't give the Pennsylvanians–or Joe Waldholtz–another thought.

Joe's thoughts, on the other hand, were more absorbed. As he would later recount to Enid, and to many others, as he walked off that ship that November night in California he had one dominating thought: *That* is the woman I am going to marry.

□□□

Joe joined the "Run Enid Run!!" ticket not long after the meeting in Newport Beach. Enid and Audrey had designs on the Pittsburgh politician. They considered him to be the perfect man for the position of campaign treasurer. As chief of staff for one of the Republican Party's biggest benefactors, he was already heavily involved in fundraising. He had contacts, and he had expertise. Plus, they knew his addition to the campaign would further secure the powerful Pennsylvania block of votes.

Audrey and Enid's chief worry was that he would turn them down because he was beyond them. They needed him a lot more than he needed them. With Elsie Hillman, Joe was working with *real* fund-raising, using a pipeline that went all the way to the top of the Bush White House. Enid and Audrey, after all, were only *Young* Republicans. Small-timers. But they wanted to make several improvements to the organization, serious improvements that took money. Joe Waldholtz was money. That was obvious just by looking at him.

They were finally able to pitch the idea to him in person at a leadership seminar in Washington hosted by the Republican National Committee in February. After listening to their spirited appeal, Joe didn't say no. But he didn't say yes either. He told them he would have to ask Elsie first. A week later he called with the news that he was their man; they could call him treasurer.

Once he had become part of the "team," Enid was surprised at how quickly, and to what extent, her new treasurer became involved with her campaign. He soon became a regular on the almost daily planning calls between Enid and Audrey, most of which took place in the evening. The three of them would hook up via conference call and discuss their campaign strategy. Joe could be reached through his answering service. When Enid and Audrey called his home in Pittsburgh they would first get an operator asking for their name. The operator would then call Joe, who, when he found out who it was, would take the call. He explained to Enid and Audrey that it was his way to screen out all the calls he didn't have time for. Another example of a rich guy spending his money.

With the time difference, it was usually quite late in Pittsburgh when his campaign colleagues called, and Joe would often interrupt the call long enough to order something to eat. "I can't decide what I'd like tonight," he'd say, conjuring up long-distance images of a short-order chef waiting by the intercom in the kitchen for his request. One night, after spilling out all the details of a particularly long and trying day at Elsie's office, the exhausted voice on the other end of the line sighed, "I'm so tired I can't even think of ordering anything from the kitchen but a grilled cheese sandwich."

From Audrey and Enid came the expected rejoinder, *"Poor baby, must be tough to be so tired you can't even ring the bell and tell the servants what you want."*

Still, for all their contact Enid had no reason to suspect that Joe had anything beyond politics on his mind; not during their conversations, not even when Joe brought up the suggestion of the three of them getting together for a planning meeting. As the Memorial Day Weekend approached, Joe said he thought it would be a good idea if the three of them rendezvoused for an organization and strategy session at a beach house he was renting in Ocean City, New Jersey. "Why not fly out and get some work done?" he had wondered.

Enid, ever sensible, demurred.

"How much work are we going to do at the beach?" she wanted to know.

"Come on," said Joe. "I'll bring my computer. I'll bring my printer. It will be great."

When Audrey and Enid arrived at the Philadelphia airport, a car and driver awaited them, ready to whisk them off to the Jersey shore.

They spent the weekend in Ocean City as planned, organizing their strategy for the Miami convention that was now less than six weeks away. The campaign was going well. Better than they had a right to expect. They had put together such a strong ticket and campaigned so aggressively that it appeared there were no serious challengers left out there. It looked for all the world that Enid Greene would be the next chairman of the Young Republicans and Audrey Merkin would be her executive director, taking over the fulltime job in Washington, D.C.

Buoyed by their head of steam, they turned their long weekend-at-the-ocean into a kind of political version of spring break. Guy Ciarocci and Chris Czarnecki came down from Pittsburgh and stayed with Czarnecki's parents in a beach house nearby. Another Pennsylvania Young Republican named Jim Crawley joined Joe, Audrey and Enid in the rented beach house. Later on, Joe's father and stepmother also joined the crowd. As the weekend wore on the mood turned away from serious and into relaxed. There were numerous practical jokes. Audrey and Enid short-sheeted Joe's bed and he howled with laughter–like a rich kid on his first night at camp. He said he'd never heard of such a thing. They unscrewed the light bulbs in his bedroom. They had water fights on the boardwalk. The more shock effect, the better. Young Republicans, flushed by the anticipation of victory, having a good time.

It went too far for Enid just once–when she walked out of her bedroom one morning and saw a pornographic magazine staring back at her on the floor. Joe and Jim were around the corner, watching for her reaction. But she was not amused. "Look, I know you're just fooling around," she said, "But I really don't appreciate this." She gave them a cold stare. They knew she wasn't kidding around, she meant it. Enid never saw any sign of pornography again.

The night before her flight back to Salt Lake City, Enid and Joe wound up talking through half of it. They'd let off a lot of steam in four days. For Enid, it all had a tremendous cathartic effect. She was a strait-laced, proper, serious-minded person, she knew that, and yet she'd been able to take a detour from all that this weekend and it had felt good. It wasn't easy, spending your days working your "real job" as the Deputy Chief of Staff for the Governor of Utah, then spending your nights running a national campaign for chairman of the Young Republicans. She rarely had a chance to unwind, but she had that chance in Ocean City and she'd taken it.

And this Joe guy had made it possible.

He increasingly intrigued her. He listened to what she had to say, he understood her, and he was constantly making her laugh. But despite all their interaction–and they'd had plenty the past ninety-six hours–unless she was completely out of touch, she was sure he'd made no romantic overtures in her direction. She found herself wondering if there might be something developing between Joe and Audrey, who was planning to stay back East with Joe until the President's Dinner the next weekend in Washington.

Of course, Enid had been given the same offer. But she couldn't afford that luxury. She was a working girl. She had a job she had to return to back home in Utah.

When she got up early the next morning, a car was waiting to take her to the airport.

□□□

The flowers sat in a vase on the coffee table in front of her. The arrangement went beyond bouquet. This *offering* in front of Enid Greene was more like a garden. The arrangement had been there to greet her when she arrived in the suite at the Ritz-Carlton in Washington, D.C., along with a card that read, "So happy you're here. Joe."

Joe and Audrey had come in moments later. Audrey had left just as quickly. A candidate might sit down now and then, but a campaign manager never rests. Now Joe sat next to Enid on the couch in the suite's sitting room. He had rented this two-bedroom suite for the three of them. As planned, he and Audrey had driven to Washington from Pennsylvania, while Enid caught a Friday flight out of Salt Lake after finishing her week's work in the governor's office. It was the first weekend in June in the nation's capital, and if you were a Republican that could mean just one thing: The President's Dinner. After the cherry blossoms and before it got too hot and humid, it was an annual rite of the summer. The Republicans came to Washington and held their biggest fund-raiser. When a Republican was in the White House (as was the case in 1991) it was called the President's Dinner. When a Republican wasn't in the White House it was called the House/Senate Dinner. From all corners of the country, the Republican Party's biggest benefactors were summoned to mingle with the party's leaders.

If Elsie Hillman, Joe's billionaire employer, wasn't the party's biggest donor, she was close. She bought three tables for the dinner, and since she had conflicting plans that same weekend she sent her chief of staff, Mr. Joseph P. Waldholtz, to Washington with orders to make sure those tables were full. Joe's first call had been to Enid Greene in Salt Lake City and Audrey Merkin in Las Vegas, both of whom graciously accepted the invitation. He arranged for a suite at the Ritz-Carlton, got them all into lunch at the vice-president's house, a reception at the White House, followed by the President's Dinner.

And, he arranged for these flowers.

As Enid looked around the sitting room that separated her and Audrey's bedroom from Joe's, taking it all in, absorbed by the huge collection of flowers, Joe leaned toward her, tilted his neck, half closed his eyes, and kissed her.

Despite the setting, the kiss took her by surprise, just as her response took Joe by surprise.

She slid back on the couch before she made her speech.

"Look, all this is nice," she said, gesturing at the flowers and the suite. "But as you like to point out, Joe, I'm *a little Mormon girl*, and I need to tell you so there's no misunderstanding. I've been through this drill before, and it won't work. I will *not* go to bed with you. I just won't."

Joe Waldholtz tilted his head back and laughed.

"OK, Enid," he finally said, his smile still as large as the bouquet in front of him, "That's fine."

Later that night, as they strolled through the streets of Washington hand in hand, it started to sink in for Enid. They weren't going to bed, but they were sure going somewhere. That kiss had opened the floodgates. Joe was more than a little interested–and so, she was discovering, was she.

They floated through the afternoon. They fairly breezed through the lunch at Dan and Marilyn Quayle's and the reception at 1600 Pennsylvania Avenue and the dinner with George and Barbara Bush at the Convention Center. They held hands under the table. Every brush, every touch, was like a shock of electricity. Those love scenes in the movies, where there's no dialogue, just a series of scenes with a man and a woman running through the surf or fields of clover or strolling down the Champs Elysees or swinging in a porch swing or frolicking in the snow, well, they didn't have anything on this weekend on the Potomac.

Enid was falling in love; and better yet, if she was any judge, so was Joe.

There were political ramifications, of course, so they agreed they should keep this new dimension to their relationship private. Enid was running for chairman of the Young Republicans, with the convention/election just a month away in Miami. Joe was her treasurer. What would it look like if people thought she had loaded the ticket with boyfriends, especially *really wealthy* boyfriends? By mutual agreement, Enid and Joe agreed they would try to keep their touching, their mutual displays of affection, and their incessant smiling, out of public view. They both understood–it went with the territory.

As smooth as Enid hoped things would go at the Young Republican's convention in Miami, they went smoother than that.

There was no opposition. Of three opponents, two dropped out well ahead of the convention and one formally announced his resignation as the convention began. Enid Greene won unopposed. The vote on the convention floor, as state after state announced their support for the candidate from Utah, was a mere formality.

Just to be sure, the night before the vote, Joe told Enid he had something for her. They were in Enid and Audrey's hotel suite–Joe's treat–in the Miami Omni Hotel. It was late. The commotion of the convention had begun to still. Joe turned to Enid.

"For good luck," he said.

"This is for you."

He held a small rectangular shaped box in his hand. Enid reached out and accepted it. She tore off the ribbon and gold wrapping paper and opened the lid. Inside, a gold ring and a gold bracelet dotted with emeralds beamed back at her. Enid was no jewelry appraiser, but this did not look like it came from J. C. Penney.

"Oh Joe," she said, her eyes bright and alive, "You shouldn't have."

"Yes I should have" he said. "You deserve it. Tomorrow you're going to win."

"Still . . ." she said, letting the thought hang in the air. They were both smiling proudly.

But of course he was right about the win. He was right about everything. This was her time, her gala, her acceptance speech. On the final evening, more than six hundred delegates crowded into the hotel's largest ballroom for a black tie banquet. Jim Pinkerton, an operative in the Bush White House, was the keynote speaker. After his address it was Enid's turn to deliver her acceptance speech. She surprised some people, including many of her close friends, by drawing on a personal experience. Normally, Enid kept a tight grip on her inner feelings. The private remained private. But in the wake of this victory she felt secure enough to open up and tell a story about her mother, Gerda Beyer Greene, fleeing to America from Denmark during World War II. "My mother shows up on these shores with fifty dollars in her purse, and now her daughter is chairman of this national political organization," she said. "To me, that's what America is!"

When she stepped down from the podium to great applause, Joe was there, the first to congratulate her, the first to wrap his arms around her, the first to tell her what a wonderful job she'd done. There were tears in his eyes. There was pride in his expression. And when he bowed, as if to say, "*Madame Chairman,*" there was something else that Enid saw and cherished–more respect than she had ever before felt. Some people are thrilled *for* you, other people are thrilled *with* you. Joe was thrilled *with* her. Enid knew that as sure as she knew Gerda had found the promised land.

□□□

Before Joe resumed his position as Chief of Staff for Pennsylvania's biggest political operative and Enid reported back to work at the Utah State Capitol as Deputy Chief of Staff for Norm Bangerter, Utah's Republican Governor, Enid, Joe and Audrey and another member of their staff repaired to Disney World for rest, relaxation, recovery, and repast.

Joe's treat.

"Just a few days to unwind," he'd said to Enid and Audrey. "We need it." He had already booked a hotel suite–by now it was becoming standard operating procedure–at the Grand Floridian on the sprawling Disney World grounds.

Once at the Grand Floridian, Joe actually went beyond unwind to physical collapse. Whether it was the pressure from the campaign or the toll exacted from working two jobs at once or whether it was just a bug from the Florida swamps, whatever it was, by the time he got to Orlando it leveled him. For two days, as the chairman-elect and her new executive director toured the Epcot Center and rode the rides at Disney World, Joe stayed in his quarters, confined to bed and room service.

Near the end of their stay, he began to feel better, however, and he asked Enid if she'd mind mixing a little business with their pleasure. He had some financial news he thought she needed to know about. No big deal, but still . . . .

When they were alone, Joe explained that he had given his gold American Express card to Audrey in Miami so she could take care of a few convention expenses and, well, she'd gotten more than a little carried away.

That Audrey was using Joe's American Express card was not news to Enid. In Young Republicans, campaigns are routinely financed by individual members of each ticket–a factor that is a big reason why many tickets go out of business before the convention. Campaigns have a way of getting progressively (and prohibitively) expensive. Not only would Audrey–and Joe, too–have chipped in for campaign expenditures along the way, they were expected to. As treasurer, Joe was in charge of campaign finances. If he was having Audrey use his personal credit card, he would also know why.

The problem, Joe told Enid, was that Audrey didn't exactly behave like a conservative when she got a tight grip on his card. Joe said she had gone on a spending spree in Miami, to the tune of nearly thirty thousand dollars.

Enid gasped. *Thirty thousand dollars!* She remembered the big push at the convention. Regardless of the lack of opposition, Audrey had been insistent that the campaign would go the distance. She had even passed out Frisbees to the delegates with their names on them. But thirty thousand dollars? How could a bunch of Frisbees and some campaign banners cost thirty thousand dollars?!

"Are you sure?" Enid asked Joe.

"Oh I'm sure," said Joe. He wore a curious grin.

"Well I don't have that kind of money," said Enid. "We're going to have to talk to Audrey and figure something out."

Joe put his hand on hers.

"Enid," he said, "don't tell Audrey. I don't see any point in bringing this up with her now that the damage is done. It's over. There's nothing we can do about it now. It will be all right. I'll talk to the trustees. They'll be upset. They'll rant and rave. But they'll cover it, I promise. Enid, don't worry about this bill."

"But Joe," she said. "Thirty thousand dollars. I mean . . ."

Joe sighed. It was the sigh of wealth, the sigh of a man willing to be patient with those who haven't lived with privilege. He had told Enid, more than once, of his family Trust, of the vast sum of money it encompassed.

"You still don't get it, do you?" he said, smiling at her gently.

CHAPTER III

Enid Greene knew a pronouncement was coming. Joe had paused; that was the tipoff. The man was nothing if not theatric. A walking, talking drum roll when he wanted to be. He was on the phone in Pittsburgh. She was on the phone in Salt Lake City. And she sensed he was about to deliver some news. She sensed right.

"I'm moving to Utah!" he finally said, the words gushing out over the long distance wires with a kind of authoritative delivery.

"I've resigned from the Bush campaign! I want to be with the woman I love!"

"That's wonderful!" Enid said. She too wanted to be with the one she loved.

She had just one reservation. She knew Joe was leaving a job as director of George Bush's presidential reelection campaign for the State of Pennsylvania. No small post. Coming to Utah meant turning away from a presidential race in a key state. She worried it might be a move Joe would resent later on. She took care to ask him point-blank about that possibility; and although Joe assured her that would not be a problem, his mind was made up, still, she worried.

But beyond that, she could not think of a downside. The man she'd fallen in love with was willing to walk away from everything to come to her side. Romantically, how could you beat it?

There were entire Harlequin romances with that as their only theme.

The news did not completely surprise her. For the last month, during their nightly phone calls, Joe had hinted more than once about dropping George Bush for Enid Greene. As executive director of the Pennsylvania Bush/Quayle campaign, his job in the election year of 1992 was clear: make sure Elsie Hillman's cousin carried the twenty-one electoral votes in Elsie Hillman's state. But as spring wore on, and the euphoria of the President's early commanding lead in the polls had given way to the sobering realization that the upstart Arkansan Bill Clinton and the Democrats were not going away, Joe told Enid he was growing more and more frustrated with the way the White House was running its campaign. He thought George Bush, even if he were the incumbent, was heading for a loss and there was nothing Joe could do about it. It was bigger than he was.

He could stay in Pennsylvania and back what was beginning to look like a loser, or he could move to Utah and back what was beginning to look like a winner.

"I'll be there the end of next week," he said, and then, before hanging up, added: "*Congresswoman* Greene."

□□□

Enid had been approached late the past fall–not long after she'd won the chairmanship of the national Young Republicans–by two Utah political activists she met through the Young Republicans, Peter Valcarce and Chuck Warren. They made an appointment to meet in her office in the Utah State Capitol, just down from the governor's office. They told her they thought she should run for Utah's second district's Congressional seat that would be opening up in 1992. Democrat Wayne Owens was the current congressman from the second district–which consisted chiefly of the heavily populated Salt Lake Valley–but he was preparing a campaign for the senate seat being vacated by three-term Republican Jake Garn. The congressional seat Owens was vacating was one the Republicans felt they could win with the right candidate. Valcarce and Warren, encouraged by her successes in the Young Republicans, told Enid they thought the right candidate was her. She obviously knew how to run a campaign and more importantly, she obviously knew how to win one.

Flattered but unconvinced, Enid tossed the possibility around in her head for a few months. She asked her parents for their opinion, as well as several politicians, both local and national, whose opinions she respected. And on the phone, she talked it over with the savviest politician she knew: Joe Waldholtz.

Joe didn't come right out and tell her she should run. He tried to approach the situation the same as Enid. He patiently helped her add up the positives and the negatives and then helped her compare both sides of the ledger. But she knew the idea excited him. She could feel the vibrations. It was obvious it was his favorite subject. It excited him as much as it excited her. If she wanted to go for it, he told her over and over again, he was one hundred percent behind her; he knew she could win, he knew she would be a great member of Congress. Joe Waldholtz was very good for Enid Greene's ego.

By late January of 1992 she made up her mind. She would run. She first called Joe and told him the news. Next she called a local Republican, Ron Wilson, and asked him if he would be her campaign manager. When he said yes, Enid '92 was suddenly, just like that, in business. For campaign headquarters, they rented the bottom two floors of a rundown office building on the corner of Fourth South and Fifth East in Salt Lake City, across the street from a Blockbuster Video. Who knew, maybe it was an omen.

She was young, just thirty-three years old, and relatively inexperienced, although the Young Republicans involvement couldn't hurt, and neither could her work in the governor's office. She could certainly make a case that she was on the right track to run for national office, even if it was a fast track.

But even if the timing wasn't exactly perfect, it seemed to Enid to be the right thing to do. Her job in the governor's office was ending, anyway. After two terms and eight years, Norm Bangerter, a popular governor with the luxury of deciding his own fate, decided he was going back to building houses. By the end of the year someone new would be in the governor's mansion and Enid, in all likelihood, would need to find a new place to work.

Besides that, she could afford it. Well, she could if she sold her house. She held the title outright to a sprawling four-bedroom, three-car garage rambler at 1456 Penrose Drive in the exclusive Federal Heights section of Salt Lake City. It was the house she had lived in since the seventh grade. Her parents had deeded it over to her seven years earlier, after they purchased a condominium in downtown Salt Lake City and decided that of their five children, Enid, who was working at the time for a large downtown law firm and was seriously dating a young man they all felt she would eventually marry, was in the best position to take care of the family home.

But the personal relationship, which continued on and off for nearly three years, didn't work out, and after that Enid decided she didn't need four bedrooms. She had been planning to scale back well before the congressional race came along, and now, selling the house made even more sense. She could use part of the proceeds to finance her campaign. When the race was over, win or lose, she figured she'd have at least enough left for a down payment on a smaller place. In house-hungry Salt Lake City, one of the fastest growing cities in the country in the early '90s, she was sure she would have no trouble finding a buyer for 1456 Penrose.

She was right on that score. She wound up selling the Penrose house to the first people who learned it was for sale: her parents.

For one thing, they had tired of condominium living. For another thing, her financier father, D. Forrest Greene, who split his time running his businesses in San Francisco, where he had held a seat on the Pacific Stock Exchange, and his family life in Salt Lake City, was planning to scale down himself, to the point where he would eventually shut down his San Francisco operations entirely. After he retired, he wouldn't be needing the condominium he maintained in the Pacific Heights section of San Francisco any longer. What he would be needing was a place big enough in Salt Lake to entertain his grandkids.

So, based on an appraisal of three hundred thousand dollars, Enid's dad bought his house back.

Beyond having sufficient money to finance her campaign, and beyond an intuitive feeling that it was the right thing to do, Enid decided to run because she wanted to. Serving in the United States House of Representatives would be, for her, a dream job. She had always been fascinated by politics, and by policy. How do you provide for people? And to what extent do you provide for them? And to what extent do you say no, that isn't the government's function? These were the kinds of questions that enthralled Enid. They had for as long as she could remember.

And while they weren't questions, she knew, that completely enthralled Joe–who, as Enid liked to say, was captivated more by pol-itics than pol-icy–he *understood* that they genuinely interested her. That counted for a lot. When the day was over, no matter how tough it might have been, no matter how many people didn't, there was Joe, on the other end of the line, who always understood.

In the end, one final reason Enid decided to run was because her political junkie of a boyfriend thought it was a good idea, too.

□□□

On a personal relationship level, Joe's coming to town had many pluses. Finally, he and Enid could put an end to a long-distance relationship that was making millionaires out of the phone company. They would be living in the same city. They could see each other every day. Joe could gauge for himself what living around Mormons was like. They could put their compatibility to the real test: daily contact.

Politically, they'd already decided they were a fit, but while Joe kept telling Enid they were a fit in every other way as well, Enid was not so anxious to throw caution to the wind and agree with him. They hadn't exactly grown up in the same neighborhood. There was plenty they didn't know about each other.

She had seen Joe in his "natural habitat" just once. He had invited her to his ten-year high school reunion shortly after the

Young Republican's convention in Miami the previous summer. At the Westin William Penn Hotel in downtown Pittsburgh they had walked into a huge ballroom underneath a banner that said WELCOME TAYLOR ALLDERDICE HIGH CLASS OF '81. There, for a night, Enid got a chance to mingle with Joe's high school classmates and meet some of the people of his youth. He had told her beforehand what to expect; that Taylor Allderdice High School was a melting pot of the very rich and the very not-so-rich and the studentbody reflected a wide range of classes. Joe said he had gone to school with children of millionaires and children of janitors. The Squirrel Hill suburb of Pittsburgh where he was born and raised had a considerable ethnic diversity, he explained, and the high school studentbody reflected that diversity. He could have attended private high school, of course, but his father wanted both Joe and his brother, Bruce, to get a solid public school education. Dr. Harvey Waldholtz didn't want his sons pampered and sheltered, he wanted them prepared to face the world as it really was.

Enid found those at the reunion to reflect just the kind of mix Joe had discussed. He had been the senior class president, he told her, and by the number of former classmates who came by to say hi she could see he was popular. He'd been a member of the cast of *Oklahoma!* his senior year; he played Jud, the anti-hero, and many people brought that up. He'd obviously had a flair for the theatrical even back then, as well as the political. Among the stories Enid heard–and heard again–was how Joe cried openly when he got the news during a rehearsal of *Oklahoma!* that President Ronald Reagan had been shot.

Other favorite stories that night centered around Joe's propensity to spend money. During dinner, they sat at a table with a girl named Sarah whom Joe had often mentioned to Enid. He had told Enid how a few years earlier Sarah–a good friend, said Joe, although never a romantic girlfriend–had her heart broken by a guy and Joe had come to the rescue, whisking her off to New York for a weekend at the Ritz, where they ordered all they could eat off room service. The bill came to more than two thousand dollars and Joe took care of it all. As Enid listened, Sarah not only verified the story of that weekend, but added even more details of her friend Joe's largesse. Finally, Joe leaned toward Enid and whispered, "Hey, don't believe everything you hear."

"Like what?"

"Oh you know," said Joe. "Nobody tries to nail you like your friends from high school."

In bits and pieces, Enid developed Joe's life story. His parents, Barbara and Harvey, divorced when he was six and, he admitted, it affected him still. His stepmother, Marilyn, tried hard but it wasn't the same. Joe said he and his father's relationship was strained and had been that way for as long as he could remember. He felt his father, a hard-working man who was still a practicing dentist despite his wealth, had always favored Joe's older brother Bruce; as a result, he didn't much care for his dad. He told Enid of family dinners when he just sat there, listening to Harvey ask Bruce about his life, his sports, how things were going in general, and never asking Joe anything. When Joe talked about it, Enid could sense the hurt.

Although he hadn't grown up with her, Joe was closer to his mother than his father. His mother had a lot of problems with her health, both mental and physical, and Joe said it was he–not Bruce–who took care of her. Joe, Enid learned, was also very close to his grandmother on his father's side, Rebecca Levenson, or, as the family knew her, Gram. Joe was Gram's pet, always had been, and she was constantly favoring him over his brother and his cousins–to what Joe said was their continual consternation. And Gram, Enid learned, had the means to do some major favoring. It was Gram who was loaded. When her husband and Joe's grandfather died she became the caretaker of the massive Waldholtz Family Trust. And even though she married again, to a man named Levenson, she relinquished none of her power, nor her affection for Joe.

But Gram was in failing health now and if that didn't leave Joe in financial straits-he said the trust was worth three hundred million dollars and his monthly "salary" alone was around

$25,000, it did leave him without much familial love. It was true–and curious, Enid thought–that Joe still lived with his father and stepmother, and their many servants, just as he had for most of his twenty-eight years. But she came to understand that that was more a practical decision than an emotional one. It was one thing to mingle with the public in high school, it was another thing to move out of a mansion. As far as Enid could figure it, Joe had left home just once, when he went to the University of Pittsburgh and stayed in the dorms. He hadn't lasted more than a year at Pitt, however, before returning to his home and going to work in politics. Politics was his first love and, as Joe continually told her, until Enid came along, his only lasting relationship.

After getting to know more about Joe and his roots, it was easier to understand how he could move to Utah at almost the drop of a hat. He had few strong family ties in Pittsburgh. And in Utah, he had Enid.

While Enid's destination–a life in politics–was the same as Joe's, she had taken a decidedly different route to get there. In many ways, her upbringing was the direct opposite of her boyfriend's. Her parents were attentive, if not doting, and her family ties were, as a result, rock solid. She could not remember a day when her mother wasn't there when she got home from school, and while it was true, her father was the quintessential workaholic who spent long hours either at the office or doing church work, she never had to guess about his affections either. He was her biggest fan.

Forrest and Gerda Greene adopted her the day she was born in a San Rafael hospital on Oct. 5, 1958 (that made her five years older than Joe). She never knew her biological parents and never felt the urge to make the attempt to find them. Her birth announcement, as penned by Gerda, said she was "selected" not "expected" and, indeed, there was nothing about her home life that ever made her feel different or unwanted. In Forrest and Gerda Greene's "second family," being adopted was the norm. Enid was the first of three adoptions. Gloria followed three years later and David another six months after that. Enid, Gloria and David grew up together, well behind their twin sisters, Sue and Randi–Forrest and Gerda's natural children who were ten years older than Enid and already off to college before Enid was a teenager.

Enid's formative years were spent in cosmopolitan San Francisco. Shortly after she was born the family moved from the Marina District near Fisherman's Wharf to Forest Hills, a more suburban section of The City where the back yards were bigger and the grass was real. The hippie movement was in full swing then but the Greenes were never candidates to join the commune–or, for that matter, to even take off their shoes. Enid's mother was a traditionalist who made sure you were dressed up when you went downtown on the streetcar to Market Street.

Enid's first passion was reading. At night she hid books under the covers so she could read after her mother shut the door and turned out the lights. When it came to unruly, that's about as extreme as it ever got. She wasn't a perfectly behaved kid but she was close. In Mrs. Jurjevich's third grade class she was crowned queen of the class for reading the most books. When she got to fourth grade she was put in a special class for the intellectually gifted. Enid Greene was the kind of girl who never complained about school, and school never complained about her.

The Greenes might have remained in San Francisco if it hadn't been for federally-mandated school busing that came along in the '70s. It wasn't that Forrest and Gerda were against racial integration. But they felt they were already living in the midst of integration, and busing, therefore, was a waste of time and money. At Herbert Hoover Junior High, where Enid was enrolled, you were practically in the minority if you were white. There were Asians, Blacks, immigrants from the Middle East. The school was already the epitome of a melting pot. When the Greenes found out that their kids would have to leave for schools on the other side of the city at seven in the morning and they wouldn't be home until five in the afternoon, they balked. That, along with what they viewed as steadily declining morals in general, prompted them to think about moving. The Bay Area just wasn't standing still. Beatniks had given way to Hippies, and not just on the corner of Haight & Ashbury. God-fearing was quickly becoming a minority alternative lifestyle. Love, peace, and, just around the corner, Gay & Lesbian Pride Week, just didn't coexist peacefully with the Greene Family values.

By 1971, just as Enid was to enter the eighth grade, Forrest and Gerda made their move. They sold their house in Forrest Hills, bought a modest condominium in the Pacific Heights section of The City where Forrest would live during the week, and moved the family lock, stock, and morality, to its new home on Penrose Drive in Salt Lake City, eight hundred and fifty miles due east. The twins were already in Utah–Randi was working on a masters degree in business education at Brigham Young University and Sue was teaching home economics at a high school in nearby Orem–and now the rest of the family was too.

In America in the '70s, you could not have found much more of a sharper contrast than by moving from the heart of San Francisco to the heart of Salt Lake City. The Greene family moved from living in the city of hippies to literally living across the street from the President of the Mormon Church (Harold B. Lee, whose house stood kitty corner from the Greene's house).

To the inwardly-centered Enid, however, there was hardly a culture clash at all. She didn't miss a stride when she got to Salt Lake. She continued to give neither her parents nor her teachers any problems. At Salt Lake's Bryant Junior High School she entered the patriotic speech contest in both the eighth and ninth grades and made the city finals both times.

At Salt Lake's East High School, the pattern of good student/no trouble-maker continued. She marched in the pep club her junior year, left plates of cupcakes on the doorsteps of the football players the night before games, worked on the yearbook staff, sang in the a cappella choir, and made the regional finals in legislative forum.

But while she was no outcast, still, she was different, and not just because, as a strict Mormon (even by Utah standards), she didn't go to the beer busts or wear her skirts short or even drink Coca-Cola. It was her interests that were different; they were more serious, more grown-up, than the other kids. She liked to talk about elections and world affairs and the environment as much as her friends liked to talk about boys and clothes and music. She liked reading more than she liked shopping.

Between her junior and senior years she was selected to spend a week on the campus of Southern Utah University and attend Girl's State–a government awareness program run by the American Legion Auxiliary. While many of the girls used the week as an opportunity to party and gossip, Enid used it as an introduction into politics. She was one of two girls selected at the end of the week to represent Utah as its "senators" at Girl's Nation the same summer in Washington, D.C. On that trip, her first to America's capital city, her political seasoning continued. At the end of her week at Girl's Nation, she was chosen FBI Director and was given a personal tour of the FBI building in downtown Washington.

The experiences at both Girl's State and Girl's Nation were positive enough that when Enid, after enrolling at Brigham Young University as a freshman for the 1976-77 school year, received a brochure in the mail advertising a leadership conference in Washington being put on by a group called the Young Republicans, she called her parents and talked them into letting her go. It turned out to be a fortuitous decision–one that absolutely locked Enid's personal course onto politics.

It was in the Young Republicans that Enid discovered a whole crowd of people exactly like herself. They talked like her, they responded like her, they were interested in the same things she was interested in. The week she spent with them in Washington, D.C. was one of the best weeks of her life. These were people who spoke her *language*.

A Young Republican *wunderkind* was born. Within a year–at the age of eighteen!–Enid Greene was elected chairman of the Utah Young Republicans. She transferred from BYU to the University of Utah in Salt Lake City just so she could better serve as YR state chairman, a non-paying position. To fund her volunteer career, she got a job selling handbags at ZCMI, a downtown department store. By her senior year she left the department store to accept a position working in the office of Dan Marriott, Utah's Republican congressman from the second district. Now, not only was she surrounded by politics, but politics was paying the bills.

After graduating from the University of Utah with a degree in political science, she returned to Brigham Young to law school and, realizing the time constraints, made a calculated decision to lay low from politics in general and the Young Republicans in particular. She just didn't have enough hours in the day. But once she was out of law school and working for the Salt Lake City law firm of Ray, Quinney & Nebeker, she was ready to get involved again. In 1984, she eagerly accepted a position as co-executive director of the Ronald Reagan presidential re-election campaign in Utah, and once again she became actively involved with the Young Republicans. Her political life was back on track.

As the '90s began, she found herself more involved in politics than ever. After seven often stormy years at the law firm, she left to take a position as Deputy Chief of Staff to Governor Bangerter. About the same time, she succumbed to the urgings of YR pal Audrey Merkin and agreed to run for the 1991 Young Republicans national chairmanship. She had made worse choices. Not only had that decision resulted in her successful race for the chairmanship, and not only had it gotten her into the race for the United States Congress, but it introduced her to Joseph Phillip Waldholtz.

□□□

The romance was nearly a year old, and nothing had really changed. Enid was still running for things. Joe was still encouraging her. And they were still head over heels about each other.

That was good enough for Enid. Not everyone liked Joe. She had come to realize that. He could be abrasive, obnoxious, biting with his wit, and, at times, a buffoon. Buffoon, she realized, isn't all that hard to pull off when you're balding, wear glasses, and weigh three hundred pounds. But for all his shortcomings (*and don't we all have them,* she often thought), Enid not only loved

Joe Waldholtz, she liked him just as much. From her point of view, what wasn't to like? All her life she had felt like the world was trying to pour her into a pre-made mold, and she could never see herself as a perfect fit. In her most candid moments of self-reflection she thought of herself as a little too chubby, a little too short; her hair a little too brown. And throw into that mix the fact that she was smart, wore glasses, and, she knew, could be hard-nosed and stubborn when she needed to be. *Not the greatest package when it comes to men*, she would think. *Especially not Mormon men.*

But she didn't like phoniness and she didn't want to change. That was her dilemma. She could have lost the glasses and worn contacts, but she didn't choose to. The Irish have a saying about being comfortable in your own skin. Enid was comfortable. In her most candid moments of self-reflection she also realized that she liked herself; she really liked herself.

And now, so did somebody else.

Remarkably.

Miraculously.

For the first time in her life, she found herself in a relationship with a man who didn't just tolerate her interests, but shared them and championed them. She found a guy who told her she was the most beautiful woman he'd ever seen, who pledged his undying love and affection, who was more emotional than she was, who wrote her notes, sent her flowers, gave her gifts even when it wasn't a holiday, held her hand, AND wanted to vote for her!

There was just one problem. A big one. Do you go ahead and marry your No. 1 fan when he's Episcopalian? And you're Mormon?

"The religion thing," they called it. For Joe, who told Enid he had been raised Episcopalian all his life, it wasn't really an issue. They were both Christians, weren't they? He didn't want to convert her. She could remain a Mormon forever, fine by him. It was also fine by him that their children would be raised in the Mormon church. Religion was not a stumbling block for Joe. He was easy. But for Enid, in a church that believed in same-faith marriages for eternity, it was.

The subject would come up periodically as they talked back and forth from the eastern time zone to the mountain time zone, or during long weekends when Joe would fly from Pittsburgh to Salt Lake and he and Enid, minus a few hours to sleep, would spend seventy-two hours together. Sometimes, Joe didn't deal with "the religion thing" with total composure. "Are you saying you would let that keep us apart?" he would say accusingly to Enid as tears sprang to his eyes. "You love God more than you love me!"

From the start, he told Enid how he felt about her, and it was unilateral and unwavering. Except for fooling around the day they "met" in Newport Beach, he never did play hard to get. They were meant to be together, that was his story and he stuck to it. It was fate. It was destiny. He didn't *think* they would be married, he *knew* it. It wasn't a question of if, only when.

The attention never waned. When he was in Salt Lake, Joe showered Enid with gifts. When he was in Pittsburgh, Joe showered Enid with gifts. She'd look up from her desk in the governor's office and there would be not just one enormous bouquet of flowers, but two. And they wouldn't be from the florists down the street. They'd be Fed-Exed from Caleb & Corolla. The most beautiful flowers in the world. Within three months after returning home from the August 1991 Young Republican convention in Miami–their first lengthy separation–Enid was the envy of every woman who worked in the state Capitol. And even if they didn't know him, Joe was the scourge of every man.

"Puts us all to shame," male members of the staff would typically observe as they rolled their eyes and walked past the flowers regularly dwarfing Enid's desk.

And Enid, make no mistake, did not mind any of it.

Later, when she had a chance to look back on those days with the clarity of hindsight, she knew what it was that completely swept her off her feet. It wasn't the jewelry, the gifts, and the flowers per se. It was the thoughtfulness behind them. Joe didn't just give her the gifts, he gave them to her when it mattered. She'd receive flowers the day after a tough assignment at work. She 'd receive a new brooch or pair of earrings out of the blue, for no reason at all. And on holidays, she never got just one present. That would have been expected. She'd receive multiple presents, with multiple cards, and the cards would be lined up in order: *Open me first, me second, me third, me fourth.* The first card would usually be humorous, and the sentiment would grow from card to card until No. 4 spilled out such tender feelings of affection that Enid found it hard to believe all of it. Could she honestly be this wonderful to someone else?

Joe's effusiveness hit high notes she had no shot at. Sometimes, Enid would smile to herself, it was as if they had done a gender reversal. He was flowery and sentimental; she was down-to-earth and wore sensible shoes. It was thanks to Joe that airport "scenes" were a regular occurrence. At the Salt Lake Airport she would put Joe onto a plane for Pittsburgh late on a Sunday night and invariably he would be in tears, crying unashamedly as they hugged about how much he hated to leave her. "I love you more than you love me," Joe would tease the dry-eyed Enid, who would laugh as if to say, "One of us has to get a grip."

□□□

Joe Waldholtz did not love Gerda Greene more than she loved him, however. With them it was a standoff. A dead heat. They despised each other equally.

It was inevitable, Enid thought. True love never runs smooth and this was proof. Her mother couldn't stand her boyfriend.

For openers, Enid's mother thought Joe was trying to "buy" her daughter. She saw the bracelets and the earrings and the necklaces and the dresses and the flowers and was not impressed. She was a quick study, this Danish transplant who throughout her life had maintained her Scandinavian accent and no-nonsense approach to life. She came to America in 1939 when she was twenty years old, riding into New York on the waves and through a loophole. Her mother was Norwegian, her father a Danish sea captain. She was born in New York City when her mother traveled across the ocean for a visit with her husband while his ship was docked in New York harbor. Her mother stayed in New York to have her baby, who was born on Mar. 3, 1919, and then waited three months before traveling back to Norway. Legally, according to maritime and U.S. law, Gerda Beyer was both a citizen of the country of her father's birth *and* the country where she was born.

Two decades later, as the Germans starting closing in on Copenhagen, Gerda took advantage of that dual citizenship and boarded the next ship for America. God bless it.

Gerda and her mother–who had divorced her father when Gerda was seven–joined the Mormon church in Denmark after coming home one day in the '30s and finding a missionary tract stuck in the mailbox. It was Mormon missionaries who accompanied Gerda on the ship to America. Before putting her on a train for San Francisco, where she was to meet her father's ship (and make his acquaintance for the first time in many years), they made sure she saw the Mormon historical landmarks in the East–the Hill Cumorah, where the prophet Joseph Smith said he dug up the Book of Mormon; the Sacred Grove, where Joseph Smith said he saw God the Father and the Son. In the Sacred Grove, located just outside Palmyra, New York, someone bit into an apple as she meditated. She shot the offender a sharp look, annoyed that someone would break the reverie. This was no timid girl.

She arrived in San Francisco on Armistice Day, 1939, with less than twenty dollars in her purse. She met her father in the harbor and then bid him farewell as he sailed the S/S Peter Lissener off to Honduras. She got a job as a governess, rented a room in Pacific Heights, polished her English, and kept the boys at bay.

She was pretty and she was alone, so she sized up the situation, took a deep breath, and took care of herself. She prided herself on a sixth sense that kept her from going out with the wrong boys, that kept her from getting in trouble, that kept her safe and secure in a world that was anything but. They didn't call it that in the war years, but Gerda Marie Beyer had street smarts, and plenty of them.

In 1992, her street smarts told her Joe Waldholtz was trouble for her daughter.

Enid, however, didn't see it that way. She felt that her mother didn't approve of Joe because he wasn't a Mormon. Pure and simple. When Joe declined taking the Mormon missionary lessons "because you're mother's a Mormon, and if that's the way Mormons act, I don't want to be one," Enid empathized with him. *Come on, Mom*, she found herself thinking, *Lighten up!*

The tension between prospective mother-in-law and son-in-law escalated quickly once Joe moved to Salt Lake–and into the basement of the Penrose house, which he wound up sharing with two other men, Greg Hughes, a friend from Pittsburgh and a returned Mormon missionary who was attending school at BYU; and Jim Clark, a member of the Young Republicans from California. All had signed on with Team Enid.

Having all those men in the house, and especially her daughter's boyfriend, did not sit well with Gerda. To help counterbalance any appearances of impropriety, she would leave her downtown condominium and drive to the Penrose House, where she would sleep upstairs with her daughter–and not just in the same room, but the same bed.

In their own way, they were all there to help Enid. She had a race to win and they were there to help her win it.

She was off to a good start. She was an unknown underdog, but so far that hadn't proven to be a problem. At the Republican convention in March she outpointed all the contenders, including the pre-race favorite, Craig Moody, who almost inexplicably folded completely out of contention. Enid was an engaging new face, a breath of fresh air, just the kind of package phenoms come from. She received forty-two percent of the vote. The next closest vote-getter, an arch conservative anti-feminist named Jim Bartleson, received twenty-seven percent. It didn't figure that Bartleson would stand a chance in the ensuing public primary in June, and he didn't. Enid won in a Republican landslide. She was headed to November.

After that was when Joe called and said he was on his way.

The general election pitted Enid against Karen Shepherd, a

feminist Democrat whose views played well in urban Salt Lake, if not in the Utah hinterlands. In a state with a Republican governor, two Republican senators, and two incumbent Republican congressmen, Karen Shepherd was suddenly the token liberal beacon waving in the haze. In cosmopolitan Salt Lake City, with its California move-ins and corporate transfers from Connecticut, the *exception* was often able to rule. Smart odds said that even if Owens was stepping down, the Democrats would retain their seat. A wily campaigner, Karen Shepherd became the heavy favorite early. Enid Greene had her work cut out for her.

It was a long and bitter race, among the most bitter anyone could remember in Utah politics. The Young Republicans had never been like this. One night Enid came home to the Penrose house to discover someone had opened the two deadbolts on the fence gate and turned her dogs loose. Another night she came home to find several teenage boys hammering dozens of "Karen Shepherd" signs in her front lawn after spraying her own signs with mustard. On yet another night, there was an abortive break-in at her campaign headquarters on Fourth South. All the while, the phones were ringing off their hooks with clandestine calls. Tipsters phoned Enid's office suggesting that Karen Shepherd was labeling Enid a lesbian in some of her speeches; and, in yet other calls, there were reports that the Shepherd camp was labeling Enid as a woman who'd had an abortion.

On the Sunday before Election Day, the *Salt Lake Tribune* ran a poll that showed Shepherd ahead by sixteen points.

The next Tuesday, Enid lost by four points.

The campaign took a terrible toll. Enid was devastated. Not as much by the loss as by the personal attacks. She had heard politics could be like this, but now she'd experienced it firsthand. It had not been a pleasant experience.

It did not help when she went to her campaign offices the day after the election and discovered a pile of unopened IRS notices. She opened them to discover that her campaign had failed to pay the payroll taxes on the employee checks!

Who knew what else had slipped through the cracks?

It was Joe who told her.

Joe hadn't officially served as Enid's treasurer during the campaign. But he wound up handling most of the books anyway as he naturally assumed many of the duties that were similar to those he performed for Elsie Hillman. And on Enid's campaign for the Young Republican chairmanship the year before. In the final months of the campaign he'd been able to take a load off Peter Valcarce, the new campaign manager after Enid relieved Ron Wilson of his duties, by paying the vendors and keeping track of the day-to-day expenses. In the cleanup after the '92 campaign, Joe approached Enid with memos concerning a number of bills he said Valcarce had failed to pay before he'd left.

"The bottom line, he overspent," Joe told Enid. "He used a lot more of your money than you'd given him permission."

One final thing, Enid sighed as she quickly did her mental arithmetic and realized the money she'd received for the Penrose house was, for all intents and purposes, gone. She no longer had a house, she no longer had a down payment for another house, and she no longer had a job. Her run for Congress had just about economically wiped her out.

Just as he'd done the previous year when he'd also been the bearer of bad financial news–when he told Enid that Audrey Merkin had overspent to the tune of $30,000 in her Young Republican campaign–Joe gave Enid his pay-and-move-on speech.

"There's no sense in making a big deal out of this with Peter," he told her. "Don't even call him. What's the sense? The money is owed. It's got to be paid. A knockdown, dragout over who authorized the expenses won't do anybody any good."

As he straightened his solid gold cufflinks, Joe added the usual rejoinder.

"Don't be upset, Enid," he said. He gave the love of his life a reassuring hug. "There's no need for that. Money doesn't have to be an issue with us. It never has to be an issue."

CHAPTER IV

As requested, D. Forrest and Gerda Greene reported dutifully to the Penrose house. Joe and Enid said they wanted to talk to them. It was the day after Christmas, 1992, a fine, clear, brisk winter day with just a skiff of snow on the ground. It had been a white Christmas, barely. Forrest allowed himself a hint of a wry smile as he walked up the sidewalk and stepped into the living room. *Visiting my own house,* he thought. Technically, it was his house again, although it would still be a few weeks before Enid–and Joe–moved out. The campaign was over. The last vestiges of the staff were leaving. Forrest Greene allowed himself another hint of a smile and a thought: Well, at least Joe will finally be out of the basement.

In all of his successful and productive seventy-five years of life, D. Forrest Greene had made everything but trouble. His nature was stopping conflict, not starting it. He was a third generation Utahn who could trace his family tree to the Mormon pioneers who, running from troubles of their own, crossed the American plains until they finally found refuge in the Salt Lake Valley, a dust bowl with one tree and no inhabitants when they first arrived in July of 1847. By point of fact, the Mormons had actually left the United States of America and entered Mexico, although two years later, following the discovery of gold in California, the "Territory of Deseret" would officially become U.S. land. Forrest's great grandfather on his mother's side, William Clayton, wrote the well-known Mormon song, *Come, Come Ye Saints,* an inspirational tune the pioneers sang to help keep them going on their 1,200-mile exodus from Missouri to the Salt Lake Valley. The song spoke of adversity and challenges, and the reward that comes to those who endure until "All is well." On virtually any Mormon's list of top hits, you could be sure *Come, Come Ye Saints* would be there. It was definitely one of Forrest Greene's favorites.

Forrest knew there was friction between his wife and Joe. He even knew why. Just yesterday, Christmas Day, had provided the latest example. Enid had opened a box from Joe and found a beautiful red wool coat inside. She'd seen the coat when they'd been window shopping a few weeks before Christmas and mentioned how much she liked it; Joe had gone back to the store later and bought the coat. But that wasn't all. At the same store he also bought her a mink coat. Forrest could only imagine how much that might have cost–and he tried his best not to. The mink had been in a box beneath the red coat. When Enid thought she was finished, she was just getting started. That was Joe. Why give one gift when you could give two? It was precisely that kind of behavior that put Gerda Greene's teeth on edge. She confronted both Enid and Joe about the mink afterward. "You give a mink coat to three people in your life," she said. "Your daughter, your mother, or your wife." She didn't say that to Enid, she said it to Joe.

Forrest knew he could change neither the mind, nor the will, of either Gerda or Joe, nor would he want to even try. But his own take on the new guy in town, and his basement, was more optimistic. Since Joe Waldholtz had come along, he noticed a spring in his daughter's step he hadn't seen before. He knew that losing the election had been the hardest thing she'd ever had to endure, and yet she came through it with her head up and her attitude strong. This man from Pittsburgh had something to do with how quickly she recovered. A father like Forrest didn't miss something like that. Joseph Waldholtz was making his daughter happy. Forrest Greene knew that, and that made him happy.

After they had all taken a seat, Joe took the floor. He thanked both Forrest and Gerda for coming and then got right to the point.

"Enid and I love each other and plan to be married," he said.

"We wanted you to be the first to know of our plans."

While Gerda Beyer Greene sat there on the couch, wearing an expression that seemed to say *He's completing his purchase*, her husband rose and shook hands with his future son-in-law.

"Welcome to the family," he said.

□□□

Never enough time, Enid Greene thought to herself as she steered her Jeep Cherokee north on Interstate 15. *Never enough time to get it all done.* It was late afternoon and she was driving toward Salt Lake City, commuting home from the Novell Corporation, a computer conglomerate with headquarters in Provo, fifty miles to the south of Salt Lake. She was back in the work force, working for Novell in its legal department. She didn't mind the commute, really. The traffic flow was in the other direction–cars filled with people from Provo who worked in Salt Lake moved north in the morning, south at night. She was always opposite, going against the flow. The drive was easy. It gave her time to think.

She was as ecstatic as ever about her upcoming marriage to Joe Waldholtz. That was the wonderful news. The not so wonderful news was that they were in that limbo land known as the engagement period. Before they could get around to setting a wedding date, they had rings to buy, families to placate, a reception to plan . . . and Enid needed to get Joe out of her basement.

Once the election was over, the campaign workers had disbanded their fraternity in the bottom of the Penrose house. Only Joe remained. And if that *arrangement* hadn't sat well with Enid's parents before, it was sitting worse now. Forrest and Gerda had never intended their family home on Penrose Drive to be the local co-ed dorm, a potential den of iniquity. A point they reminded Enid of at least daily.

As Joe told Enid just as often, his position had not changed either. They finally had a chance to be together, why should they waste half of it driving back and forth to separate residences?

They were going to be married soon anyway. Just what was the big deal?

Stuck in the middle, Enid wanted nothing more than to make her own decisions, run her own life. She was carrying more than a little hurt and anger from the '92 campaign and it spilled over into her attitude, giving her a measure of rebelliousness she hadn't had before.

Still, her mother could be quite persistent, to put it mildly, and besides, it was now *her* house. Enid had sold it back to her parents, who were waiting for her–and Joe–to move out so they could move in.

In their spare time, Enid and Joe, who had acceded to her parent's request that they delay announcing their engagement until Joe moved out of the house, were looking feverishly for a place they could call their own.

They had each found work shortly after the first of the year, Enid at Novell and Joe as executive director of the Utah Republican Party. It so happened the Utah Republicans had an opening at the top, and after one look at Joe's resume–former head of the Pennsylvania Bush Campaign, former chief of staff to well-known political operative Elsie Hillman, any number of positions with the Young Republicans–it took them no time at all to decide Joseph Waldholtz was their man.

While she often teased Joe about being a "trust baby," his insistence at leading a "normal" life sat well with Enid. She didn't want to spend the rest of her days getting her nails done, taken care of by the Waldholtz Family Trust, and neither did he. He said he wanted them both to have jobs, to be productive, and he preferred that their new house not be like the mansion he grew up in, with servants always underfoot, at your beck and call. He said he wanted to be a regular person for a change. He wanted to live like "normal" people.

A real positive, in Enid's book.

Beyond that, other things were looking up as well. Even if Joe wasn't making much headway with his future mother-in-law, he was with other members of Enid's family. He had particularly endeared himself to Enid's older sister Randi, who worked as a secretary at Mormon Church headquarters. Randi was quick to laugh and Joe was quick with a joke. It was a good combination, and it pleased Enid that in Randi Joe had found an ally in the family. It gave him an outlet and it gave her hope that one day there just might be a thaw overall.

Joe would often call Randi and the two had developed an easy rapport. Sometimes he would phone her and joke about the Mormon church. Sometimes he would do an impersonation of his future mother-in-law's voice, ranting about what a bad guy Joe was. "You know he's no good, that one," he would say in a bad Danish accent. "He's buying her, I tell you. He's buying her!"

Joe's dream home–a regular person's house, complete with a lawn to mow and a mortgage to pay–turned out to be at the bottom of an abandoned gravel pit in a new housing development called Mill Hollow on the southeast side of the Salt Lake Valley.

There would be more than fifty houses on Benecia Drive by the end of the year, every one of them stucco, but when Joe and Enid chose theirs, on lot 444 of Mill Hollow Estates, Plat D, it was the second one on the street. The view from the backyard was stunning, a full-on, full-frame look at the majestic Rocky Mountains of the Wasatch Front. Almost directly above their redwood deck, Twin Peaks, at 11,228 feet, towered high, like an enormous center piece; and just beyond were Utah's famous ski resorts. Joe got what he wanted. This was no mansion. And this was no Pittsburgh. He couldn't have been more delighted. The first time he saw the place he twirled around in the driveway; said he felt like Julie Andrews in the Sound of Music.

But if it wasn't a mansion, the house at 6691 Benecia Drive was no cardboard box, either. It had four bedrooms, a three-car garage, a spacious yard, about 3,800 square feet of floor space, and two fireplaces. Just down the street was a neighborhood park and less than a mile beyond that was the entrance to the I-215 freeway. Plenty of upper middle-class room to sprawl for Joe,

Enid, Enid's two dogs–a malamute named Sam and a Samoyed named Cheska–and her cat, Addie.

For tax reasons, they bought the house in Enid's name. It only made sense, Joe said. Unless she bought something with her own money, Enid was looking at a hefty capital gains tax liability after selling the Penrose house. Since the $240,000 price on the Benecia house was less than that she would still owe some taxes, but if the title was in her name she could use the purchase price to offset her increase and the tax hit wouldn't be nearly as big.

By selling stock she owned, Enid managed to come up with $35,000 cash, which she offered as a down payment. The mortgage company regretted to inform her, however, that a $35,000 down payment wasn't enough to qualify for the resultant loan. Her salary at Novell–a little over $50,000 a year–wasn't sufficient by itself to qualify for the estimated monthly payment of $1,750. Her income-to-mortgage ratio was too high. She needed more collateral. Enid was disappointed but not surprised. She had hoped to be able to handle the down payment herself. Joe had already done so much. He had bailed out Enid's Young Republican campaign in 1991 for $30,000 and just a few months before he had taken care of a $15,000 dollar second mortgage on the Penrose house. Enid had taken the second out years before to help a friend in financial straits and it needed to be cleared up before she transfered title to her parents.

So even if she contributed $35,000 on the down, she was still, by her own reckoning, in debt at least $10,000 to Joe (to say nothing of the jewelry, flowers and furs he'd showered upon her). Enid knew he didn't care. He repeatedly told her it didn't matter. But at the same time, they agreed they wanted to start out as equals, paying their own way. It was important to her that they do just that.

But the bottom line was, even with her $35,000, Enid still couldn't buy the house on Benecia Drive all by herself.

The only way they could swing it is if Joe added his name to the mortgage as co-obligor, meaning that even though the house wouldn't be in his name, he would still be liable for the loan.

"All you need to do is qualify," they told Joe at First Security

Mortgage, the company working with Enid to arrange the mortgage. They gave Joe an application, asked him to fill it out, and return it along with copies of his two most recent income tax returns.

"Fine," said Joe. "I'll just need to contact the trustees and have them sent out from Pittsburgh."

When the standard 1040 federal income tax forms arrived the following week, one from 1991, the other from 1992, Joe first showed them to Enid. The returns were each at least a half-inch thick. Enid idly skimmed the contents, her eye catching on line 31 on each return–the line that shows a person's Adjusted Gross Income. For tax year 1991 the return for Joseph P. Waldholtz of 6509 Darlington Rd., Pittsburgh, PA, showed an adjusted gross income of $541,565, including $248,972 in "trust income" from the J. M. Waldholtz Trust (Employer number 25-4960317) and the remainder from investment income. For tax year 1992 the return for the same individual showed "trust income" of $263,500 and an adjusted gross income of $613,979. The returns clearly showed that Joe's yearly income came from two sources–profits resulting from J. M. Waldholtz Trust investments, and his draw from the J. M. Waldholtz Trust of approximately twenty-five thousand per month.

Shortly after Joe gave copies of the 1040's to First Security Mortgage, the phone rang.

"Your loan has been approved," said the voice on the other end.

□□□

They breezed through the closing. The bank said everything was in perfect order. The title company had them sign a few dozen forms, everybody smiled, and that was that. Joe had been clearly nervous at the outset, which surprised Enid. When she asked him about it, he told her this was a big deal to him. He had never owned a house before.

As they left the title company office, Joe and Enid climbed into her Cherokee and fairly flew up Fort Union Boulevard, heading east, toward their new home on Benecia Drive. It was May. Snow still lingered high on Twin Peaks, but the grass was green and lush in the valley. There was no furniture in the house yet, but Joe asked Enid to come up to the master bedroom. He'd brought a boom box with him, and when she walked through the door he put it on the floor and switched it on.

He selected Diana Ross for the occasion. Joe loved Diana Ross, and as the queen of Motown broke into the first notes of his all-time favorite Diana Ross song, *"All of my life,"* he got down on his knees, pulled a small box out of his pocket and extended it toward Enid. She cried as she demurely accepted the package. As she expected, inside was a diamond ring. It was the one she'd admired at a jewelry shop in Pittsburgh owned by Joe's cousin.

"Please Enid," said Joe, still on his knees. "Will you marry me?" He was making it official.

Enid, while still crying and looking down at Joe, said simply, "Yes."

□□□

The next weekend, they moved Enid's furniture out of the Penrose house and moved Gerda's in. That pleased Mrs. Greene. What pleased her even more was that they also moved Joe out of the Penrose house. He went with the furniture to 6691 Benecia Drive. The plan was, he would hold down the new fort and take care of the animals until after the wedding, now set for Aug. 13, 1993, after which Enid, too, would move out of her parents' house.

They had less than three months to get everything ready.

Among the first orders of business was a quick weekend trip to Pittsburgh, where Enid could become better acquainted with her soon-to-be in-laws.

"Just do me one favor," Joe said to Enid on the flight from Salt Lake.

"What's that?"

"Please don't talk about religion around my family. They think Mormonism is some kind of cult and they're very nervous that I'm about to convert just to make you happy. I'd really appreciate it if you just didn't talk about religion at all."

"Fine," said Enid.

"Oh, and one other thing," Joe added.

"What?"

"Please don't talk about money either."

After landing at the Pittsburgh airport and renting a car, Joe drove Enid to what he announced as his "boyhood home."

"Some home," Enid said.

They drove slowly past a stunning colonial mansion, complete with grand entryway, circular drive, and sprawling grounds.

Joe sighed. "Haven't been here in a while," he said, as the car moved on.

"What are you doing?" asked Enid. "Aren't we going in?"

"Naw," said Joe. "My stepmother doesn't like a big fuss. I told them we'd meet them at the restaurant."

As he slipped the car into gear and drove away, Enid looked over her shoulder as they rounded a curve and, as quickly as it appeared, the sheer splendor that was Joe's past faded out of sight.

□□□

As the days before the wedding dwindled to a precious few, Enid noticed an abrupt change in her fiance. For months he had been nonplussed as he planned for their wedding day, the very picture of confidence. He was comfortable and in charge, the antithesis of the stereotypical non-involved insensitive male. His input was everywhere. He and Enid had sat down with her parents and agreed that, since Joe's reception plans were more extravagant than theirs, he would pick up the tab beyond what they considered reasonable. After a certain point, the father of the bride would be off the hook. Forrest Greene was liking Joe Waldholtz more all the time.

Joe was personally involved in ordering the food, the flowers, the tuxedos, the announcements. He also personally supervised the guest list, which soon stretched to more than five hundred. No sense in offending any potential future voters, that was his take. To get around "the religious thing" he and Enid agreed that they would be married by Mike Leavitt, the new Governor of Utah. She didn't care to be married by an Episcopalian priest, he didn't care to risk offending his family by being married by a Mormon bishop; so they "compromised" on the Governor. Theirs would be a state wedding. For the ceremony, and attendant reception, they secured the Empire Room in the Joseph Smith Memorial Building in the heart of downtown Salt Lake City. The Mormon church had just completed an ambitious restoration of the building, which for nearly a century had been the home of the grand old Hotel Utah. The Greene-Waldholtz wedding would be one of the first public functions in the historic "new" landmark.

All this lavishness, this extravagance, this excessiveness, Enid knew, was pure Joe; he planned a wedding the way he planned a campaign. All out. And he enjoyed every minute of it.

Or at least he *had* enjoyed every minute; with less than a week remaining, he turned anxious. His nerves, Enid noticed, began to get the best of him. He wasn't himself. He was irritable and often out of sorts.

When she asked him what was wrong, he first said it was nothing, just the usual wedding jitters, but upon further pressing she coaxed him finally into admitting that, yes, he *was* nervous–he was nervous about his parents getting together again. They'd divorced almost twenty-five years ago, when he was six years old, and they hadn't seen each other since. Joe said that when his older brother, Bruce, got married he didn't even invite his mother.

It was his mother, Barbara Waldholtz, who most worried Joe. And not just now. She was his constant worry. She and her mental problems. Joe said she was particularly prone to schizophrenia, and needed to strictly take her medicine. Sometimes she didn't. She'd been in and out of mental institutions ever since Joe could remember.

And Joe had never left her to go it alone.

He phoned her almost daily, Enid could attest to that. It was when she saw Joe at his most patient. She would hear him reminding his mother to take her medicine. Then he would ask her what kind of day she was having, and tell her to make sure she got something good to eat. Sometimes she would exasperate him and he'd hang up the phone and complain. Why didn't she take better care of herself? Why didn't she do as she was told? How many times did he have to tell her? The parent-child roles were obviously in total reversal. But to Barbara, Enid never heard Joe complain. In dealing with her, his forbearance was world class.

Joe's dedication to his mother gave Enid enormous hope and a tremendous feeling of security. *So this is how he treats the people he loves when they're down and out,* she would think. *Maybe he isn't perfect, but I'm marrying a man you can count on; a man who takes care of his mother.*

And, on the eve of her wedding day, a man worried about how his mother would hold up under the strain of a reunion with the man to whom she was once married.

□□□

In a state where weddings have not gone out of style, the Waldholtz wedding put the bulk of them to shame. The food was without end, the flowers were everywhere, and, as an added attraction, the Hotel Utah, in another form, was making its grand comeback. The caterers had advised the happy couple that a third of the guest list would not show up. The caterers were wrong. The line stretched out of the Empire Room and wound down the newly furbished corridors of the Joseph Smith Building, which was as on display as the wedding couple. When the ceremony began, the closed circuit TV system was hastily turned on so guests could watch from the outer rooms. *Everybody* was there. Except Karen Shepherd.

The bride looked radiant in white, her black hair pushed back off her face to reveal a genuine glee. It wasn't in the least bit feigned. Getting ready for the wedding had been a hassle, of course it had, isn't that standard operating procedure for weddings? And her mother could have at least attempted a smile during the wedding photos. But never mind all that, Enid Greene soon-to-be-Waldholtz was as happy as she'd ever been. She was happy to be getting married. She was happy to be surrounded by so many friends. She was happy the man she was marrying had actually *wanted* to plan their wedding. She was happy they were still very much in love.

She looked across the room to where the groom was standing, holding court, as usual, telling jokes, drawing a crowd like he always did. This was his arena; people were his element. Joe Waldholtz wasn't exactly Indiana Jones. Give him a free trip fishing for trophy salmon in Canada and he'd give it back. Make him sleep in a tent and he'd sue you. But put him in a tuxedo and turn him loose in a crowded ballroom and watch him shine.

If Enid ever ran out of passion, she was sure Joe had enough for both of them. A case in point was the previous night at the wedding dinner. They held it at the ultra-expensive La Caille, Joe's favorite Utah restaurant located below Little Cottonwood Canyon not far from their home. The guest list, limited to family and close friends, included about thirty people. Enid had gotten ready at the Penrose house and then driven to the Benecia house to pick up Joe. Joe's father and stepmother were downstairs when Enid walked in, dressed and ready for the dinner. They gave Enid a funny look and rolled their eyes in the direction of the upstairs.

"Where's Joe?" asked Enid.

"Better check up there," Harvey Waldholtz said.

When she walked in the master bedroom she found him, still in his casual clothes, and in his huge lap was a boxer puppy, in the process of being completely mauled.

Joe was like a kid on Christmas morning. He looked up, his face wet with tears. "Look Enid," he said as the puppy licked at his face, "isn't he great!" Guy Ciarocci had brought the dog from Pittsburgh as a wedding gift for Joe. Enid had heard the stories of Joe's favorite dog as a child, a boxer he'd named Mr. Rippington. Obviously Guy had too. As soon as Guy arrived from Pittsburgh he gave Joe the dog. Even if he did have a dinner party to go to, even if he was the guest of honor, Joe hadn't budged since.

"Better get ready, we're late," said Enid, trying to pick up the pace. Joe finally released his bear hug on the puppy, as tears continued to stream down his face.

That's my Joe, thought Enid, *and there are a lot worse things a man can do than cry over a puppy.*

During the ceremony, Joe, who was flanked by Guy, his best man, cried again; so for that matter did Enid, flanked by Randi, her maid of honor, who was also in tears. It was a happy, emotional time. Life had never seemed so rich. Joe's angst, so prevalent a week before, had surrendered both to the euphoria and, it seemed, to the fact that his mother and father's reunion produced no fireworks. Joe had arranged for his mother to stay in a downtown hotel, well apart from the rest of the family, and there were no embarrassing moments.

After the governor pronounced them husband and wife, Enid and Joe were maneuvered over to the side of the room to sign the marriage certificate. As they stood there, waiting for the papers, Joe turned to Enid. He was wearing an ear to ear grin. It was his drum roll look. Clearly he had big news. He leaned forward and whispered in her ear.

"It's done!"

Enid stepped back, puzzled.

"I don't know what you're talking about," she said. "What's done?"

"The five million dollar gift," he explained, the grin only getting bigger. "I told the trustees I wanted it transferred in your name today, the day of our marriage. It's your money Enid, free and clear. You can do with it what you want."

Earlier, Joe had told Enid of his intention of having the trustees from the J. M. Waldholtz Family Trust transfer a wedding gift of five million dollars into her name.

The prospect of such generosity had overwhelmed her then, and it still overwhelmed her. But at the moment, so did the curious timing of his announcement.

"Couldn't we talk about this later?" she said to her brand new husband.

□□□

To the tune of nearly three thousand dollars a day they honeymooned in Hawaii. The days flew by. They spent most of the time at the exclusive Four Seasons Resort in Maui and then eased their way back to the mainland with a couple of nights at the Royal Hawaiian on Waikiki Beach. They flew in a helicopter over the volcano on Maui and Enid snorkeled in the clear waters off the Four Season's private beach, but mostly they lounged by the pool and ate at the hotel. Five million dollar gift or not, Enid was still taken aback at how easily Joe ordered off a room service menu. *He did not look at the prices! Ever!* Six dollars for orange juice was simply not a factor.

It didn't take a psychic to deduce they were on their honeymoon. Enid glowed, Joe gushed. If Audrey Merkin had been there she'd have told them they were "still sickening." Being tucked away on a Pacific island allowed them to slow down–a few times they very nearly stopped. It proved to be good therapy for people who never did. Joe even managed to stay away from the phone . . . most of the time. They had time to talk to each other and discuss their future together. Enid wanted kids, and she wanted them soon, but Joe wanted to wait at least a year so they could cement their own relationship.

It had been nearly a year now since "their" crushing defeat to Karen Shepherd. In the months since, Joe had consistently insisted that Enid would get her strength back and want to run again. With him it was a steadfast theme, one Enid knew by heart. *She was born to lead. She was born to be in Congress. She had a lot to offer her country. Of course she would run again.*

The subject had come up often at the wedding, and Enid had shot it down just as often. She would not talk about politics on her wedding day, period.

In Maui, Joe successfully prodded her off her moratorium on the subject. He also brought up the other subject that had been taboo at the wedding: the five million dollars. He wanted to make it perfectly clear to Enid that the money was hers and hers alone–a gift from the Waldholtz Family Trust. She could do with it as she wished. She could buy a yacht, she could hire a fulltime valet, or, as Joe deftly introduced the possibility . . . she could run for Congress without having to worry about how much it was going to cost.

Earlier in the year, Enid had decided she probably would not run again. As much as she loved politics, she felt ravaged after the race with Shepherd. Ravaged and abused. She didn't know if she would ever voluntarily put herself in a position to go through that again. But sitting in a lounge chair on a pool deck in Maui, with the sun inching toward the edge of the ocean, a loving husband at her side, and a cool five million in the bank, the world didn't seem so cold. The possibilities suddenly seemed endless again. And besides, she didn't want a yacht and she already had a valet.

"I just might do it," she said.

Before the spell passed she made her concession speech–her concession speech to Joe.

"You never know," she said. "I might run again."

Joe smiled, sat back in his beach chair, and enjoyed the view.

They arrived back at Benecia Drive with *Royal Hawaiian* beach towels in their suitcases (bought legally in the hotel gift shop), semi-serious tans, and a bounce in their step. The phone rang not long after they put down their bags. On the line was a detective from the Honolulu Police Department. There had been a problem with the bill at the Royal Hawaiian, he told Joe, and the matter had been referred to the police. It seemed the American Express card belonging to one Joseph P. Waldholtz was overextended. That's the card Joe used at checkout. The hotel, then, had not been paid.

After Joe did his best to assure the officer there was a mistake, Enid took the phone. She let the detective have it. She asked him if this is how the Royal Hawaiian always did business, call the police first instead of the customer so an honest mistake could be cleared up? She asked if a file had been opened on the case. When the detective told her it had, she said she was a lawyer and demanded that it be closed. She was self-righteous, she was indignant, she was angry . . . and she was a newlywed. How dare they roll a cloud over her honeymoon!

The fact that there was a problem with Joe's American Express card was no surprise to Enid; that the matter would be referred to the police was. Enid knew firsthand that Joe had a history of problems with that Amex card. Several times while they were dating the card had been "rejected." Each time, without exception, Joe would get on the telephone with somebody at American Express and explain to them the same story. Several months before, when he was traveling extensively while working on the Bush campaign in Pennsylvania, someone had obtained his account number and rang up thousands of dollars in illegal charges. This was during the days before credit card companies made the transition to carbon-less receipts (to combat the very problem Joe had experienced). Invariably, after Joe had guided them through his account history, his charges would be authorized. Enid had seen, and heard, the routine so often she knew it by heart. Sometimes she wondered why Joe didn't just drop the Amex card altogether.

The problem with the Royal Hawaiian hadn't, in fact, been their only Amex misadventure in Hawaii. They also had a problem at the Four Seasons. After a couple of nights the front desk had called and Joe went to the front desk to straighten out the problem. He returned to their room an hour later, kissed Enid, and shook his head. "The knuckleheads," he said.

After Enid hung up on the detective from Honolulu, Joe went through a similar routine. The next day he told her he'd talked to the credit card company and everything had been straightened out–again. He assured her the Honolulu police would not be calling back.

□□□

It wasn't until the Joseph P. Waldholtzes had been home from Hawaii nearly two months that Enid decided absolutely for certain that she would again be a candidate for the United States

Congress. In the end, it was human nature that got her back in the race. When word came across the television set that Carol Nixon, an aide to Governor Leavitt, had officially announced her candidacy for the 1994 second district congressional seat, Enid just couldn't let it slide. *If she wants it, so do I*, Enid thought, and, as they say, she tossed her hat in the ring.

They made it safely through the holidays without having to gear up much of a campaign. Unlike in '92, when the seat held by Wayne Owens was up for grabs and both Democrats and Republicans lined up for battle very early, the only year-ahead positioning in the second district was among Republicans hoping to get a shot at Karen Shepherd–and they were all kind enough to each other to at least wait until the New Year to put the gloves on.

Actually, right after the New Year, Carol Nixon took her gloves *off*. After careful consideration, and one or two annoying midnight phone calls, she decided she wouldn't be running for Congress after all.

Enid and Joe were in Pittsburgh when they got the word of Nixon's decision not to run. They flew there to spend the last of the holidays with his family. Gram Levenson was in failing health and Joe thought it might do her good if he spent some time with her. They went to her bedside after they got to Squirrel Hill, a Pittsburgh suburb no more than ten minutes from the city center. Enid watched as Gram's eyes lit up when Joe came in the room. Her favorite, indeed. It was obvious. She laughed at his jokes and clearly enjoyed his company. He charmed her completely, as he apparently always had.

But if it helped her spirits it didn't help her health. Gram, the family all knew, was in the grips of dementia, sliding inexorably toward a state of total mental unawareness. All the money in the world couldn't change that.

They stayed with Joe's father and stepmother in a modest middle-class home on Darlington Drive just around the corner from Gram's. When Enid asked Joe why his parents weren't living in the magnificent mansion Joe had showed her on their previous trip to Pittsburgh, he explained that this house was a family property his father usually rented out. But with his grandmother's health failing so rapidly, Harvey and Marilyn had decided to temporarily stay in the rental themselves so they could be nearby. The house's condition seemed to validate Joe's story, and explain the rather Spartan decorating. Enid had initially found it odd that there were few pictures or mementoes on the walls, or other indications that someone had lived here for a good long time. There were no photo albums or books full of baby pictures. There was one picture of Joe when he was ten years old on the mantle and another of his brother Bruce at a similar age. Otherwise, the house was as sterile as a hospital.

There's a lot I don't understand about rich people, Enid found herself thinking. *They don't always behave the way I'd think they would behave.* She found it intriguing, for example, the way the Waldholtzes treated Christmas. They exchanged no gifts. *Maybe when you have all the money you need, you stop giving gifts,* she thought. *Maybe when you have all the money you need, you buy your own gifts.*

She didn't have long to dwell on the subject, however. They barely had a chance to settle in when Joe, upon hearing that Carol Nixon was dropping out of the race, announced abruptly, "We've got to go back to Utah. I'm not going to let the same mistakes happen again."

Even if she didn't agree with his sudden flight plans, Enid knew what Joe was referring to. It was his belief that the '92 election was lost because he left town at a key time. He'd been in Pittsburgh in early October and that's when the campaign ran the infamous "Pinocchio" ads that, political analysts agreed, seriously hurt Enid's momentum and possibly cost her the election. The ads, which ran on all the television stations, showed Karen Shepherd with a nose getting longer with every new lie she supposedly told, á la Pinocchio. The objective was to portray Shepherd as a dishonest politician who would say anything to get elected. The result was a feeling that Enid, who was derisively called "Meanid" by her opponents, had taken negativism too far.

In '94, there would be no Pinocchio re-runs if Joe could help it, and he was going to help it. So anxious was he for them to get back to Utah that they left their beloved new boxer puppy, Winston–for Winston Churchill–with Joe's parents.

"I'll fly back next weekend and pick up the dog," said Joe as he ran out the door.

Rich people, thought Enid, as she followed him to the car.

□□□

It was after their return from Pittsburgh, but before Winston Churchill Waldholtz's return–the dog was resting comfortably, they were told, in the Golden Door doggy spa–that Enid learned from Joe that he was experiencing temporary financial difficulties.

They were in the bedroom, getting ready to shut down for the day. It was the third week in January, 1994. Neither Joe nor Enid had quit their day jobs, although Enid's campaign was now fully operational, gearing up for the state Republican Convention in less than two months, where the goal, now that Carol Nixon had dropped out, was to receive at least seventy percent of the delegates. If you got that, you eliminated altogether a primary election.

Suddenly, in the midst of talking about the convention, Enid looked at her husband's face.

It was as white as ash.

"Honey," she said, "What's wrong?"

"Oh, Enid," he said, "It's my mother."

Joe's body sagged as he explained the problem. He was more disconsolate than Enid had ever seen him. His mother, he explained, had somehow managed to seriously overdraw a bank account she shared with Joe in Pittsburgh. Just exactly how it had happened he wasn't sure. There were investigators who were still checking it out. But there was evidence suggesting that his mother hadn't taken her medication and she'd gone on a spending rampage; worse than that, it was possible someone close to her had been able to victimize her by stealing her checks. The bottom line was that she was seriously overdrawn, and since Joe's name was on the accounts, he was liable.

Normally, that would be no problem, Joe explained, since,

after all, he had access to a family trust worth more than three hundred million dollars. But there was a hitch. He was prohibited from using any of the Waldholtz Family Trust money to help his mother. The rules of the trust specifically stipulated that no one who had left the family through divorce could benefit from the trust. If Joe were to use the money he received from the Waldholtz Family Trust to help his mother, he would be cut off from further participation in the trust.

Joe assured Enid that the investigators he hired in Pittsburgh would get to the bottom of what had happened and everything would soon be cleared up. In the meantime, however, he was concerned for the two women he held most dear in the world: his mother and his wife. He desperately wanted to avoid having his mother's mental problems become front page news–a certainty, he was sure, if she did not clear up her debts. And he just as desperately wanted to avoid dragging Enid through any negative publicity now that she was associated with the Waldholtz name–and her Congressional campaign was just getting started.

Finally, Joe got to his point.

"What about your dad?" he said.

"*My* dad?"

"Yes, your dad."

"What about him?"

"Do you think he would be willing to advance us enough so we don't have to go through the hassle of going to the bank and borrowing the money, which I don't think we could do in time anyway? I'd pay him back in just a few weeks, with interest."

"How much do we need?" Enid asked.

"Sixty thousand should cover it." Joe did not blanch.

Enid had to think about that one. She was thirty-five years old and she could count on two hands the number of times she had hit up her father for money.

"It's not a handout," said Joe. "It's a loan."

She was torn. She didn't want to disappoint her husband, but she didn't want to disappoint her father either. No matter how old you are, no matter how vast your reserves, nobody wants to ask their father for money.

But they were in a bind, a *temporary* bind, but still, a bind. And, like Joe said, it wasn't a handout. It was a loan.

"All right," she said finally. "But you do the talking."

D. Forrest Greene was in his study when his daughter and son-in-law arrived. He was still spending part of his time in San Francisco, but this week he was in Salt Lake City. Enid and Joe had called to say they were coming over. Forrest had no idea why. Neither did Gerda, who joined him as they moved to the family room, which sat just across the foyer from the living room. Forrest was sitting at the table, his wife next to him. Enid and Joe took seats across from them. A fly on the wall might have noted the comparison between this meeting and another one within these same walls barely more than a year before. On that occasion, Enid and Joe had been living in the house and invited Forrest and Gerda over, where Joe announced that he and their daughter were planning to be married. Now, it was Forrest and Gerda's house and in a room barely fifteen feet away Enid and Joe were requesting another audience. But in contrast to the scene the year before, this time Joe was in a suit, Forrest was in casual clothes; and while Joe was still doing the talking, this time he wasn't telling, this time he was asking.

Enid had never seen her husband so humble.

Joe still used the formal salutation for his parents-in-law; they had never requested otherwise, and he had never asked to change. He used it now. "Mr. Greene, Mrs. Greene, thank you for seeing us," he began, displaying deference as he looked downward and smiled wanly.

Joe explained the problem. He went through the predicament they were facing, detail by detail. He explained his mother's delicate mental condition, her vulnerability, his concern for her welfare. He assured Forrest Greene that he had more than ample collateral and insisted that he wanted to pay the prevailing interest rate. In spite of the hat-in-hand circumstances, Joe's presentation was masterful, an effective blend of humility and supplication.

D. Forrest Greene looked at this millionaire who had married his middle daughter and now needed $60,000 "for the short term in the extreme." He looked at his daughter, whom he loved as much as anything in the world. His pause was almost imperceptible.

"I'll wire the money in the morning," he said.

CHAPTER V

Nobody knew how much Dunford Forrest Greene was worth. Nobody except Dunford Forrest Greene.

His family didn't know. His neighbors didn't know. His children didn't know. Even his wife could only take a ballpark guess. When she was in college, Enid Greene didn't even ask if she could go on a Study Abroad program for a semester in Israel. She figured they couldn't afford it.

People on the street didn't know. People in the next office didn't know. The passengers he rode alongside for over fifty years on San Francisco's cable cars, buses and other forms of public transportation certainly didn't know. The golfers whose groups he would join at the public courses in the Bay Area, carrying his own clubs, sure didn't know.

Moreover, they'd have been surprised if they *had* known.

Nothing about him drew attention to himself or his wealth. Every day of his working life he'd gone to his various offices in the heart of the San Francisco financial district dressed in what the fashion magazines, if they'd ever seen fit to coin such a term, might have called *frugal conservative*. He wore cardigans, ten-dollar ties, twenty-dollar shirts, and leather wingtips his wife shined every week. Every five years or so he would buy a new pair of the same style wingtips. You could only half-sole a shoe for so long.

He was born in Salt Lake City on June 6, 1919, and that placed him smack in the middle of the Great Depression during his formative years. Those times left their mark. Forrest Greene knew the value of every penny that made up a dollar. He loved making them, loathed spending them.

He wasn't ridiculous about it. He didn't ration out squares of toilet paper and carve open toothpaste tubes with a razor blade to scrape out all that was left inside. He provided well for his family and was generous in a big-picture kind of way. Necessities were never neglected. He even bought nice things . . . and then he kept them. He purchased a used Cadillac in 1969, and a quarter of a century later he still had it. And not only did he hang onto his car, he made sure his wife hung onto hers. Gerda Greene bought a Buick station wagon in 1976 and put close to one hundred thousand miles on it . . . over the course of the next twenty years.

The family had stories. Boy, did they. His wife liked to tell about her husband's habit of following her around a room, turning off every light the second after she turned it on. At night he'd turn the thermostat down in the winter, up in the summer. He never passed an air conditioner he didn't want to shut off. The Cadillac didn't even have one.

His grandkids had maybe the best story about their grandfather's "frugality." When Krista, Brett and Brooke Parkinson–Sue's kids–were just little, all of them nine or under, they visited their grandparents in Salt Lake. They were delighted when they went out after a family reunion one afternoon and their grandfather pulled into a 7-Eleven for a treat. He took them inside the store and, after considerable browsing through the candy section, Brett brought a Milky Way bar to the counter, where his granddad, the big spender, already had his wallet out.

"OK kids, let's go," he shouted at the others.

"Wait, we haven't got our stuff yet," Krista answered.

"But Brett's already got this Milky Way."

"So?"

"So can't you split it three ways?"

This was the '80s. These were California kids. They knew their rights. They stomped out to the car, refusing even the Milky Way. Gerda asked them why the long faces? They promptly told on their grandfather. He wanted them to *split* a candy bar.

"Forrest," said Gerda, shooting him a look. Forrest shot her a look back and drove off, the kids in the backseat empty-handed.

□□□

But if he might not be inclined to buy you a shirt, he *would* be inclined to give you the one off his back; he was as soft as he was tight, as gentle as he was unassuming. Once, on a trip to visit Sue and her husband, Jim, and the grandkids at their home in Bermuda Dunes, California, near Palm Springs, he had–for obvious economic reasons–taken the bus from San Francisco. He finally arrived at the Indio bus station at two in the morning. He called his son-in-law Jim to pick him up. Rousted him right out of a deep sleep. When Jim got to the station he just wanted to pick up Forrest and get home as fast as possible; he assumed someone who had just traveled all day and half the night would be just as anxious. But Forrest told Jim to hold on. "There's someone I'd like you to meet," he said, and he walked him around the corner, where Jim almost ran into two Swedish girls, about twenty years old, blond-haired, and *knockouts*. They were reading a copy of the Book of Mormon Forrest had given them. "This is my son-in-law," Forrest said, making the introduction. And then the two foreign girls Forrest had befriended on the bus proceeded to tell Jim they wanted to kidnap his father-in-law, take him back to Sweden and show him off; he was the nicest man they had ever met.

Clemency was his nature. Deference was his way. He never met a person he didn't want to know better. When Sue married Jim, whose family came from California, he made it a point before the wedding reception–held in the Lafayette Ballroom in the old Hotel Utah–to conduct a little research on every member of the Parkinson family who would be at the reception. The reason was because he wanted to make them feel welcome; he said he wanted to have something relative–no pun intended–to say to each one of them.

Prior to his daughter Enid marrying into the Waldholtzes of

Pennsylvania he did the same thing. In advance of the reception–held in a ballroom just down the hall from where Jim and Sue's wedding had been–he had assembled a dossier on each member of the wedding party. Who they were, what they did, what their hobbies were.

□□□

Forrest Greene's relationship with money wasn't any less casual than it was with people. He always did his homework, leaving as little as possible to chance–and he took a great interest in his subject. In short, he made money the old-fashioned way: he hung on to it and watched it grow.

His investments were careful and calculated, for himself and for his clients. His father had been a professor of business at the University of Utah, where they named a business hall–the Mark Hindley Greene Lecture Hall–in his honor after his death in 1958. Professor Greene entitled his memoirs "A Practical Professor Speaks." His son was a practical protege to be proud of. A chip off the old conservative block.

While the Greenes' roots traced all the way back to the settling of the Salt Lake Valley, Forrest had revealed an independent streak when he set out for the Bay Area after the war. Initially it was to inquire about openings at Stanford University. But when Stanford told him there was a year's waiting list for MBA school, on account of the enrollment overload created by all the soldiers back home, Forrest decided to take a job a few miles north with Dean Witter, the investment firm, at their office in downtown San Francisco. Both he and Gerda liked the idea of settling down in San Francisco–it was where they'd met and where they'd fallen in love.

They'd fallen quickly. Theirs was a genuine wartime romance. They met through acquaintances at the Mormon church in San Francisco while Forrest's navy ship was docked in port, dated for five weeks, and were married just before Ensign Greene and the Service Force Pacific got its orders and shipped out for the far reaches of the South Pacific Theatre. It was wartime, they were in love, there seemed no sense in waiting. Forrest got a forty-eight hour leave for the marriage. A Mormon bishop performed the ceremony. They spent their wedding night at the Claremont Hotel in Berkeley. The next day Forrest was back on his ship and Gerda was off to the Federal Office Building next to the city hall in San Francisco, where, as a civilian, she worked for the Naval Reserve, handling the Commandant Budget.

That was in 1944. Two years later the war was over and Forrest and Gerda wasted no time getting their life together started. Helped by his father, whose penchant for wise investments was legendary among the University of Utah faculty (they don't name lecture halls after just anybody), they bought a middle-class house in the Parkside district of San Francisco and got down to business. The twins, Sue and Randi, came along in 1948. A decade later, long after Forrest moved on from Dean Witter and began his own brokerage firm, D. F. Greene & Company, with its very own seat on the Pacific Stock Exchange, Enid was added to the family, followed in close order by Gloria and David.

□□□

Forrest Greene didn't make a lot of money overnight; but he did make a lot of money over time. Over the course of forty years his brokerage gained a modest, if not spectacular, reputation for consistent success, while its owner's name became synonymous with fairness, courtesy, punctuality and prosperity. There were richer stock brokers on the Pacific Stock Exchange, and there were many who did considerably more volume–but there were none any more respected or consistently successful.

While the brokerage provided a steady income, it was when Forrest branched out into other business ventures that his financial portfolio really found its stride. His best move was when he became interested in a small business investment company called Continental Capital Corporation that sought out businesses that needed capital and looked worth the risk. He became a director and acquired a meaningful stock position in the company over time.

If Forrest Greene had a credo, a code he lived by, that was it: Was it worth the risk? If you were considering an investment, that was the key question you asked: Did it look *worth the risk*? That didn't just apply to finances. It applied to everything. As a Mormon bishop it was his counsel to the members of his ward. As a father it was his counsel to his family. If it looked worth the risk, take the chance; if it didn't, don't. His daughter Sue, for example, had come to him early in her relationship with her future husband, Jim. She didn't know whether to make herself vulnerable by escalating the involvement. "Look at the risk," her father had told her. "Do you think that Jim is a good risk? If you think so, then take the risk." He told all his children the same thing.

By definition, every risk isn't going to work out; otherwise why call them risks. That was certainly the case with Continental Capital Corporation's venture capital risks. Some of its investments turned sour. But many *were* worth it. Two, in particular. One was a company named KLA Instruments that developed a revolutionary system that could electronically find defects in semiconductor devices. The other was a small computer software company in Texas. With the future of the electronics and computer industries uncertain at best in the late '60s and '70s, when Continental Capital made these investments, it was a gamble to invest in either firm. By the '90s, it turned out to be sheer brilliance.

The stock prices for both went through the roof. KLA Instrument's invention wound up rendering the use of microscopes in computer repair obsolete as the San Jose-based company began selling its product to integrated circuit manufacturers around the world. As for the little Texas software firm, it was bought out by Computer Associates International, the second largest software company in the world. Overnight, its stock prices soared out of sight.

Forrest had never made so much money. His millions were begetting millions, his wealth now well into eight figures. Every other husband in America might have told his wife, "We've hit a couple of jackpots," but not D. Forrest Greene. D. Forrest Greene never boasted of his successes, not even in the privacy of his own home, not even to his wife.

□□□

As fate would have it, by January of 1994 the KLA Instruments and Computer Associates stocks were trading at or near all-time highs. Not only did Forrest have bigger financial reserves than ever in his life, he had never before had such borrowing powers. Under securities and exchange rules, stockbrokers could lend to their clients up to fifty percent of the value of their accounts. If the holdings were valued at, for example, two million dollars, the client, just by signing his or her signature, could borrow one million dollars. No financial statement was required, nor was there any repayment date stipulated or penalty for withdrawal. What this meant, essentially, is that if, for any reason, Forrest wanted to pull up to half of the value of his holdings out, he could do it simply by requesting a wire transfer or a check from the broker. In essence, his stock accounts were checking accounts.

Never before, in all his seventy-five years, had D. Forrest Greene had such instant and easy access to his money. It was as easy as snapping his fingers. If for some reason he–or some member of his family–needed the money quickly, all he had to do to get a check from the broker or give wire instructions was sign the request form, and the money was there.

□□□

Coinciding with the home runs KLA Instruments and Computer Associates were hitting out of the stock market ballpark, on Feb. 1, 1994, Joe P. Waldholtz called his father-in-law, D. Forrest Greene, for another "advance" on his short-term loan.

He had waited as long as he could.

Eleven days.

This time he told Forrest he needed "only" $24,000, less than half his original $60,000 request. The hassle with his mother hadn't cleared up as fast, or as cheaply, as he thought it would. Now there was evidence of even more overdrafts. There had been more checks working their way through the banking system, Joe explained to Forrest. She spent it all and then some. Joe was still on the hook and, as usual, his hands were tied as far as the trust money was concerned. What could he do? Again, he stressed that he didn't want to risk a lawsuit that would embarrass his mother and his family publicly, and put a damper on his wife's fledgling campaign.

"I know I'm a sad excuse for a husband," he contritely told Enid prior to again approaching her father. "I'm a disappointment in every way. I've tried everything. I just don't know what to do." But with the campaign lumbering down the runway, ready for liftoff, what alternative did they have but to turn again to family–to Enid's family? At the start of a campaign, especially, it was bad enough just to have someone see you at the bank filling out a loan application, let alone have your name become associated with lawsuits and even the hint of scandal.

Forrest, who had returned to San Francisco the week before, was in his office in the Russ Building when his telephone rang. His son-in-law was on the line. The savvy investor patiently listened to Joe's speech and hung up. He then took out a personal check on his NUVEEN account, made it out to "Joseph Waldholtz & Enid Waldholtz" for twenty-four thousand & 00/100 dollars, signed it Dunford F. Greene, and mailed it off. "I just hope this is the end of it," he said, to no one but himself. He felt sorry for Joe, and for Joe's mother and her problems. But what he was doing, he was doing for his daughter. He reminded himself of that. To Forrest, that was what made this a risk worth taking.

□□□

Enid hoped it was the end, too. She hadn't liked being a party to asking her father for money the first time, let alone the second. But he would get all his money back, plus interest. That thought made her feel better. *Hey, look on the bright side. At least I'm not destitute. I'm not hitting him up for money we can't repay.* When it came to finances, Enid Greene was fortunate and she knew it. Even if she did still have a habit of checking the right side of a room service menu, and even if she couldn't use that money to help out Joe's mother (because it was trust money) she was, after all, a multi-millionaire in her own right, qualifying on account of the five million dollars she had resting comfortably in a trust fund in Pittsburgh. Her wedding gift.

She didn't plan to spend all of it on her second try for the United States Congress. But she planned to spend whatever it took.

Did it feel good to be sitting on such a financial bedrock? *You bet it feels good,* thought Enid. *It sure does help level the playing field.* In the past, she always felt like she was running uphill, always trying to beat the odds. She was mostly a loner. She certainly wasn't one of the Utah political "in" crowd, the "beautiful people," as she called them. She had never meshed with that crowd and she knew it. She didn't socialize with them, she didn't attend their parties. She had circumvented the system, done an end-around through national affiliations such as with the Young Republicans, just to make it to the periphery of Utah power politics. So they had to deal with her, but they didn't have to like it. The truth was, she had never felt completely accepted. *Tolerated* was more like it. In the '92 race, as far as the party was concerned, she was mostly running the ball without blockers.

In politics, she knew, you had to have some cards to play the game. This was completely apart from your convictions. You had to have something that gave you a basis for support. It could be political contacts, it could be business contacts. It could even be your last name. Or, it could be money. By itself, money couldn't get you elected. Plenty of millionaires had proved that in plenty of elections. Ross Perot, for a most recent example. But as Mr. Perot had also proved, money *could* get you a bingo card; it could make them take you seriously; it could get you into the game.

Enid had a campaign staff up and running by the time the winter storms were losing their punch as they crossed the Great Salt Lake, the *Greatest Snow on Earth* reduced to common rain.

Unlike in the '92 campaign, this time Joe was officially her treasurer–in charge of the campaign finances and Federal Election Commission reports. The bucks stopped with him. Everything else stopped, at least theoretically, with Kaylin Loveland, a woman who had been a part of the team that got Mike Leavitt elected as Utah's governor in 1992 and who Enid hired as her campaign manger. Steve Taggart, another member of that Leavitt team and a longtime friend of Enid's–it was Steve who gave her the tip about the Novell job–was also added to the staff after the law firm he worked for disbanded. Steve had a new car and several other financial obligations he had assumed based on his lawyer's salary, so Enid and Joe decided to stretch the budget and pay him a wage that was not only slightly higher than the usual campaign compensation, but higher than what they were paying Kaylin–almost five thousand dollars higher. They didn't want Kaylin to know, since her name, after all, was at the top of the campaign organizational chart. As treasurer, Joe assured Enid he would make sure Kaylin didn't find out about Taggart's salary.

Running for the U.S. Congress, putting together a new house, *and* worrying about tens of thousands of dollars you're borrowing from your father can take a toll on a person. It took a toll on Enid. Worn out, if not down, by late spring she was physically sicker than she'd ever been in her life.

She finally got sick enough that she went to her doctor, who told her she had a virus and, on top of that, adult-onset asthma. The doctor gave her oxygen, pumped her full of fluids, gave her a prescription and some advice: "Slow down."

So she cut down her pace for a couple of weeks and did her best to stay out of the office, which helped her physical health . . . and then the office started to fall apart.

First it was news of a few returned checks. Nothing serious, thank goodness. A few of the staffer's payroll checks didn't clear the first time through the bank. Enid rolled her eyes. Joe might be used to having money, but he wasn't used to managing it. He had this bad habit of writing checks on accounts that didn't have money in them. She'd seen this act before. By not being able to keep their accounts straight, Joe had also bounced checks with her own family. Just the other day they'd given her brother, David, a check for his birthday and it had bounced. They told the staffers, as they'd told David, to re-submit the checks, and they cleared. Cases closed.

The most serious staff problem had to do with a deposit Joe was supposed to make in a campaign account to cover one of Steve Taggert's paychecks. Not only had Joe failed to deposit the money, but when pressed about it he lied. He said he'd tried to wire the money from an account in Pittsburgh directly to Steve's bank in Idaho. Steve checked out Joe's story with his bank and discovered it simply wasn't true. The bank had no record that there had been any attempt to wire money to his account in Idaho, not from Pittsburgh, not from anywhere. When Enid pressed Joe about why he lied, he said he got flustered because Steve had brought the subject up in the office, in front of Kaylin. "I didn't want Kaylin to know we were paying Steve more than her, so I came up with a story to end the discussion," he said. "It was a distraction. That's all I could think of. I panicked."

"Joe," said Enid. "You know we can't keep doing this."

Joe was contrite. He assured Enid he would get a better handle on managing the accounts and Enid felt–hoped–there would be no further reports of these "sloppiness" problems. And for a time, there weren't. But a few weeks later, the lid came off again, and this time with a bigger explosion.

It was late spring and still light outside as Enid, standing on the porch of what she hoped would be a future constituent's home, looked toward the street in amazement as Kaylin, her teeth clenched, her jaw set, got out of her car in front of the house, marched toward her, and said very loudly, "I've got to talk to you!"

Usually, thought Enid, it's your *opponent's* campaign manager who pulls a stunt like this.

They were in the Millcreek area of the Salt Lake Valley, high on the eastern foothills. It had been a pleasant neighborhood meeting held on an equally pleasant evening. They were holding as many of these meet-the-candidate affairs as they could. They would send out invitations throughout a neighborhood announcing a meeting for a certain night of the week at someone's home. After Enid spoke, they would serve ice cream. For obvious reasons, they called them ice cream socials.

Enid couldn't imagine why Kaylin was crashing an ice cream social like this. *Whatever it is, unless Joe's dead, it's inappropriate,* she thought. She grabbed Kaylin's arm above the elbow and steered her away from the porch, toward a hedge on the side of the property that put them out of sight of the others.

"What's going on?" she whispered.

"A lot is going on, Enid!" she said. Kaylin still hadn't lowered her voice. "There are things we have to talk about. There are FEC reports that need to be amended and they haven't been. Joe never does it. He always says he's going to and . . ."

Enid cut Kaylin off. "We're not going to talk about it here," she said, still whispering. "Not in front of these people. This is not the time or the place. Why are you behaving like this?"

As Kaylin got in her car and roared away, Enid apologized to the onlookers back on the porch, who were getting more curious by the moment. "Campaign stuff," she said, executing a you-know-how-it-is shrug as she walked to her car and drove away slowly . . . until she rounded the corner. Then she gunned the engine and headed for the office. It was late, but she knew Joe would still be there.

She walked through the door, saw her treasurer/husband/best friend at his desk, and said, "We've got a problem with Kaylin."

"I know," said Joe.

He had not yet completed a number of FEC amendments, Joe admitted, but none of them, he told Enid, were that big of a deal, and a major part of the problem was Kaylin, he maintained, who, as assistant campaign treasurer, was Joe's financial aide. He counted on her, he told Enid, and Kaylin was always leaving for Relief Society meetings at the Mormon church before their reports were finished. Joe felt Kaylin's priorities were suspect. She just wasn't doing her job. He wondered if maybe they shouldn't replace her. After the scene on the sidewalk, Enid wondered the same thing.

□□□

Kaylin wasn't through making scenes, however. The next morning after the ice cream social, she called David Jordan, a former U.S. Attorney for Utah now in private practice as a lawyer with a downtown Salt Lake City law firm. Jordan was a close friend and confidante of Governor Leavitt and although he was now in private practice–Republican U.S. Attorneys don't last long when a Democrat moves into the White House–he still traveled in the inner circles of the Republican Party; a friend who helped the Party when and how he could. When Enid got a call that same morning from David Jordan, who said he had talked to Kaylin Loveland–and also to Steve Taggart, who seconded Kaylin's concerns–and wondered if they could get together to talk, she knew she was being called in on the party carpet. There is no communication grapevine faster than a political grapevine. Good news travels fast enough; bad news travels like lightning. Between the lines the message was this: Mike Leavitt's party didn't want a statewide embarrassment on the order of the neighborhood ice cream social. They wanted to contain whatever was going on, and they wanted to contain it now.

Enid was furious. This was an internal campaign problem, they should handle it internally. Kaylin had given her no time to work anything out, and as for Taggart, he had never approached her at all!

But she wasn't so angry she lost her wits. She knew why David Jordan wanted to talk to her, and she knew she could make sure it would be a short talk if instead of marching into their meeting armed only with righteous indignation, she went in, instead, with a solution.

She and Joe huddled about what to do. The answer was obvious. They needed help on their FEC reports. The reports required by the Federal Election Commission weren't terribly complicated, but they were laborious and exacting. The FEC wanted to know what you spent, where you spent it, who or what you spent it on, what you spent it for, *and* they wanted to know where you got it. There was an entire book, at least an inch thick, that contained all of the FEC's rules. You couldn't accept any donation from anyone, including a family member, for more than one thousand dollars, for instance; and, for another, you could not borrow money from anyone, including a family member, to finance your campaign.

Money being a liquid property, it was standard operating procedure for campaigns to submit FEC reports and then, when new expenses and tallies came in, to submit amendments to the original reports. The FEC wasn't bothered if a report had to be amended; it only got bothered when it failed to receive properly amended updates.

When you didn't make your deadlines the FEC would make sure you were the first to know. The media was usually a close second.

The solution to their problem, Joe and Enid agreed, was to hire a political accountant who specialized in FEC reports. There was just one such person in Utah that they knew of, however, and he was already working for Orrin Hatch, the longtime Utah Senator. Joe said he would prefer to work with someone outside of Utah. During his days with the Pennsylvania Bush campaign he said he had worked with Stan Huckaby, whose prestigious Washington, D.C.-based accounting firm, Huckaby & Associates, specialized in FEC work. Stan Huckaby was treasurer of George Bush's presidential campaigns in both 1988 and 1992. What about Stan?

"Stan Huckaby would be perfect," said Enid. Who better to put their reports in order than the man who once did the FEC reports for George Bush himself?

□□□

As Enid suspected, the meeting in David Jordan's downtown law office was effectively defused of any unnecessary drama, finger-pointing, shouting, name-calling, and general political chaos when, at the outset, she apprised them of her new FEC game plan. Joe accompanied her to the meeting but he just sat there gloomily and said next to nothing. He was upset, he said, at constantly having his integrity questioned. So was Enid, for that matter, but she was running for Congress. She couldn't afford to be sullen and self-righteous, not with the Governor's pal sitting one chair away, not with the election less than six months away.

After a basic mea culpa to the charges of procrastination, Enid gave the Republican powers in the state capitol what they wanted with two words: Stan Huckaby. They knew of his reputation as well as she did. If his firm wasn't the best in the business, it was close to it. As they shook hands with the candidate and her treasurer, the GOP's Utah watchdogs agreed that the potential for financial embarrassment had just been, for all intents and purposes, eliminated.

After the meeting, Joe contacted the Huckaby offices in suburban Washington and talked to Keith Davis, a partner in the firm who had served as assistant treasurer to Huckaby in both of the Bush campaigns. Davis agreed that Huckaby & Associates would assist Enid '94 with its FEC reports. Enid was relieved. She was satisfied she had hired the very best, both in terms of reputation and integrity. She was further satisfied that "the very best" would forever put an end to their bookkeeping problems.

□□□

There were more financial brush fires than just the political ones, however.

Money, Enid thought with despair as she looked at the pathetic, beaten man slumping in front of her. *Money is what's causing all this.*

He was talking about killing himself–again–and she didn't like it, didn't like it a bit. This wasn't the Joe she knew and loved. This was a Joe loaded down by an avalanche of money problems and mother problems. Put the two together and you got . . . this.

"I'm better off to you dead than alive," Joe wailed. He was standing in front of her in their home. Tears were streaming down his face. His chest rose up and down as he sobbed. "I'm leaving," he finally announced as he ran out the door that went to the garage, got in his car, and drove away.

He didn't say he was leaving for good, but that's what his body language implied. That was the message between the lines. Enid didn't know if he would really end it all. He had left before, and he always returned. But how could you ever be sure? *How could you not be frantic until he returned?*

This time, thank heaven, turned out to be no different. He drove around for a while, finally answered the cellular phone when Enid called, finally backed off his threat to "crash the jeep into the cement freeway divider," and finally drove home, exhausted but alive. He couldn't do it, he said, he just couldn't leave her.

Still, the threat lingered. As Joe had explained more than once, in the event of his death, the family trust would pay a sizeable sum to his surviving spouse. It would be the one way, he told Enid, that he could do right by her as a husband.

The pressure only mounted on Joe as the problems with Barbara refused to go away. First it had been a problem with her raiding the joint account she shared with Joe. After that, Joe said, she had continued to write worthless checks even after the account was closed. That was followed by a binge spending spree on the home shopping network, carelessly sharing Joe's credit cards with the world (he had no idea how she kept obtaining the account numbers). Finally, the Pittsburgh investigators hired by Joe discovered the existence of a man who had befriended her and then conned her out of even more of Joe's money.

The number of ways Enid's mother-in-law could lose money was truly dizzying. The threat of lawsuits from the banks and credit card companies never let up, and neither did the bills from the attorney and his staff of investigators Joe had retained in Pittsburgh to straighten it all out and keep them–him and his mother–out of jail. As desperately as ever, Joe wanted to avoid any of this coming out in the open. It would expose his mother's mental illness and be scandalous for Enid's campaign. Since the family trust remained useless in this situation, the only solution Joe could come up with was to continue to lean on the generosity of Forrest Greene–either that or kill himself.

□□□

There were times when Enid wondered just when it was Joe broke the mirror.

She'd never seen such a run of bad luck. They had an inside joke about the "dark cloud" that followed them around. When they were in Hawaii for their honeymoon and the hotel staff at the Four Seasons had gone room to room, notifying them that a hurricane was coming their way and could cause some serious damage if it hit the island head-on, they looked at each other and smiled knowingly. "A *real* dark cloud," Enid said, and they'd laughed.

The American Express problems hadn't gone away since Hawaii. Joe's gold card was constantly being denied, and the discrepancy was just as constantly being cleared up after he talked to the person in charge. All Enid could deduce was that they certainly didn't communicate very well office-to-office at American Express. When Enid read in the newspaper early in the summer that Joe was being sued by American Express for an amount in excess of forty thousand dollars, she just knew it was the same old problem. The charges fraudulently put on Joe's card more than a year ago, when he was working the Bush campaign, were still being credited to him. Joe confirmed her suspicions when she brought up the subject later that day. He said the newspaper story had surprised him too, since he had never been served with any legal papers. But maybe it was a blessing in disguise. He told Enid that he had arranged to meet with American Express the next day and at least they would be able to clear it all up now that it had come to a head.

It took several months of rangling, but eventually Joe was happy to report that the suit had indeed, and as predicted, been settled. As it turned out, he did owe some back money, incurred when his mother had used Joe's card for prescriptions in Pittsburgh. But the amount was nothing to get excited about, just a little over a thousand dollars. That was all he was liable for. American Express agreed, he said, that the remainder was not his obligation. He gave Enid a copy of the papers verifying that the lawsuit had been dismissed.

Another financial problem that became public had to do with the O. C. Tanner jewelry company, a prominent retail store in Salt Lake City that sold Joe over $60,000 worth of jewelry at various times during the past year. He had charged a number of items on his store account at the time of their wedding and, since then, he'd periodically picked up a gem or two, or three, and added to his account. For Joe, jewelry shopping was like grocery shopping. He gave Enid a $15,000 pearl necklace for Christmas and the O. C. Tanner staff hadn't flinched. They were used to Joe Waldholtz, his business, and his expensive tastes. He was one of their best customers.

In May, he had issued two checks to clear up his balance. When the checks were returned from the bank because the account had been closed someone tipped the *Salt Lake Tribune* that Enid Waldholtz's husband had bounced a check. That was not correct, however, not according to Joe. The checks had not bounced, they had been returned because of a closed account. As Joe explained, he had written the checks on an account in a Pittsburgh bank. Shortly after that, thinking all the checks written on that account had gone through, he closed it and transferred the money to an account with a Utah bank. The checks to O. C. Tanner hadn't cleared, however, and *that* was the problem. He went into O. C. Tanner personally and solved the matter by paying with a check drawn on his Utah bank, which cleared.

To combat the adverse publicity that attended the story, Joe got Brent McMaster, the manager of the O. C. Tanner store, to sign a statement that said that "At no time has any check from Joe or Enid Waldholtz ever been returned to the store for insufficient funds" and "The Waldholtzes remain customers in good standing."

Enid got a copy of that affidavit, too. She put it in her campaign notebook, alongside the American Express settlement. Whenever the subjects would come up along the campaign trail–and they did come up–she not only had an answer, she had proof.

□□□

It was toward the end of the summer, after yet another threat of lawsuit aimed at Barbara, that Joe came up with a third solution to their problems: Enid should drop out of the race. If she slipped into the private sector, out of the glare of the public spotlight, they wouldn't be such a huge target. That's what Joe told her. She should just quit.

Enid was incensed. "I'm not quitting. Let them sue," she said to Joe. "Let them sue and we'll fight them. This has to stop. We've done nothing wrong."

She was in the small bedroom she used as an office on the landing between the upper and lower levels in their home. When she finished speaking, Joe walked out of the room and up the five stairs to their bedroom. The next thing she heard was Joe on the phone, talking to her father, asking him for more money. Apparently, he had re-thought that third option as quickly as he'd brought it up. This was the last time, he told Forrest, apologetic as ever. This would clear up all of his mother's problems. And if it didn't, they would just have to find another way. He could not keep asking for money like this.

By the 25th of August, 1994, seven months and four days since Joe asked Forrest Greene for the initial loan of $60,000 on January 21st, he had made nine more such requests, most of them by telephone when Forrest was in San Francisco, and more than half of them when even his wife didn't know he was calling. All together, he had asked for $653,000 to help out his mother. And his father-in-law had given it to him.

□□□

Resiliency. Joe and Enid both had enormous reserves of it. And that was a good thing in the summer of '94. As tough as the times sometimes got, their powers of recuperation kept proving superior. Give them a few hours and they were ready to run another marathon, no problem. The sun always came up the next morning, figuratively as well as literally. They were still together, they were still madly in love, they had a comfortable home with plenty of food in the pantry, Winston and the other animals were in the back yard, and they were doing what they loved–politicking. Between the adversity, and sometimes during it, they found plenty of time to enjoy themselves. There were many times when they would laugh uproariously about how ridiculous their lives sometimes got, about that "black cloud" they believed was assigned to follow them around.

Yes, Joe would sometimes threaten to kill himself, but not because he hated life–because he loved his family. At least Enid knew that was his motivation. If he died, he could provide for her.

That's why his threats scared her so much. She knew he loved her and she worried how much he could take. He tended to fatigue so fast, to fall apart so easily. At the office he could turn into a real whiner when the hours got too long or the problems too many. Enid just wasn't sure where Joe's breaking point was.

Then again, give him a few hours to recover and he was always back, cracking jokes, delivering biting satire, holding court. He could bring the office to a standstill with his imitations of Karen Shepherd. Joe tended to live life to the fullest, with immoderation and extravagance. A large man who lived large. His powers of shopping were legendary. Sometimes he would go to lunch, for instance, and swing by a men's clothing store on the way home "just to pick up a tie." By the time he was through, he would have a dozen ties laid out on the counter, always made of the finest silk, always a hundred dollars or more each, retail, and he would take them all. That was his style. Joe never bought just one of an item. If he liked a pair of shoes, he would buy a pair in every color. A shirt. Same thing. And he liked to take audiences along on his sprees. Enid remembered one of Joe's famous "runs" when he took half the campaign staff with him to Circuit City, where he loaded up on a big screen TV, a VCR, a stereo system and several other electrical items that caught his eye. Then he used the staffers he'd brought along to help him carry everything out to the car.

When Enid would come in the door at home and see her husband assembling one of his new toys, or walk in the office and hear him going off on Karen, she would smile and think, *he's not suicidal anymore.* That always gave her solace. That gave her hope. She was getting to know Joe more and more; she realized that a man who was sensitive enough to give her four cards on her birthday, a man who could cry at a supermarket opening, was also sensitive enough to have his occasional dips into the valley of despair. A real mercurial man. Enid had her own emotional ups and downs, but unlike her husband, she tended to keep them to herself. She was a shy person by nature. If she was going to fall apart, she preferred it to be in private.

As for facing problems, she preferred to attack them head-on. Do what had to be done and move on. Act, don't react. It gave her an aura of no-nonsense toughness and made her no stranger to conflict. That was why, when she worked for the governor, they tended to give *her* the adversarial assignments. The favorite newspaper quote she ever read about herself had appeared during one such case. She was sent by the Governor to deal with a group of Native Americans who were perturbed over the way they were being treated by the Government. She had done her job, which was to defend the Utah State Government, and held her ground firmly. Afterward the newspaper reported the reaction of one of the Native American leaders: "Who is this white woman who is telling us what to do?" The quote thrilled Enid. She took it as a high compliment.

□□□

It was a good thing the Waldholtzes were resilient. Because as rough as the spring and summer financial storms had been, between juggling the staff problems and the Barbara problem, by the time September came along, those seemed like the good old days.

Now, Joe announced, the family trust, including the money Enid had received as her wedding gift, was frozen. He would still be getting his monthly allotment of twenty-five thousand a month, but that was it.

This was the worst news of all. For the campaign, the timing threatened to be catastrophic. The money that came from the Waldholtz Family Trust affected their professional lives as much as it affected their personal lives. It was the primary funding behind Enid's campaign. There had been a few outside donations, but precious few. The donation solicitors Enid had brought onto the staff had not worked out very well. She had been patient with them, she had a five million dollar reserve. That kind of money helped develop a lot of patience.

But now, Joe was informing her she didn't have her five million, or at least she didn't have access to it. As they stood opposite each other in the campaign headquarters late one night, each by their desk in the office they shared, Joe explained to his wife that it was his cousin Stevie's fault.

Cousin Stevie was Steven Slesinger, the oldest son of Joe's aunt. Steve and Joe, like Joe's brother Bruce, were Rebecca Levenson's grandchildren. Along with their parents, they were the "family" that, in varying degrees, participated in Gram's vast trust.

Cousin Stevie, as Joe called him, had always been jealous of Joe's relationship with Gram. Joe had explained the family dynamics to Enid more than once. He was Gram's favorite, always had been. Cousin Stevie had never liked it, and with Gram now almost senile, he was starting to cause trouble.

Enid had met cousin Stevie once in Pittsburgh. He hadn't seemed hostile toward Joe back then, but now it was apparent he was acting hostile enough. He was contending that Joe–or someone, cousin Stevie wasn't being specific–was inappropriately taking funds out of the trust. That was preposterous, Joe said. He said Stevie was miffed because Gram had given Joe a bigger monthly income based on a number of successful investments Joe had made for her. That's all it was. Good old fashioned jealousy and envy. The trustees wouldn't have to look very far until they saw the truth. But until they did that, just to be safe, Joe said the trustees had called to say they were freezing all the funds in the trust until they conducted a thorough investigation. On top of everything else, that meant that Joe wouldn't be able to get the money coming from investments he had cashed in–money he was planning to use to pay back Forrest Greene. How was that for irony? Joe's mother's problems had finally subsided. The charlatan who stole her money was in jail, the banks and lawyers and investigators had been paid off, the bank accounts were closed and square, the sainted D. Forrest Greene was next in line, and now . . . this.

Worse–way worse in the short term–it meant Enid wouldn't be able to access any of her money, either.

It was early September, the election was less than two months away, and the two richest people Enid Greene knew–herself and her husband–didn't have a dime to turn to.

□□□

They ranted and raved about the unfairness of the trustees. Joe was, as usual, fatalistic, and Enid was beyond upset. "Those trustees of yours who are supposedly looking out for your welfare don't do anything but give us problems," she said. "You need money for Barbara, they're no help; now cousin Stevie's making accusations, and they put everything on hold. Haven't they ever heard about due process? About innocent until proven guilty?"

Joe just sat there, numb. Occasionally he'd launch into trust mumbo jumbo. Enid would have gotten more technical with him if trusts weren't such a mystery to her. In law school she almost flunked the course. Trusts was by far her worst subject. How about that for irony? She passed by about two percentage points. When she graduated from law school she wasn't sure exactly what kind of law she was going to specialize in, but she knew it wasn't going to be trusts.

Mostly they fumed about what this meant for the campaign. If they were going to win, they needed to make a major push and they needed to make it now. They had spent $700,000 to get this far and while they felt they had closed some ground on the incumbent, Karen Shepherd, they were also sure they hadn't closed enough. The truth was, they were stagnating, and both Enid and Joe knew it. They still trailed Shepherd in the polls, and, depending on what polls you wanted to look at, they weren't that far ahead of the independent challenger, a self-exiled Republican and big spender himself named Merrill Cook. If you wanted to believe Cook's own polls, he was ahead of Enid and about to overtake Shepherd. But the stretch run was coming and they were confident they could still catch Shepherd and leave Cook well behind with a good September and an even better October. They couldn't, however, if they had no access to their money. Shepherd and Cook would be spending like mad. For Enid and Joe, the maddening part was that they would soon have access to their money again, no doubt in a matter of weeks; days even. The timing of this trust fund freeze couldn't have been worse.

Soon enough, the ranting and raving gave way to reality and they both stood there, silent, looking at their desks. They were trapped. Enid absent-mindedly tapped her fingers and then started to pace. Finally Joe said something.

"We have to go to your dad."

Enid swung around.

"What!"

"We're too close," said Joe. "We've got to."

Enid was apoplectic. She didn't know where to start. This wasn't a private money crisis, as had been the case with Joe's mother. There were FEC rules against borrowing money from relatives to bankroll a run for office. You can't do it. Period. You could get a thousand-dollar donation and that was it. Forrest Greene had donated his thousand dollars long ago, at the start of the campaign. As far as the election was concerned, he was maxed out.

"We can't go to dad," Enid said. She reminded Joe of what she thought he knew. "It's against the FEC rules." Enid remembered her '92 campaign, when she sold her house to her father to finance her run. To get money she could in turn contribute to the campaign, there had to be a sale of something of real value—something like her house. There had to be an exchange of assets.

"There has to be some kind of a sale of an asset," she said. "He can't just loan us money. He can only give us money for *something*. There has to be an asset, Joe. There has to be something of value."

"We could assign him your interest in the Trust," Joe said.

Enid thought about that, but said, "No, it's in litigation. It might considered too risky. . . too speculative."

On the other side of the room, Joe did not miss a beat. The words were out of his mouth almost before Enid finished speaking.

"I've got some real estate in Pittsburgh," he said, "and it's just about through probate. We could use that."

"What are you talking about?" said Enid.

"Real estate. In Pittsburgh. A relative died and left it to me. She didn't have any children of her own but she was close to Gram, and Gram said she should leave it to me. She wanted to make sure it went to somebody in the family."

The property still had to clear probate, said Joe, but he'd been told that process was just about complete. When it was, the parcel of property already had a willing buyer waiting–a willing buyer with $2.2 million in cash.

"We're married," said Joe. "So half of that's legally yours."

Enid's mind raced. If they gave her father an assignment of real estate proceeds then maybe it would qualify as a legal transaction. They'd be off the hook. They could get the money from her father and, in turn, give him an interest in the proceeds of the sale of the property in probate, with its ready and willing buyer. It would be exactly like when she sold her house to her father.

She turned back to Joe.

"You've got to check this out with the accountants," she said, meaning Stan Huckaby and Keith Davis, their FEC specialists, specifically. "And check it out with the lawyers of the trust. We've got to make sure this is absolutely legal. Otherwise we can't go to dad."

Two days later Joe said he had checked with everyone involved. The deal had been cleared. He assured his wife that they had all given them a green light, Huckaby, the lawyers, everybody. This was legal. They were playing within the rules.

That night at home, Joe called Forrest in San Francisco, and explained the situation to him. Enid got on the phone after Joe got off. She was emotionally spent. The roller coaster ride had gone on long enough.

"Dad," she said, "we've checked it all out. It's legal. I would never expose you to any wrongdoing."

On the first day of September, nineteen hundred and ninety four, D. Forrest Greene, his financial portofolio now including $1.1 million in proceeds from a sale of Pittsburgh real estate he had never seen, sent a wire transfer in the amount of $187,000 to the First Security Bank account of Joseph P. Waldholtz & Enid G. Waldholtz. On the 12th of September he sent a check from his account at Wells Fargo Bank to the same two individuals for another $150,000, and on the 19th of September he sent another wire transfer to First Security Bank, same account as before, this one for $381,000. In nineteen days, he sent Enid and Joe $718,000.

The race was still on.

□□□

All by itself, money can't buy votes. Not legally anyway. But money can buy the services of people who can get you votes. For their stretch run the Enid '94 campaign elected to spend its money on just such a service.

When Eddie Mahe arrived in Salt Lake City he didn't *look* like the cavalry coming over the hill. But looks can be deceiving.

A shadow of a man, barely five and a half feet tall, with a perpetual crewcut, a wardrobe consisting of short-sleeved shirts and hush puppies, and a slight speech impediment, Eddie caused nary a head to turn when he walked into Enid's campaign office. He had agreed to talk to Enid and her staff about their "situation" during a layover between flights. He had been in Montana, where he was consulting on a senatorial race, and was on his way back to Washington, D.C., where he lived and where the offices of the Eddie Mahe Company, a "strategic communications company," were located. By the '90's, the Eddie Mahe Company dealt primarily with businesses, corporations and other organizations seeking help on plotting strategy. But the company had made its name, as had its founder and namesake, in the political arena, successfully plotting strategy for politicians–make that *Republican* politicians. Candidates helped by Eddie Mahe–and his equally renowned partner, Ladonna Lee–didn't always win, but they usually did. A former deputy chairman of the Republican National Committee, Eddie moved into political consulting in the mid '70's and quickly gained a reputation as an astute forecaster, a man who could tell a campaign what to do and when to do it. His successes were consistent enough that they had long ago stopped asking why. "Yoda," they called him, after the all-wise gnome in the *Star Wars* movies, and not just because of the physical resemblance. He could tell which way the wind was blowing before it even started to blow. In a political world woefully short on legends, Eddie Mahe was one.

On October 2nd, 1994, when Enid Greene, a student of Republican politics since she was eighteen years old, saw Eddie Mahe himself walk into her campaign office on the corner of Second South and Fifth East in Salt Lake City, she *did* turn her head. She suddenly felt like cheering. If she could have hand-picked a consultant, she would have hand-picked this one.

It had only been by a sheer stroke of luck and coincidence that Eddie and Enid had come together. A few weeks earlier, during a regularly scheduled conference call with GOPAC, a Washington, D.C.-based campaign service organization, Michael Levy, Enid's campaign press secretary, had talked personally with Eddie. GOPAC is an arm of the National Republican Committee that assists, free of charge, Republican candidates seeking Congressional seats. In the final months before the 1994 national elections, GOPAC organized weekly conference calls, featuring guest consultants, that were open to any campaign in the country. On the day Levy joined in, the great Eddie Mahe happened to be the guest consultant. It also happened that no one else phoned in that day. Levy had Eddie all to himself. Before they were finished, he talked Eddie into dropping by the Salt Lake office on his upcoming swing out West, "to take a look and see if you can help us."

□□□

It was on a Sunday morning the first weekend of October that Eddie Mahe and Ladonna Lee were met at the Salt Lake Airport by Michael Levy and driven to Enid's campaign headquarters just east of downtown. They had agreed to "investigate" only. There were no promises. Eddie and Ladonna only did one or two political campaigns a year anymore. The bulk of their time was spent in the business world, where the money was, and in bipartisan pursuits. It was their firm, for instance, that had done all the consulting for the United States World Cup organization that successfully won the hosting rights for the 1994 World Cup, soccer's world championship tournament.

Eddie and Ladonna did all the rest to pay the bills; they did political campaigns because that was where their hearts still were. If they thought they could help a good Republican–and for Eddie and Ladonna, the phrase was redundant–then they would give it their best shot. Since they were both natives of Colorado, they preferred to help out Western candidates. That boosted Enid's odds.

They held the meeting in the campaign conference room. Soon, Eddie had poster paper taped up everywhere–his usual working style–as he emphasized point after point. The key members of Enid's staff were there: David Harmer, the campaign manager (he replaced Kaylin Loveland after she left early in the summer following the ice cream social outburst), Levy, and, of course, Joe. They gave Eddie input and he gave them output. After about two hours, Eddie and Ladonna had a plane to catch. On his way out the door, Eddie said he could see the campaign was in trouble; then, to everyone's relief, he added that he thought he and Ladonna could help. If Enid '94 wanted them, the Eddie Mahe Company was theirs. Enid's spirits rose immeasurably. The dark cloud didn't *always* follow them around.

As they shook on it on the way out the door, Eddie asked, "How much are you guys willing to spend?"

Enid looked at Joe and Joe looked at Eddie.

"Whatever it takes," Joe said.

□□□

They spent a million dollars in five weeks, the Eddie Mahe Company's fee of twenty-five thousand dollars (plus a win bonus), a mere pittance of the grand total. Mainly, Eddie told them where to spend the rest, and Team Enid did as it was told. Eddie's genius was in analyzing data collected from polls and other research and determining exactly what voters needed to be targeted, where, and how. He didn't need to be on site and in fact was frequently out of the state working with other clients. But whether he was physically in Utah or not, he conducted daily meetings with Enid's staff every morning, sometimes with Eddie in a hotel room hundreds or thousands of miles away. Eddie Mahe was a man who *could* be in two places at the same time.

They sent out "selective" mailers, targeting people in specific socio-economic ranges with messages Eddie said they needed to hear. They went on the offensive with Shepherd and Cook, turning their own words against them. They used the mass media on every front, utilizing television, radio, the newspapers, and direct mail. They were also careful. They never released a television ad they didn't "focus group" first, testing it with a sample audience to make sure it wasn't offensive or counter-productive. There would be no repeat of the "Pinocchio debacle" of '92 if they could help it. But they also didn't pull any punches–this was no light-spirited campaign–or spare any expense.

They certainly could afford it. With money not a problem, the campaign expanded in all directions. Every inch of space in the rented headquarters building was filled, upstairs and down. When more help was needed to man phones or lick envelopes, more help was hired. When the van the campaign was leasing broke down, Joe leased a Lexus.

Daily, almost hourly, they could practically feel the momentum shifting. Enid sensed it as she traveled around the district, giving speeches, shaking hands, and making her final push. It was a tough race. Three-way races usually are. She did her part. She wound up debating Shepherd and Cook well more than a dozen times. In between she was doing audio tapes and shooting TV commercials. She became adept at changing clothes in a truck. Just before the election the campaign got a boost when Newt Gingrich, the longtime Congressman from Atlanta, Georgia, flew to Salt Lake City and gave Enid his endorsement. The Shepherd camp scoffed at that one. For Karen Shepherd, Vice President Al Gore had come to Utah and all Enid could come up with was the House Minority Leader.

Eddie's strategy called for the campaign to hit its highest gear slightly sooner than was typical. He had his reason. He knew that the Salt Lake City *Deseret News* routinely released a poll conducted by Dan Jones & Associates, a reputable polling company, on the Sunday before Election Tuesday. Because of the Cook factor in the race–and make no mistake, both Cook, a millionaire, and Shepherd were spending in the million-dollar neighborhood themselves–Eddie reasoned that it was paramount that Enid be ahead of Cook in that final *Deseret News* poll. Even though Cook was an independent, he had previously been a Republican. Both he and Enid were seen as conservative candidates. In many ways, they paralleled the roles of George Bush and Ross Perot in the '92 presidential election, where Perot, as his momentum mounted, tended to drain votes away from Bush.

If Enid was ahead of Cook in the final Dan Jones poll–a poll that would be compiled from interviews conducted nearly a week before the election–it made sense that she would drain votes from him as the conservative voters headed for the polls. A conservative is a conservative, and, Eddie reasoned, there would be a tendency for voters to jump on the winning ticket. As for Shepherd, no one expected to make much of a dent this late in the game in her support group, but since the polls consistently showed her hard-core Democratic backing to be only slightly more than a third of the voters, it stood to reason that whoever emerged from the conservative pack, Enid or Cook, would be the one with a chance to overtake Shepherd.

Excellent reasoning, as it turned out. When the *Deseret News* released the Dan Jones poll two days before election day, Shepherd and Waldholtz each had a projected thirty-seven percent of the vote, with Cook back at a projected twenty percent.

The stage was set.

□□□

The ballroom at the Marriott Hotel in downtown Salt Lake City was packed with balloons, bunting, bands, and plenty of smiles the night of Tuesday, November 4th, 1994. Election night. This wasn't Republican Heaven, but it was close. The polls had closed long ago in the East, and the results were pouring in. Cheer after cheer resounded through the Marriott–the official Republican gathering place on Election Night–as those results were announced. Republicans were winning everywhere. It was quickly becoming apparent that for the first time in forty years the Grand Old Party would control both the House of Representatives and the United States Senate. The American people were sending a message: They wanted the conservatives to have a crack at things in Washington. They wanted less government, not more. It was time for a change.

Enid won going away. She collected forty-six percent of the second district vote, a full ten percentage points ahead of Shepherd's thirty-six percent and twenty-eight points ahead of

Merrill Cook's eighteen percent. Eddie Mahe's projections had been right on. Cook's hardcore supporters had stayed with him, but that was all. The rest clamored over to Enid's side, giving her more than enough votes to put Shepherd out of office.

In Utah, a traditional Republican stronghold, the news of the re-taking of the second district's Congressional seat was the biggest of the election. "Waldholtz Leads Tuesday Night Massacre," said the headline in the next morning's *Salt Lake Tribune.* "GOP Freight Train Runs Down Shepherd," said the headline in the *Deseret News.* The subhead added: "Fed-up Conservatives Tap Waldholtz." Next to the text was a picture of Enid kissing Joe.

Enid hadn't dared get her hopes up. The '92 race had taken any such notions completely out of her. The day of the election she continued in perpetual motion, to keep occupied if nothing more. At rush hour, both morning and night, she waded into the streets of Salt Lake, doing "honk and waves." She and Joe didn't arrive at the Marriott–where the Utah Republican Party had rented the hotel's biggest ballroom–until a little after seven in the evening. The polls would close in less than an hour. As they were walking down the corridor toward the ballroom, Janie Clayson, a reporter for KSL Television, rushed toward Enid and ushered her into the service corridor.

"Our projection at 8 o'clock will be that you're our new congressperson," she said excitedly, anxious to be the first bearer of good news.

Still skeptical, and a bit dazed, Enid emerged back into the hallway, where Joe was waiting.

"Is it bad?" he asked.

"No," said Enid. "It's good." And Joe started to cry.

As the ballroom turned into a full-scale celebration, Enid still hung onto her reserve. The infamous and erroneous "*Dewey Beats Truman*" headline the Chicago Tribune prematurely ran in 1948 kept running through her mind. Even after Orrin Hatch, who had easily won reelection, stood at the podium and declared victory, Enid followed him and said, "We're not declaring victory yet."

Reporters and supporters alike gave her a hard time about it but she held stubbornly firm, her resolve only fading, and eventually eroding entirely, as the night wore on and the totals, although not yet complete, became more and more convincing.

Her family was there. Her campaign staff was there. Her volunteers were there. All of her Republican allies were there. As Enid went from media interview to media interview, from spotlight to spotlight, she soaked it all in.

She thanked them all and hugged them all until, suddenly, it was after midnight and she and Joe piled into the Cherokee and drove home. Enid's mind was racing. In her best fantasies, she hadn't imagined one quite like this night. One of her most satisfying moments had been when her dad, who'd flown up from San Francisco, gave her a hug and said, simply, "Congratulations." He wore a contented smile throughout the night, and for the stoical Forrest Greene, that was as demonstrative as it got. But Enid knew it was a grand night, too, for her dad.

We did it, we really did it! Enid thought. *We had more problems than any ten campaigns and we still pulled it off.* She felt so much vindication. She had never stopped believing in herself, or in Joe either. She felt they had both been unfairly maligned, both by people close to them and by people who didn't know them at all. Even tonight, they had been maligned. Merrill Cook had actually called Joe "A Nazi" on camera. But that hadn't spoiled the night. Nothing had. Nothing could. They had survived it all. They had survived the problems with Joe's mother, and the problems with the frozen trust. Survived them and then some. For the past couple of months, in fact, money had been no hassle at all. The money for Enid's campaign was easily accessible, now that her dad had been assigned the sales proceeds of the real estate in Pittsburgh. Joe hadn't had to bother Enid about anything since that transaction. Money was no problem. It was amazing how much everything had calmed down. Joe had quit threatening suicide. He had become confident again. Everything had just taken off. The tide had turned.

And now, the Waldholtzes were going to Washington.

They fell into bed that night exhausted. Enid couldn't remember ever being more tired, or enjoying it more.

The next morning, after Enid did more interviews over the phone, Joe approached his wife with a victory gift. He'd wanted to give her this memento last night, he said, but his superstitions wouldn't let him. He didn't want to jinx anything.

She looked inside the jewelry box and saw a pearl pin, set in gold, and shaped in the form of an elephant.

The perfect gift for a Republican congresswoman. The perfect gift from the perfect husband.

CHAPTER VI

Newton LeRoy "Newt" Gingrich walked purposefully toward the table of the new congresswoman, as if every eye in the room was on him.

These days, Newt Gingrich walked with a purpose everywhere. For the past two weeks, ever since the Republicans had wrested control of the House of Representatives, wherever he went, a spotlight went with him. He was on all the news programs and all the talk shows. The press was ever-present. Overnight, the life of this congressional lifer was turning into an open book. Almost literally. He was negotiating a book deal with a New York publisher calling for an advance in seven figures. Newt Gingrich, Georgia congressman, was a man in demand.

That was outside Washington. Inside Washington, it was even more intense. As the new Speaker of the House, Newt had benefits to confer and gifts to pass out. His breast pocket was filled with assignments for the nineteen different House committees that were now, suddenly, in the domain of the Republicans. Where there were two seats on a nine-seat committee in the past, for example, now there were five. Life in the majority. In a democratic government, there is nothing like it. Newt and Dick Armey, the Texas Republican who had become the House's Majority Leader, the new second in command, were making friends fast and fast friends.

Enid Waldholtz, the newly-elected Republican congresswoman from Utah, rose as the Speaker approached. She didn't know whether to call him Mr. Speaker, Mr. Gingrich, or to just simply genuflect. But when he said, "Hi Enid," she said, "Hello Newt."

"How are you?"

"I'm fine. How are *you?*"

"Great," said the Speaker as he subtly turned Enid away from her table so that what he had to say would be heard in private.

"This is not an offer. I'm just thinking out loud, but I'm wondering how you'd feel about working on Rules."

"I know you're newly married," the Speaker went on, not giving Enid a chance to reply before adding, "and Rules requires a lot of extra hours. You're at the Capitol late many nights. I wanted to throw this by you so you could toss the idea around with your husband. You know, get his reaction . . . Think about it, OK?"

Enid Waldholtz was stunned. *A freshman on the Rules Committee*? They didn't put freshmen on Rules. There hadn't been a Republican freshman on Rules in 80 years. There hadn't *ever* been a freshman woman on Rules.

Would I be interested? Newt Gingrich wanted to know if I'd be interested in working on Rules!?

She looked around the room for her husband. They were in Statuary Hall, adjacent to the Rotunda, deep within the corridors of power in the United States Capitol. They were the Republican freshman class of the 104th Congress, comprising seventy-three men and women who would take office in less than six weeks, and they had just been treated to a candlelight dinner. During dinner, Enid and Joe had sat at a table with, among others, Bob Michel, the outgoing minority leader. Newt, whom Enid had met when he helped her campaign in Utah, was at the next table. All during dinner Enid got the impression he was staring at her. *Like I'm some new species of beetle,* she thought. But then, after dinner, he surprised her with the little teaser about the Rules Committee.

She located Joe and hurried over to him.

"Joe, you won't believe what just happened," she said.

"Newt just asked me if I wanted to be on Rules!" She rushed on, not waiting for a reply. "And I'm supposed to ask if it's OK with you!"

Joe Waldholtz's face lit up. "That's wonderful!" he exulted, his expression confirming what Enid already knew. She didn't have to ask if it was OK, not with this husband. This wouldn't interfere with their home life. It would enhance it.

The candlelight dinner in Statuary Hall kicked off nearly three weeks of orientation for the United States House of Representatives' first-timers. The one thing they all had in common were victories two weeks previous in the nationwide general election. Of the eighty-six in the Class of '94, an overwhelming majority of seventy-three were Republicans. Added to the one hundred fifty-seven Republicans who had succeeded in winning re-election, that meant the Grand Old Party had gained majority control of the House: 230 Republican seats to 204 for the Democrats (with one Independent). It had been awhile. The last Republican majority had been in 1954. Even when a Republican was in the White House–Richard Nixon, Gerald Ford, Ronald Reagan, George Bush–the House of Representatives had steadfastly remained in the clutches of the Democrats. But now, that had all changed. Now, it was the Republicans who had their shot at running things; and, with the spirit of a bench-warmer finally getting to start the game, they were determined to make the most of it. "Newt's Warriors" weren't about to take the opportunity lightly.

Such was the atmosphere during freshman orientation, where the nuances of the House were explained to the newcomers. Enid, one of seven women in the group, by no means owned the only comeback success story of the group. She was surrounded by them. Giant-killers, the press called them. There was George Nethercutt from Washington state, who defeated no less than the sitting Speaker of the House, Tom Foley. There was Michael Patrick Flanagan from Chicago; he'd defeated the veteran Dan Rostenkowski. There was Stephen Stockman from Texas, who had taken on Jack Brooks, the head of the Judiciary Committee, and knocked him off. There was Frank Riggs from California; he won in '90, lost to a Democrat in '92, and had come back to reclaim his seat in '94. And there was Jon Fox from Pennsylvania, who, like Enid, had lost in his initial try for the House in '92 but had come back to triumph in '94, defeating Marjorie Margolies-Mezvinsky, whose "yea" a year ago had been the deciding vote for the Clinton tax increase. Knocking off Mezvinsky had been particularly sweet for the Republicans.

Everywhere, there was the fresh look that comes with a fresh start. There was 29-year-old Randy Tate from Washington State. There was Steve Largent, the ex-football star, from Oklahoma. And there was California's Sonny Bono, the former flower child, former husband to Cher, and now a soldier in the Republican Army. Next to Newt, Bono was trailed by the most television cameras.

They were all huddled together during orientation, housed at the Hyatt Hotel that sits at the foot of Capitol Hill, a small army of politicians on temporary hold just a block from their final destination. All they had to do was wait until the people currently occupying their seats vacated the building.

Even if she wasn't yet official, Enid, like most of the others, already had her game plan in place, and it began with getting the best committee assignment available–and plenty *were* available.

Almost a month previous, she'd started sizing up the lay of the new Congress. The day after the election she drove to Farmington, Utah, and met with Jim Hansen, flush with victory himself in the wake of winning his fifth consecutive race as Utah's Representative from the first district. They talked at Hansen's cabin in the foothills. Enid asked Hansen's advice about what committees she should try for. The first thing Hansen said was, "They don't put freshmen on Rules," so they ruled that out immediately. The Rules Committee–a thirteen member group that examines every potential rule before it gets approval to go to the floor of the House–rarely drafts first-timers, partly because it requires a solid working knowledge of the House's regulations and procedure, but mostly because it is one of the most powerful of the committees and is traditionally filled by representatives with a great deal of seniority. It is the Rules Committee, typically made up of nine members of the majority party and four members from the minority party, that decides what does and doesn't make it to the floor of the House, and, once it's there, how much time a bill will be debated; and it is Rules, unlike all the other committees–which come under the province of the Committee on Committees–that falls under the personal jurisdiction of the Speaker.

The Rules Committee is one of four House committees termed "exclusive," meaning if you're on one of them, you can't be on any of the others. Of these big four–Rules, Ways and Means, Energy & Commerce, and Appropriations–Enid and Hansen decided her best shot was at Appropriations. There hadn't been a Utahn on Appropriations in so long no one could remember if there had *ever* been one. With all the new seats available to Republicans, now might be the time. And in its own way, Appropriations is as powerful as Rules. The Appropriations Committee authorizes expenditures set up by the budget. It controls the purse strings of Congress. If you don't get a check cut by Appropriations, you don't get one.

Even before the formal orientation period, Enid was busy setting up her own groundwork, doing her own orienting, as it were. Less than seventy-two hours after the November election, she and Joe caught a flight to Washington, D.C., where they milled around the House side of the Capitol and she introduced herself to as many of the new conservative power elite as she could. She met Armey for the first time, and John Boehner, the House Republican Conference Chair from Ohio; and Bob Livingston from Louisiana, whom Newt had already appointed as the new chairman of the Appropriations Committee, an appointment that had shaken things up early, since Livingston had been chosen over several Republicans with more seniority. Enid let it be known that she was available for any and all assignments, and that Appropriations was something she was particularly interested in. The news got around, although one longtime representative got it slightly turned around. He thought Enid wanted to be on the Agriculture Committee. Knowing she represented the most urban district of Utah, when he saw her in the hall one day he asked her about that and she corrected him. *Appropriations, not Agricul-*

ture. As he was leaving, he asked, "Just what crops do they grow in Salt Lake?"

"Children," said Enid, and the lawmaker laughed and laughed. The rookie from Utah was making her mark. She was making it quickly.

On that same mid-November trip, she and Joe looked around the greater D.C. area for a place to live. A friend of a friend knew a realtor who agreed to show the Congresswoman and her husband around. As ordered, the realtor set a blistering pace as she attempted to show them in a short amount of time a quick sampling of what was available. As with all members of Congress, the Utahns explained that they would be going back and forth between "home," so they were looking for a place reasonably near the airport, reasonably close to the Hill, in a reasonably safe neighborhood, and nice. The realtor had heard the rundown before. That's what they all wanted. Usually the new ones would look around a little and then settle in Arlington, Virginia, just across the Potomac River from the District of Columbia, or they would settle in The District itself. If they got re-elected they would sprawl out later; airport proximity tended to become less and less important the longer your tenure and the more advanced your case of Potomac Fever.

What the realtor hadn't heard all that often was the exchange between *this* member of Congress and her spouse.

"How much do you want to spend?" she asked her husband.

"Oh Enid," he said impatiently, "you know it doesn't matter."

They first looked across the river in Virginia, where the schools are good and the trees are everywhere. Somewhere beyond McLean they cruised around a two-acre estate with a huge house, a pool, and tennis court. For $2 million, Joe was tempted to buy on the spot. But they talked about it and pulled in their reins and returned to reality. Maybe they *could* afford it. You didn't have to scrimp when Joe's monthly draw from the family trust was slightly more than $25,000 a month, but that wasn't the point. The point was they weren't coming back here to replicate Mount Vernon or to live like the Jeffersons. They were coming to Washington to work. Enid hoped to land a spot on one of the four major committees, and that could mean long hours and late nights, and regardless, her top priority–*their* top priority–was The Job. She didn't need a forty five-minute commute even if a mansion was waiting at the end of the ride. She needed something close and handy, and *rented.*

"If we get past the re-elect, then maybe we'll think about buying," she said to her husband.

That's when the realtor turned back to the east and drove across Key Bridge, leading them into Georgetown, home to kings, presidents, embassies and Elizabeth Taylor. This was close, this was convenient, and this was reasonably safe. It just wasn't cheap.

They saw a place in Foxhall, slightly beyond Georgetown proper, just east of the Georgetown University campus, that Joe liked. It had an elevator and a big stone fireplace and a lot of size. But it struck Enid as cold, so they looked on. Then, on their last stop before going to the airport they walked through a townhouse in the heart of Georgetown that the brochure said was once "the residence of Henry Kissinger." It was large for a townhouse, over 3,000 square feet on five levels, with a small walled-in courtyard off the lowest level, and, significant for an area with a dearth of such a luxury, it had a one-car garage.

"This could work," Enid said, sizing up the possibilities. It had three bedrooms, meaning if and/or when they had a baby there would be room for both the baby and the nanny they would need to hire to care for the baby. It had a safe outside play area–another baby plus. The garage meant they wouldn't have to park on the street. Barring traffic problems, it was fifteen minutes from the Capitol and fifteen minutes from the airport, tops. True, the neighbors were right on top of you, but this, after all, was the East. In Utah they would have called it a box. In Washington they called it a townhouse and charged thirty-eight hundred dollars rent–a month.

And it had been good enough for Kissinger.

"I think we'll take it," said Enid, ending any thoughts Joe might have had of the Foxhall place.

After flying home to Utah, she called the agent and they agreed to a two year lease. The house Kissinger once lived in—they'd be living there too.

□□□

Once their shopping spree in Washington was behind them, Enid and Joe stopped in Salt Lake only long enough to pack their beach clothes. Then they were off to Hawaii.

They had been going nonstop for almost a year, and prior to launching into what assuredly would be more of the same, they elected to return to Maui, the scene of their honeymoon, for a rest before the renewal of their relentless pace. They rented a suite, stayed a pampered week, ordered rich food, made daily excursions to the hotel spa, where Joe tried a new scrub or massage every day. Enid may have been in charge of house selection, but Joe remained in command of picking the hotel, and spending their money. Enid would have preferred another stay at the Four Seasons, where they spent their honeymoon. Not only was it a fabulous five-star resort, but she saw something poetic and symmetrical–as well as sentimental–about returning to the same pool and private beach where, just a little over a year ago, she had been able to draw a breath deep and clear enough that she had decided to run for office again. The therapy provided by the Four Seasons and a terrific marriage: that was the unbeatable combination that brought her back.

Joe gave thumbs down to the Four Seasons, however, saying he preferred trying someplace new. Enid thought it curious that Joe, who was ordinarily given to sentiment, would want to switch, but she let the thought pass. Joe's "someplace new" turned out to be the Grand Wailea, next door to the Four Seasons. *Close enough,* Enid thought. The views and setting were virtually identical. And the Grand Wailea's spa, it turned out, was even better.

□□□

When freshman orientation began the first part of December, it was a tanned and relaxed Enid Waldholtz who learned the do's and don'ts of Congress. She learned about the Rules of Order, about the various traditions, about the process of governing.

And she learned that she indeed would be serving on Rules.

The morning after bringing up the "possibility" at the Statuary Hall dinner, Newt Gingrich saw Enid in the hallway.

"Still want to be on Rules?" he said almost in passing, posing a question that was tantamount to asking an actor, "Still want to play Hamlet?"

"Absolutely," said Enid.

"Good, we're announcing it at noon," said the new ruler of the House. He was obviously taking to his role very quickly.

Just like that! thought Enid. *Two months ago they were saying I was unelectable and now I'm a majority member of one of the most powerful committees in the United States House of Representatives.*

She was a quick study at orientation, so quick that the process got a little tedious, and then, to make it longer yet, they threw in an overnight trip to Baltimore to please the Heritage Foundation. Membership has its privileges, but it has its obligations as well. Finally they got around to the logistics of the office, which meant actually choosing a physical office. There are three office buildings that flank the south side–the House side–of the United States Capitol and comprise the headquarters of the members of the House and their staffs. They include the Rayburn, Longworth and Cannon Buildings, each named after House Speakers of days gone by and each maintained by the taxpayers of the United States of America. And while you can lobby for committee assignments and other perquisites, the assigning of offices is strictly on a seniority basis. It doesn't matter how tight you are with the Speaker. The longer in office, the higher the pick. New members draw for those offices left over.

Enid was close to last to choose her office location. She wound up on the fifth floor of the Cannon Building, a.k.a. "The Penthouse." And while it's true that the fifth floor is indeed the top floor of the Cannon Building, it's also true that most of the elevators only go to four.

Enid was joined on the penthouse level by others of the 104th freshman class. Around the corner was California's Sonny Bono, next to her was Tom Latham of Iowa. Newcomers all of them, newcomers looking forward to a long Washington future–and lower floors.

Just before the end of freshman orientation and a trip to Utah for the holidays, while riding in the elevator, an aide from one of the lower offices offhandedly asked an Enid staffer what office Congresswoman Waldholtz had received. When the staffer answered, "515 Cannon," the aide, a Hill "lifer," smiled. "That's where John Kennedy started out," she was told.

So she'd leased Kissinger's house and moved into Kennedy's office . . . she was ready to govern.

□□□

Despite its inconvenient location, the fifth floor office of Utah Congresswoman Enid G. Waldholtz proved to be no problem for the employees of Ridgewell, one of Washington's finest and most exclusive caterers. The waiters expertly carried their trays of smoked salmon and stuffed artichoke hearts to room No. 515. It was January 4, 1995, swearing-in day for the 104th Congress, and one's wife only gets sworn in once every two years, that was Joe Waldholtz's attitude. He had called Ridgewell's and ordered their top-of-the-line service with generous quantities and a promise of generous tips.

Enid and Joe had offered to pay the way for any members of their respective families who wished to come to Washington for the swearing-in ceremony, held at noon in the Capitol rotunda. Most of them took them up on it, staying at rooms in the downtown J. W. Marriott Hotel, where Joe set up a tab. The relatives were thrilled, the ceremony was flawless–and so was the food by Ridgwell's.

The office reception, which immediately followed the swearing-in ceremony, was open to family, friends, constituents from Utah, neighboring office staffs, and anyone else who happened to wander in. These traditional "first day" parties were being held in virtually every other congressional office in the Cannon, Rayburn and Longworth buildings, although, in most cases, with considerably less opulence than in the Waldholtz office.

It certainly created a grander mood than two days before, when Enid and Joe had flown to Washington from Salt Lake City fully expecting to spend their first night in their Georgetown townhouse–only to discover the furnace wasn't working. It was nearly midnight when they turned the key in the door that would usher them into the Washington phase of their lives. But as soon as they realized–and this didn't take long–that it was actually colder *inside* the house, they were back in their car. They drove to the end of 34th Street, checked into the Georgetown Holiday Inn, and, although deservedly indignant, laughed yet again about that little black cloud that *wouldn't leave them alone.*

The next day they called the landlord to complain. They were paying roughly a hundred and twenty-five dollars a night for the townhouse–and that was *before* you figured in utilities–and they thought that ought to include a working furnace. By the next afternoon, the furnace was fixed.

□□□

Unlike most of the one hundred and three Congresses that preceded it, the 104th Congress allowed, oh, maybe thirty-five minutes for lunch.

Whereas swearing-in day had traditionally been a day for pomp, ceremony, and catered finger food, now it was a day to, as Newt put it, "Make a statement." The Republicans were bound and determined to hit the road running–to demonstrate their seriousness at righting forty years of Democratic wrongs. Newt scheduled more than a dozen votes for the first day, all of them after the noon swearing-in ceremony. As a consequence, Enid was more of a passerby than a participant in her office party. She would trot over from the Capitol, manage a quick hello, agree that, yes, it *was* a magnificent ceremony, and then trot back over to the floor for another debate or vote.

The Hundred Days had begun.

The idea behind the Hundred Days was to send a loud, clear statement to Americans that now that the Republicans were in control, they intended to get something done! They fully intended to complete their Contract with America. The strategy behind both the well-publicized Hundred Days and the accompanying Contract With America was to produce a dizzying amount of reform legislation *and* an image of hard-working, dedicated public servants.

Amid much fanfare, and under the gaze of network cameras, the Contract had been revealed to the public in a ceremony on the west front steps of the U.S. Capitol a little over three months previous, when, on Sept. 27, 1994, 367 Republican candidates for Congress assembled together. Four by four, these Republicans–a mixture of current Representatives and others, like Enid, hoping to be elected–walked up the Capitol steps and took turns signing the Contract. The performance received considerable air play all across America. In Utah, the footage centered on candidate Enid Waldholtz putting her name on the line.

In their Contract With America, the Republicans outlined a "blueprint for action" should they assume a majority position in the House after the November elections.

In summary, the Contract pledged to "restore the bonds of trust between the people and their elected representatives" by bringing about sweeping changes in policy. On the first day of the 104th Congress alone, the new Republican majority pledged to pass eight "major reforms," ranging from hiring an independent auditing firm to search for waste, fraud and abuse in the Congress to requiring committee meetings to be open to the public. During the first Hundred Days of the 104th Congress, the Contract further pledged to bring a number of hard-hitting bills to the floor of the House, bills that included an aggressive anti-crime package, a balanced budget amendment, and term limits on politicians.

On Nov. 4, 1994, Election Day, the American people, by and large, bought it.

On Jan. 4, 1994, the Republican Congress set out to do what it had promised.

In the 208-year history of the House of Representatives, there had never been a first day quite like it; or a first *Hundred Days*, either. And as the Republicans were soon to discover, as with jumping off a bridge, once they got started, even if they wanted to, there was no turning back.

□□□

Between the fourth of January and the fourteenth of April, nineteen hundred and ninety five–exactly one hundred calendar days–Congress, as promised, kept emergency room hours. The mood fluctuated between frenzied and panicked. It had been since 1954 that any Republican had been involved with House leadership, which meant that exactly none of the current Republicans suddenly sitting in power had any experience with what they were doing. Then there were the Democrats, who were neither happy about turning up the pace on the treadmill nor reluctant to drag their feet every chance they got on the passage of any Republican-generated bills. The end result: nothing went as smoothly or as quickly as the Republicans would have preferred, adding hours to every day and frustrations to every hour. Some days did not end. There were times during those Hundred Days when a session would begin at ten in the morning and end at ten the next morning. And then they would start all over again.

The members of the Rules Committee, especially, were constantly in motion. Newt was right about those extra hours. Since Rules meetings sometimes convene only after the day's business had been completed–so they could have everything ready for another round in the morning–the committee meetings often didn't begin until it was nearing, or well after, midnight. The pace was close to nonstop.

And Enid Waldholtz loved every minute of it.

She loved her new life. She was perfectly content to stay late. She was happy to throw herself into her work. She read every bill before it came to a vote. She made every vote. She studied the rules of parliamentary procedure. She enjoyed just walking through the Capitol. She soaked in the history that surrounded her. When the buzzer went off throughout the Hill, announcing a vote, and traffic cops literally stopped traffic at all the intersections surrounding the Capitol so the Members could get to the floor, it sent a thrill through her. She was one of them. A Member. She *belonged.*

She loved it even more when she discovered she was pregnant.

□□□

They were nearly a third of the way through the Hundred Days when she knew for certain. She took the home pregnancy test twice, just to make sure, and twice it turned pink, for pregnant. Her first clue had come a couple of days before, when she and Joe had been in Utah. They'd been out with a realtor, looking at houses near downtown Salt Lake City. Joe was on a crusade to sell the Benecia Drive house and move into a bigger house closer to the airport. While they were riding in the car Enid felt an unfamiliar queasiness in her stomach. She whispered to Joe that she thought she might be pregnant, but he recommended they wait until they returned to Washington to buy the home pregnancy test. "Somebody would see you buying it here and then it would be all over the news," he said. "They watch everything we do."

So she waited, and as soon as they touched down in Washington she went to the Safeway up the street and bought the kits.

Enid was as excited by the news as Joe was frightened. He was visibly unsettled. When Enid asked him, "What's the matter?" he said it was just that he had a hard time picturing himself as a father; and picturing them both as parents. It wasn't exactly the reaction she had hoped for, but Enid didn't push it. She was content to let her husband ease into the reality of it all. They had agreed it was time to start their family. For her, it was everything she wanted. She could not have been more thrilled.

They had been trying to have a baby for the past couple of months. Enid had acceded to Joe's request for a year's "transition" into their marriage, and ever since the year was up she had abandoned all precautions, hoping nature would take its course. She was thirty-six years old and that number was not going down–she couldn't pass legislation to change that.

She had hoped, in her best case scenario, to be pregnant in time for the baby to arrive in August, while Congress observed its traditional recess. Her due date missed that, but only just. The doctor said the baby should arrive some time during the third week of September. Conception had occurred around Christmas.

To keep the news out of the press, Enid and Joe agreed that they wouldn't tell anyone, with the exception of their parents, until she had at least gotten past her first trimester, a date that would roughly coincide with Easter break and the end of the Hundred Days. Enid became particularly adept at camouflaging morning sickness. During the crisp Washington winter mornings, while Joe drove up Independence Avenue toward the Hill, she would hang her head out the passenger window, gulping in great volumes of twenty-five-degree air. By the time she arrived at her office, she appeared fresh and ready to go–around the clock if need be.

□□□

Joe Waldholtz didn't just have money; he knew how to spend it. He wasn't just rich, he had rich tastes. His closet was lined with ties by Hermés, shoes by Ferragamo, and dozens of expensive suits. If he wasn't wearing his Rolex watch he was wearing the Baume & Mercier, or, if he were dressing down that day, maybe the Tag Heuer. He wore designer socks, solid gold cuff links, sometimes dotted with rubies; he slept on satin sheets, thought nothing of pouring Perrier into the dogs' water bowl, thought even less than that of phoning up La Caille while in Salt Lake, or maybe Bistro Francais of Georgetown, for takeout, and would use his cellular phone even if he were standing ten feet from a regular phone. A consumer of the highest order. A friend to retail. A man who never asked, "How much?"

His art tastes were particularly refined, and when his wife won the appointment as the Representative from Utah's second Congressional district, Joe knew just how he wanted to show off that refinement.

Within weeks after they landed in Washington, Joe's brainstorm was hanging all over the walls.

"I want to showcase Utah artists for the nation," Joe had told Enid. "We can hang their work both in your offices and at the townhouse, and people can gain an appreciation for western art."

Enid's response, if not quite matching her husband's enthusiasm, was, "Why not?" The art was beautiful, and, as Joe explained further, with time, good art only increased in value.

In concert with an art dealer he befriended in Salt Lake City named Clayton Williams, Joe soon accumulated a sizeable collection of Western art. By the time he and Enid arrived in Washington the collection numbered well over two dozen pieces, including several Kent Wallis's, LeConte Stewart's, Maynard Dixon's, with the odd Alvin Gittins, Larry Wade and Richard Murray thrown in. There were also some renderings by Williams, himself a professional painter, one of which went up behind the bed in the master bedroom of the Georgetown house. It was entitled "Rural White House."

Williams had opened a gallery in Salt Lake City–Williams Fine Art–after his retirement; and he became Joe's pipeline to the Western art world. When a new shipment would arrive at the gallery, Williams would phone Joe. They kept each other happy, and in business.

The crown jewel in Joe's collection was an oil entitled "Fishing in Yellowstone Lake" by Albert Bierstadt, which Joe hung in the dining room of the Georgetown house. Bidding on Joe's behalf, Williams had picked it up at a hospital charity auction for $36,000. When he gave it to Joe he told him it was worth twice that. One of the Maynard Dixons was worth $20,000, another was valued at twice that. The rest of the pieces ranged in value from a thousand to ten thousand dollars. In all, the Joe Waldholtzes had over $200,000 worth of Western art to showcase in Washington.

And showcase it they did. In Enid's outer office in the Cannon Building, Joe opted for a LeConte Stewart, a Jim Norton that featured a cowboy herding cows across a stream, and the $40,000 Dixon entitled "Washoe Wickiyup." In Enid's own office he made a statement by hanging a huge Michael Coleman oil of a Rocky Mountain peak, along with a farm scene by an M. Savitsky, and one of the Wallis pieces.

It wasn't the National Gallery, but by contrast it was. The wall decor in the Utah Congresswoman's office contrasted markedly to the wall decor in the offices of her colleagues that surrounded her. Next door, in Tom Latham's office, there was an erasable greaseboard that said "Congressman Tom Latham welcomes you to Washington, D.C.," followed by a huge fifteen-figure number announcing the Public Debt as of that very day. On the other side, in the offices of Rodney Frelinghuysen of New Jersey, there were two pictures of Abraham Lincoln and a caricature of an Eagle carrying the stars and stripes. Two doors down from that, in room 512, Representative Sonny Bono of California's office decor featured a poster from the Southwest Arts Festival in Indio in 1989 and a U.S. Geological Survey of the 44th Congressional District, California. Farther down the hall, Representative Mark Souder of Indiana's office greeted visitors with a poster from *Rudy,* the movie. In the race for most elegantly decorated congressional office, the Waldholtz office faced no real competition.

For Enid Greene Waldholtz, who had grown up under the frugality of Dunford Forrest Greene, Joe's spending habits seemed at first outrageous, but over time they moved into the realm of amusing and finally became standard operating procedure. Enid was not the kind of spender Joe was, but she was proving to be a fast learner. To Joe, spending came as easily as breathing, and not just on himself. As often as not, he was spending his money on someone else, his wife being exhibit A. If she needed it, she got it. If she didn't need it, she also got it. One day, during the height of the '94 campaign, she walked outside the campaign office and Joe tossed her a set of car keys. He motioned toward a new Jeep Cherokee Limited in the parking lot. "It's yours," he said. It was essentially like her old car, also a Cherokee, but with more options, nicer wheels, and about 90,000 less miles. Joe hadn't traded in the old Cherokee, either, he'd tossed those keys to Aaron Edens, one of the staffers on the campaign. Just gave him the car.

Enid saw him extend such charitable gestures on a regular basis. In 1993 there had been a big news story in Utah when a deranged young man named Cody Judy had attacked Howard W. Hunter, the president of the Mormon Church's quorum of the Twelve Apostles, while he was speaking at Brigham Young University. A number of students sitting nearby jumped onto the stage to the Mormon leader's aid. One of them was a student from Pittsburgh named Greg Hughes who had worked with Joe during a previous campaign in Pittsburgh and had lived briefly in the basement at Penrose Drive during Enid's '92 campaign. In the ensuing scuffle, Hughes broke his hand. When Joe discovered Greg didn't have medical insurance, he wrote out a check and paid for every cent of Greg's medical bills himself.

It was nothing, Enid knew, for Joe to see a transient on the street and quietly slip him a twenty. Once, when Joe learned the wife of a friend couldn't accompany her daughter on a school choir trip to Italy, he bought the airplane ticket for her.

Joe spent money when he didn't have to, Enid knew that too. He showered it on himself–during his legendary "tie runs" he would buy a dozen ties at a time; drop a thousand dollars, easy, without even thinking–and he showered it on people he liked. He was always doing something for Guy Ciarrocci, his best friend. Guy's father had died when Guy was sixteen and Joe told Enid that on his death bed Guy's dad asked Joe to "take care of Guy when I'm gone." Not only did Joe personally bankroll Guy's campaign to win the election for state chairman of the Pennsylvania Young Republicans, but Enid often heard Joe on the phone talking to Guy's mother–cheering her up. And when he wasn't doing that he was buying funny cards and sending them to her in the mail. *That's the Joe I fell in love with,* Enid would remind herself.

The kind of person who even takes time for his friend's mother!

He wasn't a Mormon. But he was an Episcopalian, and, while hardly a regular attender, still essentially loyal to his faith. Several times Joe and Enid attended Episcopal services in Salt Lake City, where Joe would coach Enid when to stand up and sit down and otherwise make it comfortably enough through the services that it looked as if she belonged. Peter Eaton, the assistant rector, adored Joe; particularly when he would write a check to pay for the flowers for next week's service.

He showered things on his wife more than any of them. As Mrs. Joe Waldholtz she quickly accumulated a jewelry collection sizeable enough to make you realize why rich people carry insurance. She had dozens of bracelets, watches, rings, necklaces, earrings, strands of pearls, and pendants in one form or another, and the collection was ever expanding. Her wedding ring was valued at $22,500, she had a watch that cost $25,000, a Cartiér watch valued at $3,700 and a Breitling watch that went for a mere $1,750. She had two strands of cultured pearls worth close to $15,000. Each. She had a Fabergé egg pendant worth $2,500. She had earrings she could have traded straight across for a new Jeep. She had emeralds, sapphires, pearls, rubies, gold, silver, beryl and diamonds. All this, and she'd known Joe for less than four years. Imagine where the collection would be in forty years!

And she didn't buy a single piece of jewelry herself! Over the years, one by one, step by step, Joe brought them home and they found their way into her jewelry box. It was that way with her wardrobe, too. In Washington, Joe became such good friends with the buyer at the Neiman Marcus store in nearby Chevy Chase that the buyer would call him whenever a new shipment of dresses came in. He would ask the buyer to set aside anything she thought Enid would like, and when they got a free minute, he would herd Enid down to the store, where he would sit in a chair and encourage her to buy *everything*.

It would be one thing, Enid would often think to herself, *if he were running us into the poorhouse. But it's his money, and if this is how he wants to spend it.*

The only guilt Enid could admit to was feeling like she was dominating their married life. It was always *her* career, *her* pregnancy, *her* staff, *her* schedule. Joe had put a promising political career of his own on hold for hers, and that gave her some pause. She wanted him to be content too. She wanted it to be *his* money. She was glad he had it. She didn't want to hassle him unduly about how he spent or managed it.

She made other accommodations in their relationship where she could, all in the name of striving to keep a balance. Even though she discovered she was allergic to boxer puppies, for instance, she let Winston sleep with them in their bed–at least she did until the rash got too bad. And she tried not to nag. If Joe wanted to do something a certain way, even if she disagreed with it, she was determined to let him.

He wanted to handle their bills, for example. At first that was foreign to Enid. She'd been single the first thirty-five years of her life. She was accustomed to handling her own bills. But Joe insisted and she yielded. He also liked to handle the mail. He would sort through it and parcel out to Enid what was hers. He was like that with the telephone answering machine too. Which was fine with Enid. As much as Joe loved the telephone, she didn't.

But mostly, she tried to bite her tongue and not to nag when Joe spent money unnecessarily. His family had a huge trust, with a staff of trustees overseeing the money, and she wanted him to know that she understood that was his domain. The wealth as well as the hassles all that wealth sometimes created. When he would come home and say, "I want to buy this Kent Wallis for twenty thousand and the trustees said OK," she would let it go at that.

He could be eccentric. In their Georgetown townhouse, just after the Hundred Days, Joe was calling remodelers to give it a once-over. He ordered new wiring, a fresh coat of paint in several of the rooms, new carpet, and he upgraded the security system and the intercom.

"Joe, we're *renting* this place," Enid had said in the beginning. "You don't do this to a place you don't own."

"We might buy it," Joe had answered, non-plussed, and after reconsidering her outburst Enid let it go. *If his family has lots of money and this is how he wants to spend it, OK by me*, she would think. *If it makes him happy to have freshly painted walls and recessed lighting, that's fine.*

The only thing they couldn't buy, it seemed, was time. They never seemed to have enough of it. But even in that regard, the money helped. When the Hundred Days and the pregnancy and the weekend trips to Utah effectively froze her out of the normal operating hours for furniture stores in Washington, Enid simply stopped by *Crawford and Day*, a high-end furniture store in Salt Lake where she and Joe had bought the furniture for their Benecia house. She gave the designers the measurements for the rooms in Georgetown, pointed to a variety of couches, love seats, lamps and end tables she liked, and asked them to ship it across the country to 34th and Reservoir Streets, Georgetown. Surely and not so slowly, she was getting the hang of her new lifestyle.

□□□

More than that, she was getting the hang of her new job. In truth, Capitol Hill was her home. She would pass through the Georgetown townhouse after dark and leave early the next morning; the house in Salt Lake saw her less than that. Most of the time she was in office, literally. She was proving to be a quick study, a Congresswoman Who Was Noticed. For a first-termer, especially, she was cutting a noticeable swath. First Republican freshman on Rules in eighty years. First woman freshman *ever* to sit in the Speaker's chair and conduct Congress (she performed that task one day in the late spring when Newt was out of town). *Congressional Quarterly* called her a "Freshman to Watch." Her pregnancy got her added attention. She was a guest on MacNeil/Lehrer; on CNN's *Crossfire Sunday*, she debated longtime Democrat Congresswoman Pat Schroeder about, among other things, prayer in schools and The Contract; and on CNBC's *Donahue & Pozner*, Phil Donahue and Vladimir Pozner politely asked for her comments on welfare and, before taking a call from Muncie,

Indiana, made jokes about the days on the bed being numbered for Winston, the Waldholtz's boxer dog. "He'll be losing his benefits when the baby comes," said Pozner. "I don't know about that," said Enid. "But he will have to get off the bed." Bantering on national television with well-known commentators. All heady stuff for a freshman member of Congress.

Not only was she doing her part on the Contract With America, but she was making headway in other directions. She put together an amendment with Matt Salmon from Arizona for a welfare bill designed to make it easier to enforce child support across state lines. On her own she introduced a gift ban bill. The legislation, officially H. Res. 134, called for "severe restrictions on the ability of Members of Congress to accept gifts, meals or trips from lobbyists."

"While the majority of my colleagues hold themselves to high ethical standards, imposing strict guidelines will do away with even the appearance of impropriety and help restore public confidence in Congress," Enid said in her press release of May 9, 1995 that announced H. Res. 134. She was quickly turning herself into the conscience of the House. Earlier she had served public notice that she would not accept her congressional pension, she would personally pay for the entire cost of her health care plan, she wouldn't use the Congressional franking (free mailing) privilege except to answer direct inquiries from constituents, and she would only accept a salary of $89,000, the amount of the salary paid to House members in 1989 prior to Congress authorizing its own inflation-adjusted regular pay increases. By 1995, those cost-of-living raises had elevated congressional pay to $133,600 annually. Enid promised to donate the extra $44,600 to charity. She wouldn't accept full salary, she promised, until the budget was balanced.

And if all that wasn't enough to grind the teeth of other members of Congress–at least those without a trust-fund spouse–she also pledged that she would cut her staff's allowable operating budget of about $900,000 by twenty-five percent.

Whatever she was doing, it seemed to be working. Maybe she hadn't ever been Utah's favorite politician, but back here they *liked her.* Jerry Solomon, the Chairman of the Rules Committee, would routinely seek her out for counsel. Newt Gingrich would do likewise. When her pregnancy advanced to the point that it was getting more and more difficult to make the ten-minute trek from her office to the floor for meetings and votes, Newt came to Enid's rescue. There was a small, windowless cubbyhole of a room deep in the bowels of the Capitol that had long been used by Tom Foley, the former Speaker, for solitude and to listen to music. Newt had some spare furniture moved in–a couch, a refrigerator, a small desk for a telephone, and a television tuned to C-Span–and presented the door key to Enid. Now she had her own Capitol retreat, and wouldn't have to walk so far to vote.

Anyone who doubted the relationship between power and popularity need only look at Enid to be convinced.

People were always doing nice things for her. In mid June, her pregnancy quickly nearing the end of its second trimester, she was summoned to what she was told was "an emergency meeting of Republican women in the Speaker's office." But when she walked in she found herself the guest of honor at a surprise baby shower hosted by Congresswoman Susan Molinari of New York. There were refreshments, gifts, balloons, and blue and pink ribbons draped all around Newt's office, spilling over and around the wall-sized oil painting of George Washington and the full-scale Tyrannosaurus Rex skull that sits as the room's centerpiece. Toys for the baby-to-be included a "stick elephant" and a t-shirt that said "Future President." A poster-sized "guest list" on the wall that read "Love, Your Aunts and Uncle" was signed by Enid's fellow Congresswomen and also, at the bottom, by "Uncle Newt" himself.

□□□

Not that life inside room 515 of the Cannon Building was a constant sea of tranquility. With the blistering Hundred Day pace and a rookie congressional staff to break in–let alone a rookie congresswoman who happened to be pregnant–there was plenty of chaos, with dissension thrown in for good measure. The adversarial relationships that had been an Enid staple during her campaign wound up surviving the journey to Washington just fine.

Enid's biggest staff problem was with her Administrative Assistant, David Harmer. From the start, the two didn't see eye to eye, which would have been fine under other circumstances, but under these circumstances, one of them was the other's boss. When Enid said "jump," instead of "how high?" Harmer usually said "first tell me why?"

As Washington power struggles go, the one between the Congresswoman and her AA was hardly out of the ordinary. Such clashes of ego are common at the top. And normally, such a power struggle is quickly resolved: The one with the power stays, the one without the power leaves.

But Harmer stayed, and primarily for one reason: Joe. Joe liked David Harmer. It was Joe who lobbied for Enid to make him her campaign manager after Kaylin Loveland's early departure, and it was Joe who pushed Enid to make Harmer her Administrative Assistant in Washington.

Enid thought this odd for the simplest of reasons: Not only did she have a hard time getting Dave Harmer to do what she asked him to do, but . . . *Joe knew it!* He had a ringside seat. He knew how upset Enid got over "David did this" or "David didn't do this" during the campaign. He knew the relationship was not made in political heaven. He knew she and Harmer argued constantly, because Joe was often listening in. When Enid screamed at her new AA for nearly an hour, at long-distance rates, from the telephone in their hotel suite in Honolulu–because while Enid and Joe were away for their island R & R, Harmer tried to make staff assignments contrary to what Enid wanted–Joe sat next to Enid on the bed and heard the whole thing . . .

. . . And still he backed Dave Harmer.

Enid and Joe had a succession of intense arguments–easily the most intense of their married life–over *another man.* David Harmer. Enid wanted to fire him, Joe wanted her to keep him.

And she couldn't figure out why.

Joe's loyalty to Harmer was especially confusing to Enid because whenever Harmer didn't do something, it was usually Joe who did. The staff came to Joe with problems as much as they came to Harmer. It was like they had two parents. When one doesn't work, try the other. And the thing was, from Enid's viewpoint, Joe tended to be their favorite. Joe was always telling Enid about taking care of problems David had created.

Joe became Enid's favorite as well. In many ways, *he* became her AA. It was Joe, not Harmer, who organized a daily folder for Enid that contained the essential things she needed to do that day. At night it was Joe, not Harmer, who would brief, and sometimes badger, the Congresswoman. "Just do these three things tonight, and you can go to bed," was his constant refrain. Joe Waldholtz was Enid's eyes and ears, and conscience. He was her righthand man, not David Harmer.

Finally, overriding Joe's protests, Enid let Harmer go. As Congress was breaking for the Easter holidays, she put her AA on thirty days probation. He was as good as gone and she knew it. Sure enough, ten days later, Harmer faxed a letter of resignation to Enid and Joe's home on Benecia Drive in Salt Lake. In the letter, he thanked Joe for what he had done for him and said he hoped they could continue to have a positive relationship in the future. To Enid, he said nothing of the kind.

Joe got even more work after Harmer's exit, but he didn't seem to mind. Enid asked him to work with Mike Hogard, the office manager, and put together a progress report for her on her office budget. It was something she'd asked Harmer for and never received. Now they were three months into the year and she didn't know where they stood.

Joe was not happy. "That was dumb, your promise to cut the office budget by twenty-five percent," he told his wife. "You've put us in such a box now you can't afford to go out and hire a good Administrative Assistant."

"Smart or not," Enid answered, "I did it and I've got to live by it."

Joe was right, of course. She was limited by her budget reduction pledge. So she didn't hire a new AA. Instead she and Joe organized a "management team" consisting of Linda Toy, the legislative assistant; Kate Watson, the press secretary; Enid Waldholtz, the Congresswoman; and her non-paid but ever-present husband, the independently wealthy Joe Waldholtz.

As awkward as it sounded, it worked–both for Enid and for Joe. As May gave way to June and June gave way to July, the morale in the office seemed to pick up. Part of it was the workload that had lessened in general on the Hill, now that the Hundred Days was over. But a bigger part of it, Enid felt, was her husband's willingness to absorb the work load and help out whenever possible. Just like at home, he took the calls and handled the mail. She honestly didn't know what she would do without him.

□□□

By early summer, Joe's back finally gave out. Not figuratively. Literally.

He was still handling the office problems well enough, but his own back was another story. He'd had trouble with it for some time, but nothing so serious it couldn't be covered over by pain pills. By early summer, however, even the prescription medication wasn't working. On a flight to Salt Lake City toward the end of May the pain hit its apex. The next morning Joe was in LDS Hospital, where doctors examined MRI scans that had been taken in Washington. They didn't just recommend surgery, they ordered it. They told Joe it was his only real option. Have the surgery and relieve the pain, or live with it the rest of his life. He didn't even go home. He checked into the hospital and prepared for back surgery two days later.

Enid cancelled their plans to return to Washington and began a rotation between her district office at the Federal Building in downtown Salt Lake City and the hospital. She slept in the hospital the first night Joe was there, right next to his bed. He told her he was frightened and he didn't want to be alone.

The doctors had given Joe no undue cause for alarm. On the contrary. They were upbeat and optimistic about what the surgery could accomplish. It had few downsides, they told him. Not only did it give Joe reasonably high odds of a full recovery, but there didn't seem to be any real dangers of further complications.

Still, Joe could not relax. He talked excessively of dire consequences, starting many of his sentences with "If I don't make it . . . ."

Enid tried to reassure him the best she could, but Joe's fatalism was persistent. It was as if he were talking himself into thinking that he was going to die. He told Enid repeatedly that she would be "taken care of" when he was gone. "The trustees know how to get hold of you," he said. The good old aptly-named trustees. It was funny, Enid thought–Joe spoke of "the trustees" who monitored the family trust so often that although she had never met any of them, she still thought of them practically as family. She knew many of their names and often she heard Joe talking to them on the telephone. She asked Joe for their phone number that night in the hospital, just because–because, well, you never know–but Joe had shaken her off. He'd simply replied, "Don't worry, Enid, they'll call you," and she let it go at that. She didn't want to stir him up any further.

The second night, with surgery set for the next morning, Enid, after making a requisite appearance at that night's Governor's Ball at the Salt Palace, walked into the room and found her still-fatalistic husband with tears running down his face. He told her he spent the afternoon writing two letters, one to her and one to their unborn daughter, who they had already agreed they would name Elizabeth.

"I want you to promise me you'll read these tonight, before you go to sleep," he said, waving the letters in the air. Enid took the letters from his hand as Joe wiped at his tears.

"I love you so," he said.

"And I you," his wife answered.

Not wanting to drive to the south part of the valley only to return the next morning, she spent that night just up the road from the hospital at her parent's home. As she settled into the bed she'd slept in as a child, she pulled out the letters and began to read. She read her letter first:

My Darling Enid:

What a difficult letter this is to write–especially to you. As I sit here tonight while you are at the Governor's Ball I am watching old tapes of Election Night and swearing-in day. What an incredible journey we have had together.

You have a tremendous destiny to fulfill, and I fully expect to be a part of that. But, my darling Enid, if that is not to be, I will never rest knowing that you walked away from your dream which really is our dream. You must run for re-election and then for the Senate when the time is right. I see you so clearly as Vice President. I know you don't, but I do. And you must know that I will always be with you every step of the way. Somehow you'll know that I am there for you. Somehow you will.

My tantrums of pain aside–for which I really must ask your forgiveness (although I know you know how bad the pain is), I want you to know that you are absolutely everything that I want in a wife. You are the perfect person for me. If I don't make it through this operation, you need to know that you gave me everything I wanted. Always. It was (being your husband) the greatest honor and joy that I could ever have.

I want you to go on living your life, Enid. You are a bright and beautiful woman who deserves to have a husband. I hope that in time you will meet that special, lucky person and that you will have a fantastic life together.

I am going to ask one thing that I probably shouldn't–but I hope you might consider marrying the second time only for time and not eternity. I know that this is a lot to ask, but, you see, I plan to say "yes" if they really ask me because I want to spend eternity with you.

This isn't shaping up to be the poetry I had hoped for. It was not so easy to write and cry and heave and hurt my back! It was kind of like a "Lucy" episode!

Tell Elizabeth about me, when she's old enough to understand. I am going to write her a letter too, but I wanted to write them in the order that I order my life in. You have always come first. You will always come first. I adore you, Enid. Make those dreams come true. I love you.

Forever,

Joe

P.S. Please, please take care of Winston as we did together since he came to us. I need to know that you will keep him, keep him safe and love him and take care of him.

Next, Enid picked up the letter to their unborn daughter.

My Elizabeth,

How amazing it is to love someone before she is even born. I write this letter to you, my precious daughter, facing what should be a very easy and uncomplicated surgery for a little disc problem in my back (As I finished that last sentence I had to run and throw up–from the steroids they have me on to reduce inflammation. But ask your mother about my legendary throwing up problems–you too would have a real laugh out of them!)

There are many things I am proud of in my life–your incredible mother and the success that she is–and you–knowing what great things you will achieve in your life.

I am sorry that I wasn't strong enough in body to see you born, to take those first days with you–and yes to even change your diaper–something I know your mother thinks I may not do–but deep inside I am sure she knows I would have shared in your life with her as your beautiful mother as I did with everything in our lives. Your mother is a tremendous sharer even if I teased her about it.

Most of all, I wanted to watch as your mother and I grew as a couple and dealt with the great joy and change that you will bring in our lives. I wanted to see you take your first steps into the great, wonderful world ahead for you. You see, Elizabeth, you can do ANYTHING you want to do–You can be ANYTHING you want to be–and you are lucky to have the finest example of right from wrong, of good from evil, of moral from immoral, and, most important to me, of Republican from Democrat.

Politics was a pretty big part of your mother's life and mine, too. She'll tell you how we met, how silly I was, and how truly special a life together your mother and I had. I don't believe two people could share so much over a short period of time. Those years were the best of my life and I know that together, you and your mom will build a life together. I hope that your mom will marry again, because she shouldn't be alone. I wouldn't want that. Your mother will make the right choice for you and for her.

If you want to honor me, you can do that by doing one simple thing–honor your mother. ALWAYS. I know there will be times it will seem silly and you might not like it, but by honoring, listening to and loving your mother you will become the person that I know you should be. Help your mother and learn from her.

You are so blessed to have some truly special grandparents on the Greene side of the family. Their love, strength and wisdom has taught me a lot in life. Your grandparents on the Waldholtz side are good people who have had their share of tremendous advantages coupled with family and health problems that your mom can explain to you later in life. My grandmother, Rebecca, was a noble woman who worked and worked to build upon the empire that was given to her. Your mother is now steward of all of that. I know she will do well.

There are others in my life who I hope someday you can meet. I have a most treasured friend who lives in Philadelphia, Pa. His name is Guy. I hope someday you can have a friend like that. He is closer to me than any brother could be. I know that he and his wife Chris will be a big help to your mother.

Elizabeth, if you ever truly begin to wonder what is important in life–I hope you will think not of inanimate objects and other material possessions, but of family. Who is a rich man? It is he who is content.

As I write this to you now, I know your mother is in Church–

praying for me and our family. Go to Church with her–learn from it. You can't ever go wrong by listening to your mother.

As for me–as I said earlier, honor and respect your mother. Nothing could make me happier or more content and at peace. Always talk with her, ask her advice and know that she alone has your best interests at heart.

From me comes some light-hearted advice —

1. If anyone asks you if the Waldholtz-Shepherd feud is over because your father is gone, tell them NO. NEVER! (Your mother can explain that to you).

2. Never buy a Shepherd dog–only Boxers. They were my favorite.

3. Register and vote Republican. Just do it. (That was an old Nike shoe ad from the 1990s).

4. Do not marry anyone related to, or who supported, Karen Shepherd. In fact, just stay away from anyone with that name to be safe. (Smiley face). It is much too long a story for this note. But it is a really, really long story. And one that you should hear.

I will watch over you, my Elizabeth. I will watch you live your life and grow up and achieve what you want to achieve.

I know I must sound like a broken record but remember this about me–if you only remember one thing —

Honor your Mother.

I love you, Elizabeth,
Daddy

Enid set down the last of the two letters and, with tears rolling down her face, stared at the ceiling. *That sweet man,* she thought, *that dear sweet man.* She thought of how it was her husband who had made her pregnancy so bearable. It was Joe who would help her trudge up all the flights of stairs in the townhouse after a fourteen-hour day in Congress, and then, as she fell into bed, it was Joe who would go back downstairs to the kitchen and heat up some soup, put it on a tray with some bread, and carry it up to her. It was Joe who was always checking with her staff if she'd eaten "anything decent" that day. It was Joe who stayed by her side until the last vote was counted every night, whether it was two in the morning. Then they would turn out the lights, close the office door, and without fail hold hands as they trudged down the hall toward the elevator. It was Joe who kept her on track, who buoyed her up, who told her to set her sights high, she could do whatever she wanted to do.

Yes he could be abrasive, yes he could whine, yes he had a temper. If you were on the wrong side of his biting wit, it could really sting. It was true, he had been at his worst the past couple of weeks. As the back pain heightened, so did his impatience. Yes he could be sloppy and haphazard, and yes he would speak his mind–about David Harmer, for instance–and not back down an inch. But he never held a grudge, ever, not with his wife, and whatever his shortcomings, he cared. Enid knew that as sure as she knew anything.

Enid smiled at the thought of Joe lying in the hospital, watching those "highlight" videos–*her* highlight videos–and writing those letters, tears streaming down his face. He was a big, big baby. He wasn't going to die! He thought he was, of that she was sure. But he was going to be fine, she was sure of that, too, and they'd soon be back together, living out their dreams. Joe Waldholtz would always be there. Above and apart from everything else, he was loyal. That's the sentiment that rang loudest from those letters from the heart. "Honor your mother," he'd told Elizabeth, over and over. "Share with her as I did." *What a husband I have,* thought Enid as she turned over and went to sleep.

□□□

She was right. The doctors were right. Everybody but Joe was right. The surgery was a complete success. He did live.

He fought it tooth-and-nail to the finish, however. He'd asked that Enid be allowed in the recovery room, "just in case," and she'd made her way there just minutes after he came out of surgery. Barely half conscious, Joe saw her and she reached out and held his hand. At that moment a nurse rushed over. No one but doctors, nurses and patients are allowed in recovery, and she asked

Enid to please leave. Patients don't even know who they are, let alone who anyone else is, as they emerge from the anesthetic.

But the nurse supervising Joe had been watching this husband-wife scene and she intervened. She'd noticed something. When Enid took Joe's hand, he calmed down noticeably. He was quite agitated, with a heart rate well beyond normal; "fighting the anesthesia," they called it. But when his wife appeared, he stabilized. "You can stay," the nurse said to Enid, smiling. "You seem to have a powerful effect on him."

Joe walked out of the hospital a free man–free from back pain, his recovery just short of miraculous. He still needed to take pain medication for a while, and it would be a good idea, the doctors told him, to take off a few pounds (few as in at least fifty), but the surgery had done its magic and the chronic, debilitating misery was gone. Within a couple of weeks he was back on his feet, being, as Enid put it, "her old Joe." The energy was back in his step, the laugh back in his voice, the passion back in his dreams. Enid couldn't have been more pleased, or relieved. On Father's Day, she mimicked a Joe tradition and gave him multiple cards. The first was humorous, the second more serious, and the third was deep affection. In that note she answered his sentiment from the hospital:

Dearest Joe —

You are the man who is greater than my dreams. I never could have imagined that life could be so sweet, so full of joy! I knew you would come through surgery because I know we belong together always, and that our life adventure together has just begun.

You are my life, Joe. My life has sense and meaning because of you. I am a better person because of you. And I know our daughter will be the better for having you as her father–to lean on as I do.

Love always,
Enid

Joe responded with a card of his own. On stationery next to a poem entitled "I Am Faithfully Yours in Love Forever" he wrote:

My darling Enid,

The months of waiting have turned into weeks. I can't tell you how excited I am to be a father. I only hope that I can measure up to her mother! I know you will be a fantastic mother. I meant what I said in the letters I wrote at LDS–Elizabeth has a perfect example to follow.

I love you, Enid, with all of my heart. I always will. Together we will be great parents and a great family. Maybe a great First Family.

I love you forever,
Joe

CHAPTER VII

They were at the White House, about to have their picture taken with Bill Clinton, when she decided she couldn't take it any longer.

She was going too fast, too hard, too long. She couldn't handle the pace. It wasn't healthy, for her or the baby.

It was July, it was Washington, it was hot, it was humid, and Enid had an epiphany of sorts. She'd been Superwoman long enough. She was into her seventh month and she needed to listen to what the doctors were telling her, and, more importantly, to what her own stomach and feet were telling her. She needed to back off! She couldn't make every fund-raiser, every breakfast speech, every weekend trip back home. She just couldn't.

What they were doing now, the President's Picnic, was a perfect example–and, for her, the final straw. Along with hundreds of other specially invited guests from inside the Beltway, the members of the 104th Congress were invited to the south lawn of the White House. The President's Picnic was a rite of Washington summer.

Enid balked about going in the first place, but Joe insisted. "Come on," he prodded. "Do it for posterity. Get your picture taken pregnant next to Bill Clinton." Amused at the thought, and with himself, he laughed.

So she went, against her will, and now she was hating life because her feet were swollen, she felt dizzy, the heat was almost overpowering, and the presidential receiving line was taking *forever.*

As soon as the photographer snapped the photo, she turned and thanked the president; then she and Joe shook a few hands as they made their way to the exit. The next morning her fears were realized when she looked down at her ankles and they were still swollen. *Not* good news. Before, a good night's sleep had always reversed the swelling.

Her doctor told her she had toxemia, a normal enough complication during pregnancy that causes your body to retain fluids. But a complication nonetheless. The doctor's advice was to slow down, take it easy, get her feet up. He gave his OK for her to continue working, within reason, until the end of July. But in August, when the House recessed for the entire month, he wanted her off to Utah, away from the humidity and hustle of Washington, and straight to bed. Enid took that as an exaggeration, the bed part, but the doctor's no-nonsense attitude scared her enough that she immediately began to cut back on her schedule. There was a major event at Lake George in New York state hosted by the National Republican Congressional Committee that she cancelled. There was a big fundraiser for Newt Gingrich, also in New York, that she'd previously committed to. She uncommitted. If it wasn't basic, absolutely essential congressional duty, it wasn't on her agenda.

□□□

As Enid slipped into her congress-and-baby vacuum, Joe took over even more command of her affairs than before. He had been her eyes and her ears, now he was also her motion sensor. For anything–or anyone–to get to her, it had to get past that sensor. The President had the secret service. Enid had Joe.

He was virtually omnipresent. The Congresswoman's lead blocker. Not that a spouse's fulltime presence was unprecedented on Capitol Hill, or even that unusual. A most recent example was Heather Foley, the wife of Tom Foley, Newt's predecessor as Speaker, who had served as her husband's chief of staff; as with

Joe, it was strictly on a non-paid basis. A kind of taxpayer bonus. Like the art hanging on the Waldholtz walls.

With his wife's pregnancy, and his emergence as a member of the office "management team," Joe gave up completely on his plans of seeking outside employment in Washington. His days were spent exclusively in room 515 of the Cannon Building. He did not restrict himself to any one area in the suite of three offices; his forte was running interference for his wife. Phone calls to the office asking for the Congresswoman? They were to first go through Joe. Mail? Through Joe. Staff problems/questions/concerns? Through Joe. Federal Express and other overnight courier deliveries? Through Joe. The air Enid breathed did *not* come through Joe, but that was about it. If they'd drawn up an organizational chart for Enid Waldholtz's congressional office in the summer of 1995 it would have showed Enid at the top of one page, her staff on another page, and Joe on yet another page, the one separating the Congresswoman and her staff.

□□□

So it was that when the *Salt Lake Tribune* launched an investigation into discrepancies between Enid's 1994 and 1995 federally-mandated financial disclosure statements, Joe knew about it well before his wife did.

After hearing about the investigation from *Tribune* reporters Dan Harrie and Tony Semerad, Kate Watson, Enid's press secretary, gave Joe the news at the end of June. Joe insisted that Kate not tell Enid. "The baby," he said, and his meaning was obvious. They shouldn't do anything that might unduly upset Enid this late in her pregnancy. And if there was anything that *could really* unduly upset her, Joe reminded Kate, the media was right up there on the list. Particularly the *Tribune.* Utah's largest newspaper and Enid had a *history.*

It dated back nearly three years, to the crunch days of the '92 Congressional campaign when Enid and Karen Shepherd were jockeying to replace Wayne Owens. The campaign heated up, as most all campaign races do, after Labor Day, with the general consensus being that although Shepherd was leading, this one was still up for grabs.

Then, with less than a week to go before the election, the *Tribune* released a poll that showed Shepherd ahead by sixteen percentage points–the political equivalent of a five touchdown lead in the fourth quarter.

When Enid wound up losing to Shepherd by less than four percentage points on Election Day, she was livid, blaming the loss, at least in part, on that *Tribune* poll. It was her contention that the voters, by their own irrefutable voice, revealed just how far off the *Tribune* poll's numbers had missed the mark. That left Enid and her supporters to wonder how many voters inclined to cast their ballots for Enid had lost interest, thinking the race was lost, and hadn't even bothered to vote?

She'd hung on to her bitter feelings about the *Tribune* and carried them with her into the '94 campaign, when what she saw as a similar "poll discrepancy" happened. In a poll released just after Labor Day gauging the three-way showdown among Shepherd, Enid and the independent challenger, Merrill Cook, the *Tribune* showed Enid running third, not only well behind Shepherd, but Cook too.

This time, Enid's campaign had secured its own pollster, Neil Newhouse of Public Opinion Strategies. When Newhouse, a man nationally-recognized in the polling field, saw the *Tribune* numbers he told Enid they differed markedly from his own research, which showed Enid just a few points behind Shepherd and well ahead of Cook. Enid, in turn, asked Newhouse if he would try to determine why there was such a wide range between his numbers and the *Tribune's*.

Newhouse's research didn't have to go very deep. The news story in the *Tribune* accompanying the poll explained that the *Tribune's* polling samples included, completely above board and on purpose, people either not likely to vote or not registered to vote. Newhouse explained to Enid that most polls either throw out those people or give them virtually no weight. Otherwise, the poll isn't as likely to reflect an accurate forecast of what will happen when people actually *vote.* When Enid asked Newhouse if he would state that in a press release, he agreed that he would. The press release went out the next day.

The morning after the release of that press release, the editor of the *Tribune,* Jay Shelledy, phoned Enid at home. The two had never met in person. Shelledy informed Enid that the reason the *Tribune* included a percentage of non-registered voters (about fifteen percent) in its poll was as a prod to spur voter registration. He further informed Enid that, because of her inflammatory press release, the *Tribune's* polling service, Valley Research, was considering suing her for libel.

"I meant everything I said in that release," Enid told the newspaper editor. "I'm prepared to stand behind every word of it. If your pollster wants to sue me, let's go." To which Shelledy replied, "Until you apologize, you and I are through talking."

The editor was true to his word. Enid Waldholtz did not hear from Jay Shelledy again, nor did he hear from her. They had established their positions and they were sticking to them. When, in subsequent research, Enid learned that it was Shelledy who instructed Valley Research as to what samples he wanted and it was Shelledy–and not the newspaper's usual political writers–who wrote the front page stories about the polling results, her distrust heightened. Enid Waldholtz did not trust the *Salt Lake Tribune*.

□□□

Just as Joe had forecast, when Enid finally learned, days after the rest of her management team already knew, that she was the target of a media investigation by *The Tribune,* she was livid. And when she learned that the newspaper had hired an accountant to assist the reporters, she went beyond that.

"An accountant! Jay Shelledy's hired an accountant!" she looked at Kate and Joe, the bearers of the news. "We *are* special, aren't we?" The sarcasm was dripping from her voice. "How many other candidates get to have an accountant go over their books?"

But she was not concerned.

For one very good reason: she had this base covered, and she knew it. Enid knew that she had personally gone over every line of her federal financial disclosure statements, both in 1994 and 1995. The biggest job had been in 1994, the spring after she and Joe had married. They'd sat down together at the kitchen table at their home, pushed everything off the top–the salt and pepper shakers, the napkin-holder, the flower centerpiece, everything–rolled up their sleeves and gone to work. The better part of two days it had taken, but they'd dotted every *i* and crossed every *t*, she was sure of it.

Financial disclosure statements were required so that the employers of federally elected officials–namely, the U.S. taxpayers–could have a way of checking whether their public servants were working for somebody else. If you were being bought, set up, taken care of, or otherwise financially maintained by someone or something that could conceivably cause a conflict with your job, it theoretically would be disclosed.

Enid also knew that the point behind a financial disclosure statement was *not* to reveal the exact net worth of a politician. The FDS's were not another Forbes 400 list. The public didn't have a right to know how rich you were, or weren't. What it did have a right to know was where your assets were coming from; to know you hadn't sold your soul to the highest bidder. In fact, when the media would speculate as to an elected official's net worth based on an FDS–and such speculating was common–it was an inside political joke just how far off they often missed the mark. Part of the reason was because there were certain assets an official did not have to reveal. If you were part of a "blind trust," for example, you didn't have to disclose any information about the trust. All you had to do was check the box that said you'd verified that the trust "qualified" as blind. The other part of the reason was because you didn't reveal exact amounts in your FDS, you only revealed ranges of values. In the area of "assets," for example, the disclosure form listed a number of boxes lettered A through H, with box A reflecting assets of zero to five thousand dollars and box H reflecting assets of a million dollars or more. Each letter in between had its own range. The range for box G was half-a-million to a million dollars

It was box G, Enid learned, that was giving the *Tribune* something to dig at. Joe told her that the G box had been checked on both her 1994 and 1995 statements, reflecting assets ranging in value between half-a-million and a million dollars. But since it was well-publicized, not to mention acknowledged in FEC reports by Enid herself, that she spent $1.7 million dollars on her '94 campaign, the obvious question was; if she didn't have that much money herself, then where did all the money come from? If it came from the private assets of other family members, including her husband or her wealthy father, that would be a violation of federal election law.

The answer, Joe further explained, was as simple as the question: they had checked the wrong box. Enid should have checked box H–reflecting assets of a million-plus. That's the box that accurately reflected the value of the five million dollars Joe had given her on their wedding day–the money that by and large had financed her campaign.

Enid was aghast that it had happened. In 1994, after she and Joe finished their marathon work session on the kitchen table, they had talked about how glad they were the value categories stopped at one million "and beyond." As Joe had told her on numerous previous occasions, the Waldholtz Family Trust–which he said qualified as a blind trust–was worth "hundreds" of millions of dollars. On top of that, and in addition to Enid's five-million dollar wedding gift, Joe had personal assets that totaled up well beyond a million dollars in value all by themselves. He explained that some of his money was tied up in a variety of longterm investments, some was invested in U.S. Savings Bonds, and he also had some non-monetary assets, including a family heirloom coin collection locked away in a safe deposit box in Pittsburgh and was worth between a quarter and a half-million dollars. The coins, Joe said, included several U.S. Mint originals. They had been handed down from Waldholtz generation to generation. His grandfather had given them to Joe, insisting that they stay in the family.

There is no way they would have knowingly not checked the million-plus box. But somehow–and this was the only thing Joe could think of–when he transferred the check marks from the working copy he and Enid had done in pencil, he must have messed up and checked the wrong box. Enid hadn't caught that. As a matter of fact, she hadn't had the chance. She'd signed a blank FDS sheet the day the form was due, May 15, 1994, as she rushed out the door for a campaign obligation. Joe's job was to transfer everything over from their working copy to the form she signed, drive down Fort Union Boulevard to the post office, and mail the official report to the Clerk of the House.

I wish Joe hadn't checked the wrong box, but anyone can make a mistake, Enid thought as their meeting ended. *But that's what this is and that's all it is. Joe's mistake. This amounts to a clerical error and nothing more.*

As for the 1995 FDS, which they had submitted less than two months previous, the explanation was equally simple: In copying the basic check marks from the 1994 form–virtually all of their "values" had remained the same–they had again inadvertently checked the wrong box.

In both cases, it was what is known as a "correctable error," and that's all this media witch hunt amounted to. A clerical mistake. They needed to check box H, not box G. Case closed. The *Tribune* could move on to other vendettas.

That's what Enid told Kate and Joe.

Joe cleared his throat.

"Well," he said, "it's not going to be *quite* that simple."

The issue behind the *Tribune's* inquiry, he explained, was one of documentation. It was all well and fine to acknowledge a mistake and say the wrong box was checked, but what the reporters really wanted to know, now that they had their antennae up, was if Enid indeed had the money she said she had. To answer that, they wanted her to show them evidence that she did.

"So let's show them," Enid said.

Now Joe looked worried. He explained why. The remainder of Enid's wedding day gift, about four and a quarter million dollars, was in a liquid investment account managed by a firm called TWC Ready Assets. That was the good news. The bad news was that, as Enid knew, everything associated with the Waldholtz Family Trust was in a frozen state at the moment pending the settlement of family infighting instigated by Joe's cousin Stevie. Because of that infighting, a number of trustees had recently been fired and a new set of trustees was just now getting up to speed. The bottom line: He was having trouble getting the documentation as quickly as the *Tribune* wanted it. The reporters had set an arbitrary deadline for Friday, July 7th, and Joe didn't think he could meet it.

Friday, July 7th, was tomorrow.

□□□

When Tony Semered and Dan Harrie ran, as scheduled, their front page *Salt Lake Tribune* story about Enid Waldholtz's Financial Disclosure Form discrepancies on Sunday, July 9th, it could have been worse. But the reporters bent over backwards to be fair. Both Enid and Keith Davis, the lead accountant who handled Enid's campaign books for Huckaby & Associates, were quoted liberally and accurately in explaining the error in checking the wrong category of value boxes. Further, it was duly noted by the reporters that Enid and Joe's explanation for failing to provide corroborating asset documentation for Box H was mainly due to the time constraints caused by the July 4th weekend.

Still, the reporters had hardly become apologists for the Waldholtzes. Their article also accurately reported that the Congresswoman had so far produced no evidence to back up her claims; there was a good deal of justifiable editorial censure on that point. And now that it was all out in the open, not only was the *Tribune* waiting for such documentation, but so was every other major media outlet in Utah. Until Enid provided evidence of the source and existence of her wealth, she could be sure they wouldn't let it rest.

And that wasn't all. The magnifying glass looking at her financial disclosure forms had expanded its focus to include amendments that hadn't yet been made to the Enid '94 Federal Election Commission reports–amendments needed to explain in greater detail the sources of the already-reported \$1.7 million in campaign expenditures. In Washington, Huckaby & Associate's Keith Davis was ready to file those amended reports on Enid '94's behalf, but he too needed documentation. As Davis explained to Joe, Huckaby & Associates had a firm policy that its clients provide as expeditiously as possible any and all pertinent records necessary to authenticate the information disclosed on the FEC reports. The original Enid '94 FEC reports had been filed in the summer and fall of 1994 without corroborating documentation because Joe didn't forward those reports to Davis until the day they were due. Since the FEC has no provision for tardiness–deadline extensions are simply not allowed–and since the FEC reports (like personal income tax reports) don't require accompanying documentation–the accountant forwarded the Enid '94 reports to the FEC based on Joe's word only.

But now, as Davis waited to begin preparing the amendments to those filings, he needed–and was prepared to wait for–bank statements, cancelled checks, deposit slips, donor receipts and a number of other items that Joe, the campaign treasurer, had promised to deliver, but so far hadn't actually delivered.

The *Tribune* kept its accountant, Gary Petersen, on retainer, set yet another deadline, for August 16th, and, when August 16th came and went with no word from Joe, the press was ready to pounce. But then, as if he'd strung them along just long enough to show who was boss, Joe announced that he had received from Ready Assets the document they'd all been waiting for. He agreed to fax a copy of the document to Greg Engeman, the director of Enid's district office in Salt Lake City, where the fax would be available to be examined by the *Tribune* accountant. But if he was going to expose this information, the media would have to play by his rules, Joe stipulated. He insisted that no reporters could be present while the accountant examined the document and no copies could be made. Only the accountant would be allowed to examine the document and take any notes he desired–and then advise the media.

As advertised, the facsimile arrived in Engeman's office,

where Gary Petersen, acting for the *Salt Lake Tribune,* personally reviewed a "Ready Assets" account certificate. What the accountant saw was a document that included the Congresswoman's name and address in the upper right hand corner and the amount of $4,238,682.90 listed next to the box labeled "Total Investments." There wasn't much more to it than that. There was no address or phone number of the Ready Assets office, or other details. As Engeman supervised, Petersen looked at the document for maybe forty-five seconds, tops, and took no notes. He then set it down and gave it a thumbs up. "Looks fine to me," he said to Engeman.

□□□

In spite of the disclosure of the Ready Assets document, the pressure never did let up. Not really. The evidence that Enid had $4.2 million dollars of her very own still didn't explain why her FEC amendments–which required more extensive documentation–hadn't been filed.

Now the media wanted to know where the $4.2 million came from. No one would be completely satisfied until Enid and Joe delivered documentation with detail.

In the meantime, everyone slipped into their roles. Like hounds on a hunt, the reporters, print and electronic, tightened their focus and increased their scrutiny. As Enid's press spokesperson, Kate Watson kept them at bay as best she good. Ladonna Lee, Enid's political consultant (the services of the Eddie Mahe Company had been maintained since the '94 campaign), helped Kate with behind-the-scenes counsel and strategy, which mainly amounted to "hang on and wait." As for Keith Davis, that's all he could do as well. Joe, the man they were all waiting on, kept coming up with updates and excuses, but almost none of the financial documentation they needed to close this chapter.

In a truly dizzying run of bad luck, red tape, and bureaucracy, something was always going wrong. The dark cloud Joe and Enid joked about had turned into a grade four tornado. You name it, it happened to Joe. The trust switched banks and the new bank couldn't get the account information from the old bank. When the bank finally did send the statements, Federal Express lost the package. When the package was traced and found, it finally got delivered but was lost at the office. Then a roll of microfiche with valuable information was destroyed in a fire. Then the fax machine garbled important reports on their way from Pittsburgh *and* Salt Lake City. Everything except "the dog ate it."

But as hot as it got in the summer of '95, Enid Waldholtz, Congresswoman, managed to walk unruffled in the eye of the storm. The gusts swirled all around her, but barely touched her. For four reasons. First, she was insulated on every front, mainly by her husband. Second, she was convinced of her innocence. Third, it was the media doing the attacking and as a matter of personal principle she didn't pay attention to the media anyway. And fourth, her far and away top priority was her pregnancy.

As much as the reporters were bugging Kate and Joe for answers, Enid's doctors were bugging her to back off. Her self-imposed slowdown after the President's Picnic wasn't enough. The symptoms of toxemia increased. By the time she got to Utah the first of August for the month-long congressional recess, her Salt Lake doctor ordered her to air-conditioned house arrest. Her blood pressure was particularly worrisome. The doctor hooked up a computerized monitor in her home that, along with other vital signs, periodically checked her blood pressure. If there was an event that she absolutely, positively needed to attend, she went; otherwise, she didn't. For Enid, the August recess would live up to its name. Doctor's orders. Everything was on a need to know basis, and, as far as she was concerned, other than the baby being all right, there wasn't much she really needed to know.

□□□

Certainly there was no need for her to know, during her eighth and ninth months of pregnancy, that she and Joe had almost as many creditors as constituents.

The problems with the momentary freezing of Joe's family's trust had created some momentary money problems. But what, Joe asked, was the sense in telling his wife? Anyone who tried, he suggested more than once, should be prepared to be able to live with it should Enid lose the baby.

It was incongruous that a man who wore $2,500 cuff links could be ninety days overdue to the florist, the plumber, and the furniture store; and it was inconceivable that a man who wore one hundred and twenty dollar designer ties could bounce checks to the phone company, the grocery store, and the water company. But if the people calling to demand payment on the office telephone and using the office fax line *to put it in writing* could be believed, it was true. If Enid Waldholtz's staff, right down to the ninety-day interns, knew anything in the summer of '95 they knew this: Joe owed money to a lot of people. A lot of very angry people.

Kate Watson sat back and watched in astonishment as Joe juggled the calls, the faxes, the demands, the outright threats. She fielded one call herself from an irate creditor who said if payment wasn't received by two o'clock that afternoon, a suit would be filed at 2:01 in the Washington, D.C. Superior Court. Kate reported the threat to Joe–but not, of course, to Enid–and, since Kate never heard of any lawsuit, she assumed he actually paid that bill.

Sometimes Joe would use young office staffers to run his financial errands for him, or help him pay his bills. He'd send one of them to the credit union to make a deposit. He'd send another to a store with a check. He regularly used the personal American Express credit card of Aaron Edens–the young legislative assistant he'd given Enid's old Jeep to at the end of the '94 campaign. He ran up nearly $40,000 on the card. Edens was enthusiastic at first, because he earned frequent flier miles every time his card was used, and because Joe made the payments on time. But then Joe started missing payments, and when American Express began hounding Aaron about them, his enthusiasm quickly waned.

Joe went to the top of the staff and used Kate to straighten out a problem with his water bill. The water had been shut off at the townhouse and Joe asked Kate if she'd go to the water company–

you had to go in person on a shutoff–and pay to have it turned on with her own personal check. He promised he would pay her back. He explained that it was the landlord's fault. They were supposed to pay the water, they hadn't, and they weren't in town. It was all just a big mistake. But after standing in line at the water company for nearly two hours, when Kate paid the bill they showed her a bounced check–from Joe Waldholtz. So *that* was why he couldn't use one of his own checks. When she confronted Joe about the discrepancy, he said that in his haste to avoid having the water turned off he paid with a check on an account he'd closed. Joe had as many reasons as he had bills.

Kate and the office manager, Michael Hogard, kept track of Joe & Enid's "top 12" creditors. Kate's personal favorite was the catering company Joe had used when he threw a party for Enid's staff to celebrate the end of the Hundred Days. Congressional and senate staffs all over the Hill were having such parties, celebrating the end of fourteen-hour days. They were typically pizza bashes, catered by Domino's, and held in the staff offices after work. But not Enid's. Not with Joe planning it. Joe held it at the Georgetown house, replete with tuxedoed waiters carrying trays of all the food you could care to eat. "When you're used to the kind of money I'm used to," Joe said to Kate as he snared an oyster off a passing tray, "you just can't do pizza."

But the check he sent the caterers bounced.

Through it all, Joe remained outwardly undaunted; the very picture of a man with enough reserves to pay late fees for eternity. Joe liked to tell Kate his "money stories." He told her he'd never walked in the grass in his bare feet until he was 21. He'd never packed his own suitcase the entire time he was growing up. He'd never fixed his own lunch. Kate, who felt a certain kinship to Joe–they were the same age, 32, and were both hopelessly addicted to politics–had never heard such stories. She didn't come from great wealth herself, but her parents were well enough off that they'd sent her to Ashley Hall, a private girl's school in South Carolina where Barbara Bush, among others, had attended. She'd been around people with a lot of money, and they differed from Joe in two ways. One, they never talked about their money, and two, the rich people she knew would have ordered the pizza.

Still, she didn't know if any of them came from the kind of money Joe came from. "Kate, you don't understand," he told her one day, sprawled out on the couch in Enid's office, his two hundred dollar Gucci suspenders bulging at the waist, "that trust is worth *four hundred and fifty million dollars!*"

□□□

It can get wearisome running interference for a millionaire deadbeat. By late July Kate Watson was weary. A ten-year veteran on the Hill who started out working for Newt Gingrich, she thought she'd seen it all. She hadn't. Besides having to deal with the financial disclosure and FEC amendment problems, she also had to deal, constantly, with the "creditors" as they disrupted the usual office work. The media, for whatever reasons, hadn't caught onto that story yet: *"Waldholtzes Owe The World."* Sometimes you luck out. But how long could Enid's good fortune–if you could call it that–hold?

Out of concern for the baby and because of the natural tendency to shy away from wedging in between a husband and wife, Kate didn't want to bother Enid. But she had to turn somewhere. She turned to Ladonna Lee.

As a spinmaster, Ladonna was as good as there was in Washington. The yin to her esteemed partner Eddie Mahe's yang, Ladonna's strength was common sense. Ladonna worked in color, not black and white; she added bedside manner to practicality. As the Eddie Mahe Company's consulting work with Congresswoman Waldholtz had switched more to public relations and fundraising, Ladonna had taken over the lead from her partner. She was great at hand-holding.

Like everyone else who had been following the Utah news, Ladonna already knew about the FDS and FEC concerns. When Kate apprised her of the problems with overdue bills and bounced checks as well, she sized up the overall situation and went to work. A good consultant tells the client not to just expect anything, but to be *prepared.*

To Kate's relief, Ladonna agreed with her that the potential for a media disaster was considerable and that, baby or no baby, something should be done now. The spinmaster determined that Enid needed to be prepared for scrutiny on each of the three "situations," namely the FDS reports, the FEC reports, and the creditor problems. To that end she prepared three preferred "press responses"–each designed to head off a crisis at the pass in the eventuality that any of the three should became a major topic on a slow August news day.

The first response addressed the financial disclosure forms and the TWC Ready Asset Account. "Make the document readily available," advised Ladonna. "Don't keep it hidden. Tell the press it's here and ready for examination by everyone. Case closed."

The second response addressed the delay in amending the FEC reports. Ladonna recommended basically a mea culpa ("my fault, I am to blame"). "Tell them it's been a crazy time, you can't do all things. You've hired an accountant. You're giving him everything he needs. It's being taken care of as we speak. Case closed."

The third response addressed the problems with the bills and the bounced checks. Ladonna's recommendation was to acknowledge that there had been some problems in the past, they had all been cleared up, and that they would hire an accountant to handle paying their personal bills in the future.

After preparing the responses, Ladonna arranged for a meeting to present them in Enid's office with Enid, Kate and Joe all present. They met in late July, just before the congressional recess. As was her custom, Enid read through each statement with a sharp eye and a red pen. On the first two she nodded occasionally and made several corrections, mainly having to do with grammar and tone. Her body language signalled that she agreed with what Ladonna proposed.

Then she got to the third.

Her face grew red and her voice grew shrill as she threw down the paper in disgust.

"This is NOT true," she said. "I pay my bills!"

There was a bated stillness in the room. Only the hum of the air conditioner could be heard. Ladonna shifted from one foot to the other as she looked first at Joe . . . and then at Kate . . . and watched incredulously as neither of them said a word to correct their leader.

□□□

Acting upon Ladonna Lee's advice, the Eddie Mahe Company resigned from Team Enid in early August. The scene in the Congresswoman's office had troubled Ladonna greatly. She usually didn't feel helpless, but she had on that occasion. She couldn't tell Enid that, as a matter of fact, she *didn't* pay her bills. Or, more to the point, Joe didn't pay them. She had no first hand evidence of that herself. She didn't receive the faxes from angry creditors, she didn't field the phone calls. That was Kate and Joe's area, and yet, she had seen them remain silent as stumps, both of them, as they listened to Enid's protest. Ladonna suspected that Kate, even if she was Enid's press secretary, was uncomfortable going over Joe's head since Joe, after all, was Enid's husband and self-appointed protector. Kate didn't want to kill the baby.

But Joe just stood there too, and that unnerved Ladonna. In this business you needed trust more than you needed anything. Joe needed to play it straight–with her, with Enid, with everyone.

So she resigned.

Joe, worried that the resignation would somehow leak to the press, called Ladonna with that lament. But Ladonna was quick to allay his fears that it would be leaked by anyone from her company. "It does no one any good to go public with this," she'd said, and let it go at that. Privately, she hoped the resignation might act as a wake-up call for Joe, a man, it seemed, bound and determined to dodge responsibility at all costs. Also privately, she wasn't too sure that it would.

□□□

In another office in Washington, across the Potomac River in Alexandria, yet another member of Team Enid was also growing weary and getting ready to throw in the towel.

Keith Davis had worked at Huckaby & Associates for hundreds of clients and he knew he had never been even close to this frustrated. The man who had filed all of Enid Waldholtz's FEC reports was ready and waiting to file the necessary amendments–but he was being kept in a continuous holding pattern. All the information for the amendments would be in order, he was sure, based on the detailed information Enid's husband/treasurer, Joe, had verbally given him concerning their financial circumstances and history. According to the information coming from Joe, they hadn't even come close to breaking any federal election laws. Enid had used her own money, plain and simple. But Davis needed the records that backed that up . . . and all he got were assurances that the records were on their way.

The maddening part–especially for an accountant–was that at this point the amendments definitely fit in the preferred category of "preventive medicine." They were completely voluntary. The Enid campaign was merely, on its own, filing updated reports to correct bookkeeping errors made during the height, and heat, of the campaign. As long as these amended reports got filed in a timely fashion, great. There would be no complicated problems with FEC audits or MURs (Matter Under Review), the bane of all campaign treasurers and bookkeepers. The feds love it when you do your corrections before they have to *tell you* to do your corrections.

But day after day, as he sat as his desk in Alexandria, Keith Davis kept waiting . . . and waiting . . .

Finally, in mid-August, about the same time as Ladonna's resignation, and as Enid sat at home in Utah, hooked to a blood pressure monitor, Davis sent a memo to Kate Watson that contained a comprehensive list of everything needed to amend the FEC and Financial Disclosure reports. At the end of the memo he added, "If we don't have this information by September 30th, we will no longer work for Congresswoman Waldholtz."

□□□

Meanwhile, back at the obstetrician's office at LDS Hospital in Salt Lake City, Enid reported for her regular weekly checkup on the last Thursday of August. She and Joe had driven to the doctor's office from their house that morning. After the appointment Enid thought she might stop by the office to sign a couple of papers. The next day they would be flying back to Washington, where, in approximately three weeks, she planned to have the baby. She had been a good girl, she was prepared to tell the doctor. She had kept her head down and her feet up, but she was getting awfully tired of Ricki Lake.

She and Joe had bickered on the way to the doctor's office. They had been verbally sparring more and more the past several days. Enid wondered if she was turning into a nag; partly because Joe kept telling her she was, partly because she knew it was true. She couldn't help it. She knew Joe needed to collect all the financial documents necessary to clear up those "clerical" errors with both the financial disclosure and FEC reports, and she knew he hadn't done it. He was always *doing* it, but he never got it done. That's what bugged her. "Just get it done!" had become her slogan, just as "Back off, I'm doing the best I can," had become Joe's.

He had a point. In some ways, Joe did do it all. He was a regular one-armed paperhanger these days. When he wasn't coordinating the business between the congressional office in Washington, D.C. and the district office in Salt Lake City he was doing the grocery shopping and running the household. All the while, Enid lay around, trying to keep the baby comfortable. Enid had never been any good at lying around anyway. She could work up a good case of feeling guilty if she ordered dessert at lunch. In spite of knowing full well just *why* she had gone horizontal for much of August, she felt guilty anyway.

They stopped bickering when the doctor ushered them into his office. They stopped *everything* when the doctor told her she was going to have the baby NOW!

They didn't let her call her office, they didn't let her go home and pack a suitcase and get her toothbrush. She was back in LDS Hospital, where just two months ago she held Joe's hand as he came out of back surgery. This time he was holding her hand. "Hang on," he kept telling her. Tears filled his eyes.

Her amniotic fluid level was dangerously low. That was the problem. Enid's due date was still twenty-two days away. Close enough. The doctors were taking no chances.

They made her as comfortable as they could and began the process to induce labor. Enid gave Joe a list of the things she would need in the hospital and he was off. When he came back, he ran into a news crew in the hospital lobby. Word had spread fast. Utah's Congresswoman was about to deliver. Film at ten.

The baby didn't make its entrance until the next afternoon, checking in about six p.m. on the 31st of August, 1995. She was on her way to a smooth delivery until halfway down the birth canal she simply became stuck. After half an hour she hadn't moved and began to go into distress. The doctors went to Plan B. Elizabeth Waldholtz would be born caesarean.

She came out quiet and slightly blue, but she came out, that was the important part. The doctors handed Elizabeth to a nurse who wrapped her in a huge bundle of blankets and hustled her off to an observation room where she spent her first night breathing extra oxygen. The next morning Elizabeth Greene Waldholtz was proclaimed good as new.

In the meantime, Elizabeth's mother had experienced problems of her own. No sooner had the doctors told her "Your baby's a girl and she's fine," than they followed it by adding, "Now we're going to put you back to sleep."

Enid had no time to agree or disagree. Within moments she was anesthetized and the doctors went about removing a cyst about the size of a softball they'd found on one of her ovaries. They couldn't save the ovary and they'd have to send a sample off to pathology.

The next thing Enid knew, Joe was standing in front of her bed. He was beaming. He told her he just changed Elizabeth's first diaper. He'd gotten the "honor" while Enid was in recovery. Enid finally got to hold her baby when they wheeled her to the observation room. It was close to midnight. They managed to close out August together, mother and daughter, if only barely. It had been some month.

□□□

The media "covered" the birth of Elizabeth from all angles, and Enid knew that would be just the start of it if she wasn't careful. She was the first congresswoman in twenty-four years to give birth while in office and only the second in the history of the House. She wasn't about to give her critics a chance to complain about how long it took her to get back to work. To that end she and Joe hired Kristin Jones, a nurse from the hospital's newborn unit, to live with them at their home for the first few days of Elizabeth's life. Kristin taught Enid how to care for her baby, and gave her the opportunity for optimum rest. After Labor Day, Congress would be back in session. Enid planned to be there as soon as possible thereafter.

Proving that they really do have hearts, members of the media had backed off Enid during August–until she had the baby. But it wasn't twenty-four hours after Enid arrived home from the hospital that they were back. This time it wasn't reporters from the *Tribune*, it was a television reporter, Rod Decker of KUTV, Salt Lake's CBS affiliate. Decker called Enid's office in Washington, D.C., where he asked Kate Watson if she would pass along a message to the Congresswoman. He apologized for the timing, so soon after the delivery of Elizabeth, but word had just come in that the Democrat Congressional Campaign Committee was going to file an ethics complaint against Enid on the basis that she hadn't documented the assets she used to fund her own campaign. Apparently, those guys read the papers too.

Enid was in her bathrobe in the kitchen when Kate called. Kristin was upstairs with Elizabeth. Joe was behind his wife on a bench near the kitchen door.

"If the Democrats really want to attack me one day after I'm out of the hospital, let's go," Enid said to Kate, her agitation showing.

"Kate," she continued. "Call Rod Decker and tell him to give me two hours. It will take me that long to shower and wash my hair. Then he can come out to the house and talk to me. And fax me a copy of the Ready Assets account, the one we got for the Tribune. I'm going to show it to Decker and we're going to put this to bed once and for all."

Kate said "Fine," and hung up.

Less than five minutes later Kate called again. This time her tone was different. She'd lowered her voice.

"Enid," she began, "are you sure you want to show Rod Decker that statement?"

"Of course I do," said Enid.

"There's something I have to tell you," Kate went on, still speaking measuredly, not at all like the usual upbeat Kate.

"So tell me," said Enid.

Kate proceeded to tell Enid that just recently Aaron Edens had come to her and confessed that two months ago, over the July 4th break, Joe had asked him to forge a document that was titled "Ready Assets" at the top and showed an account balance in Enid's name in excess of four million dollars. According to Aaron, Joe had sent him a copy of one of his old Merrill Lynch financial statements and instructed him to take that statement to a Kinko's copy center, change the name and amounts, and create a new document. Joe told Aaron he needed it "to show the Tribune." Aaron had actually gone to a Kinko's and begun the forgery, but in the middle of the project his conscience got the better of him and he decided to quit. He called Joe and told him he didn't think it was right and he wouldn't do it. He'd kept the news to himself until the end of August, when he heard Joe had finally acquired the long-sought-for Ready Assets document. It was then that Aaron confided in Kate. For her part, Kate had kept the news to herself because of Enid's rapidly approaching due date. But now, she felt her boss ought to know.

Enid absorbed this news so evenly that later she guessed it was the pain pills that kept her so under control. She hung up the phone and slowly turned around to face Joe, who she knew had heard every word of her end of the conversation. When she began saying "Aaron did what?" and "Aaron said what?" she sensed Joe freezing up behind her.

When she completed her pirouette her husband already had tears running down his face. His skin color was ashen, as white as the kitchen walls surrounding him. She wondered if he might pass out.

Before she could speak he'd already said, "Enid, I'm so sorry."

In great gushes his explanation rushed out of him. Yes, he'd asked Aaron to forge a Ready Assets document. Yes, it was wrong. Yes, he was glad Aaron never did as he'd been told. But he'd been so desperate. He hadn't known what else to do. The money was there, but it was the 4th of July and he couldn't get anyone to help him. The transition of the trustees was going on at the time and everything was a mess. The people at Ready Assets wouldn't help him without the trustee's OK. He explained that to Aaron. It wasn't a lie what they were doing. The document would be telling the truth; the same as the real document would tell. It's just that they couldn't access the real thing right then, and there was that damn deadline.

The bottom line, Joe told Enid, "Is I couldn't stand to watch the *Tribune* hurt you. They're out to get you, we both know that, and I couldn't just sit there and watch it happen."

As luck had it, Joe explained, the *Tribune* backed off and waited, and it was almost a month later that the trustees finally sent the Ready Assets document they needed. The authentic one. That's the one they showed the *Tribune's* accountant, who, Joe reminded Enid, had been more than satisfied it was legitimate.

"Are you swearing to me the one we showed the Tribune is real?" said Enid.

"I swear it," said Joe, still sobbing.

"Please Joe, stop it!" Enid said finally. She looked at the penitent hulk of a man falling to pieces in front of her. "Stop crying. I believe you. Now let's call Kate back and get that document."

Two hours later, Rod Decker was on their doorstep. He and his camera crew were invited in. Twenty minutes later they emerged with a videotape that aired that night on the Channel 2 news. It revealed a closeup of the Ready Assets account–its first public showing–in the name of Mrs. Enid Waldholtz, displaying "total investments" of $4,238,682.90.

While holding Elizabeth in her lap, Enid watched the newscast with relish. This was vindication in living color. Proof of that came when Decker told her that the Democrats, even before the document was displayed on the air, had reversed their field and decided not to file a complaint against the Republican Congresswoman from Utah.

Two days later the Waldholtz family, now three members strong, arrived at the Salt Lake Airport loaded with baby bags, suitcases, and more than a dozen mover's style boxes filled with "Joe's documents," containing all of the papers, he told Enid, that "would make Keith Davis's day." They weren't just returning to Washington, they were returning *armed.* As soon as they got to Washington, Joe promised Enid he would sort through those boxes and produce for her what she'd asked for: A bound set of papers that would contain every financial documentation they needed to clear the air, and the Waldholtz name. It would be a bigger version of the folder she'd once carried with her during the campaign that contained the papers that exonerated Joe from the O. C. Tanner and American Express slander.

"I want a big book that I can just open and show people whatever they want to see," Enid told Joe. She managed a smile. The baby was safe. Joe was bringing his boxes with him. Washington was delightful in the fall. They were going back to work. Life was sweet again. They were survivors, still.

"The Democrats and the media," said Enid, the smile disappearing momentarily as she shook her head back and forth and spoke aloud the names of their avowed enemies.

"Yeah," said Joe. "The bastards."

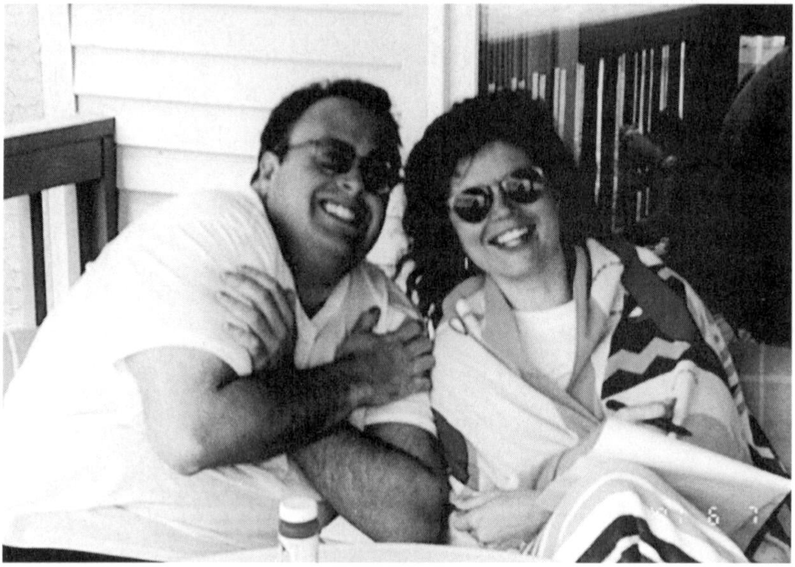

Joe and Enid take a break to mug for the camera during their "planning session" at the Jersey shore during Memorial Day weekend, 1991.
Photographs provided by Audrey Merkin.

Joseph Waldholtz's yearbook picture his senior year in 1981 at Taylor Allderdice High School, Pittsburgh, Pa.

To the senior class at Taylor Allderdice High, it was "President Waldholtz."

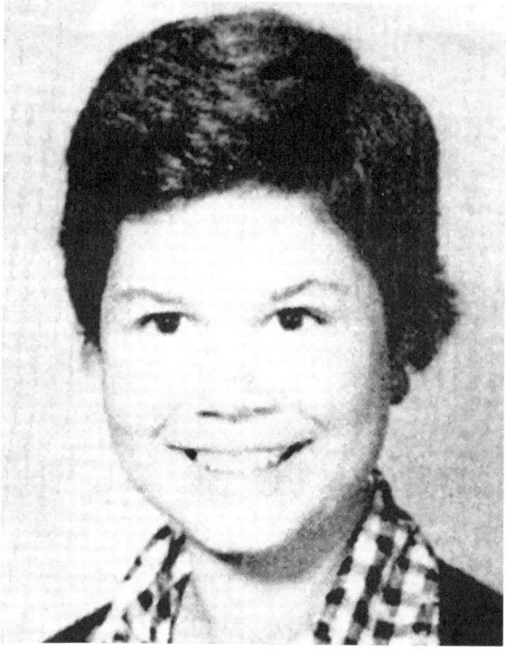

A young Enid Greene.

Enid and Joe in the kitchen at the Jersey Shore beach house, 1991.

Thanksgiving Day, 1993, Mr. and Mrs. Joe Waldholtz were barely returned from their honeymoon.

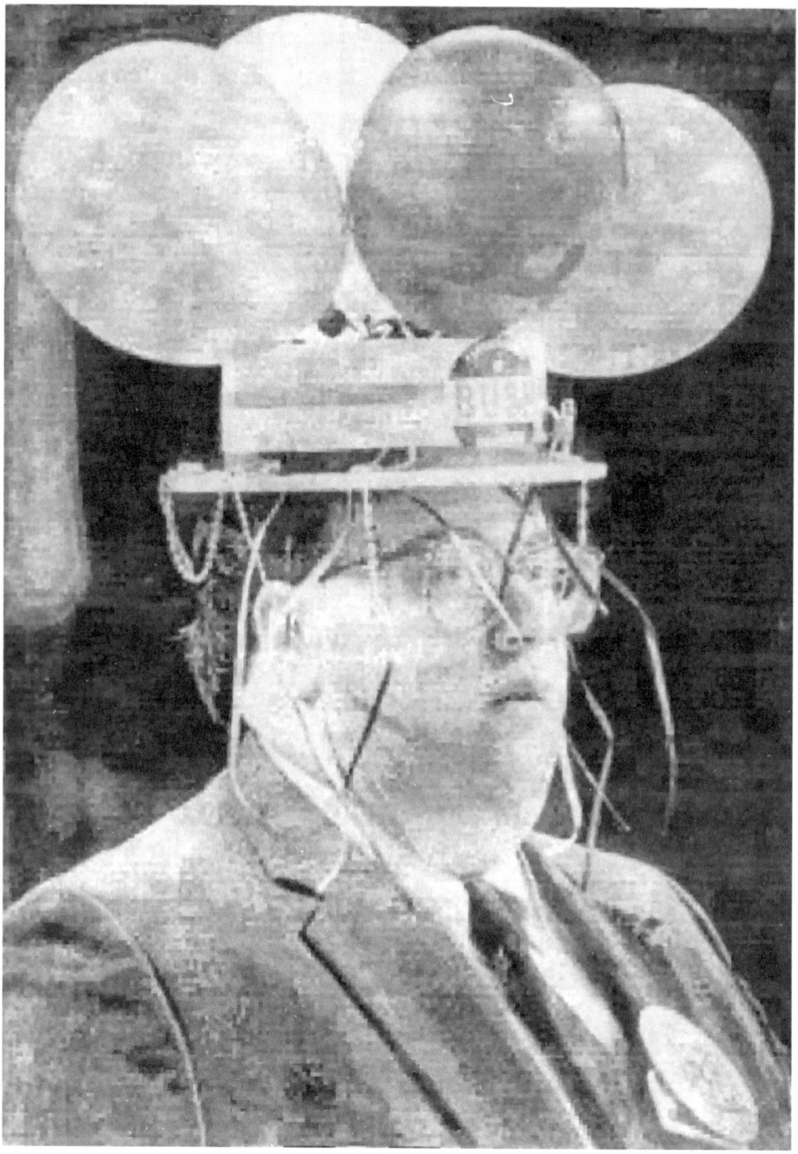

Joe at Republican Convention in Dallas, Texas, 1988.
AP photograph.

The house Joe grew up in, at 6509 Darlington Drive in the Squirrel Hill suburb of Pittsburgh; he told Enid it was a family rental.
Photography by Lee Benson.

Family support: Krista Parkinson, Randi Greene, Gerda Greene and Jim Parkinson stump for Enid.

On Christmas Day, 1994, neither Enid nor Joe could hold back their smiles as they awaited their first days in Congress.

Joe's "Sound of Music" house on Benecia Drive in the Salt Lake foothills.
AP photograph.

Victory kiss!
Photography by Gary McKellar, Deseret News.

Election Night, 1994: Joe beams as Enid receives her due.

Kissinger's old place at 1671 34th Street, Georgetown. The Waldholtzes rented it for $3,800 per month.
Photography by Lee Benson.

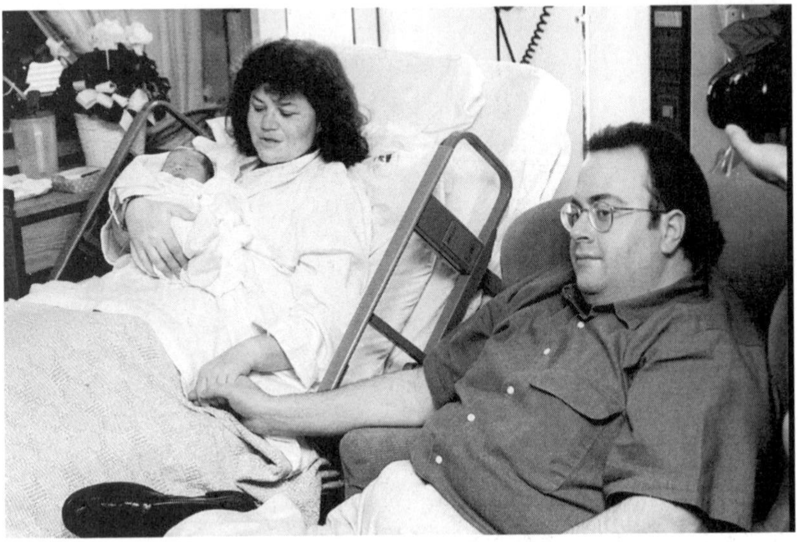

Shortly after Elizabeth's arrival, the whole family gets together.
Photography by Gerald Silver, Deseret News.

Through it all, Gerda and Forrest Greene stood by their daughter.

On the day Elizabeth was blessed, Forrest was front and center, while Joe hid behind Enid. Matt Parkinson and his mother, Sue, are at the right.

Enid and Newt during her '94 Campaign.

Enid and Joe face the Press together.

The man in the middle—Enid's brother-in-law Jim Parkinson.
Photography by Tom Smart, Deseret News.

Memorandum

To:	Mr. D. F. Greene c\o East-West Co.
CC:	Mr. and Mrs. Joseph P. Waldholtz
From:	The Waldholtz Family Trust
Date:	September 21, 1994 [computer file date]
Subject:	Assignment Letter and US Attorney Infomation

Mr. Greene, we apologize for the delay in sending the materials to you. Joe and Enid asked that we send you the assignment of the real estate and the letter from the U.S. Attorney. We apologize for the delay and the confusion.

If we can be of further assistance, please give us a call.

Thank you.

This Memorandum, printed from Joe's personal computer, documents a communication from "The Waldholtz Family Trust" to "Mr. D.F. Greene." One of the two actually existed.

Merrill Lynch

CMA Cash Management Account Monthly Statement

Summary Page

April 1994

Account No.	Taxpayer No.	Page	Statement Period
[illegible]	[illegible]	[illegible]	03/25/94 TO [illegible]

Your Financial Consultant	Office Serving Your Account	Questions?
FERN G SCHWARTZ	[illegible]	Call Your Financial Consultant
(412) 566-[illegible]	PITTSBURGH PA 15222	OR 1-800-[illegible]

MR JOSEPH P WALDHOLTZ
6691 BENECIA DR
SALT LAKE CTY UT 84121-3487

Account Status

	As of 03/25/94 31	As of 04/28/94
Ready Assets Account CMA MONEY ACCOUNTS	$0.00	$0.00
CASH $1,901.42	$1,901.28 $4,234,781.48	-$37,[illegible].60
TOTAL	$1,901.28	-$37,[illegible].60
[illegible]	[illegible] $4,238,482.70	[illegible]
[illegible]	$[illegible]	[illegible]
[illegible]	[illegible]	[illegible]
[illegible]	$1,901.00	$0.00

Dividend and Interest Income

	This Statement	Year to Date
DIVIDENDS (REPORTABLE)	$2.30	$27.27
Total Dividend and Interest Income	$2.30	$27.27

EFFECTIVE YIELD FOR THE PERIOD 03/25/94 TO 04/28/94
CMA MONEY FUND: 3.08%

Account Activity

Credits	This Statement	Year to Date
INVESTMENTS SOLD	$0.00	$0.00
DIVIDEND/INTEREST INCOME	$2.30	$27.27
FUNDS RECEIVED	$8,700.00	$143,700.00
OTHER CREDITS	$7,472.20	$47,423.20
TOTAL CREDITS	$16,174.50	$191,150.47
Debits		
INVESTMENTS BOUGHT	$0.00	$0.00
CMA CHECKS	$15,853.11	$60,442.70
VISA GOLD CARD TRANS	$0.00	$0.00
INTEREST CHARGED	$91.17	$99.34
OTHER DEBITS*	$39,570.00	$168,035.00
TOTAL DEBITS	$55,514.38	$228,577.04
Net Activity	-$39,339.88	-$37,426.57

*Includes Fee Charged

CMA NEWS

INTRODUCING THE NEW FREE MERRILL LYNCH CERTIFIED CHECK SERVICE. SEE NEWSLETTER FOR MORE INFORMATION.

YOUR CMA ACCOUNT CAN HELP MAKE IT EASIER FOR YOU TO PREPARE FOR RETIREMENT. SEE YOUR NEWSLETTER FOR DETAILS, THEN CONTACT YOUR FINANCIAL CONSULTANT.

April 1994

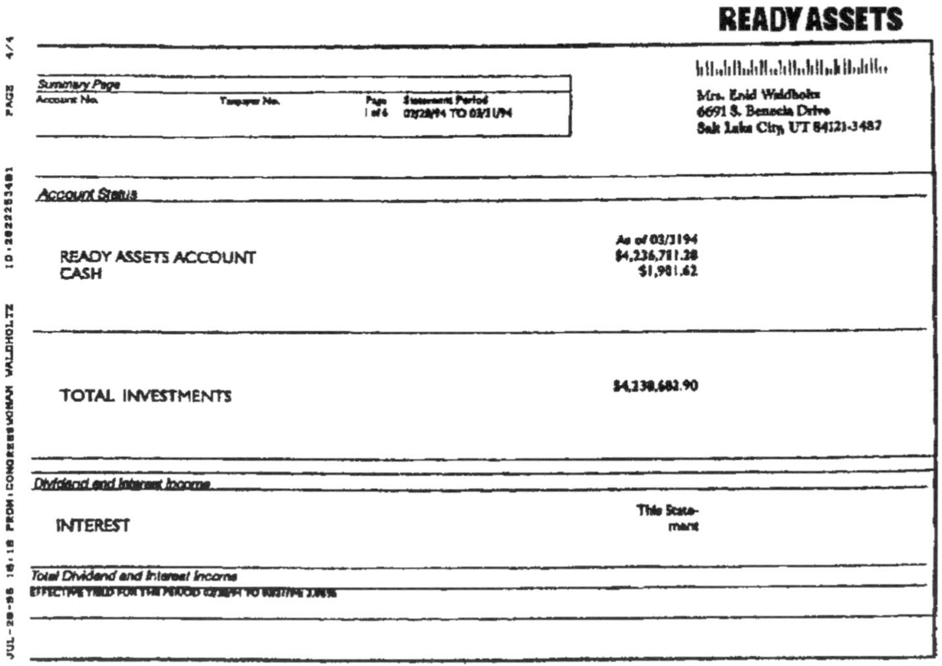

JUL-28-98 16:18 FROM:CONGRESSWOMAN WALDHOLTZ ID:2022253481 PAGE 4/4

READY ASSETS

Mrs. Enid Waldholtz
6691 S. Benecia Drive
Salt Lake City, UT 84121-3487

Summary Page

Account No.	Taxpayer No.	Page	Statement Period
		1 of 6	02/28/94 TO 03/31/94

Account Status

	As of 03/31/94
READY ASSETS ACCOUNT	$4,236,711.28
CASH	$1,981.62
TOTAL INVESTMENTS	$4,238,682.90

Dividend and Interest Income

	This Statement
INTEREST	

Total Dividend and Interest Income

EFFECTIVE YIELD FOR THE PERIOD [illegible] TO [illegible]

These documents, discovered after Joe's departure, show Joe's instructions for transforming a standard Merrill Lynch statement into a "Ready Assets" statement. Both the name of the company and the amount reflecting "total investments" are fictitious, but Enid's name and address are correct.

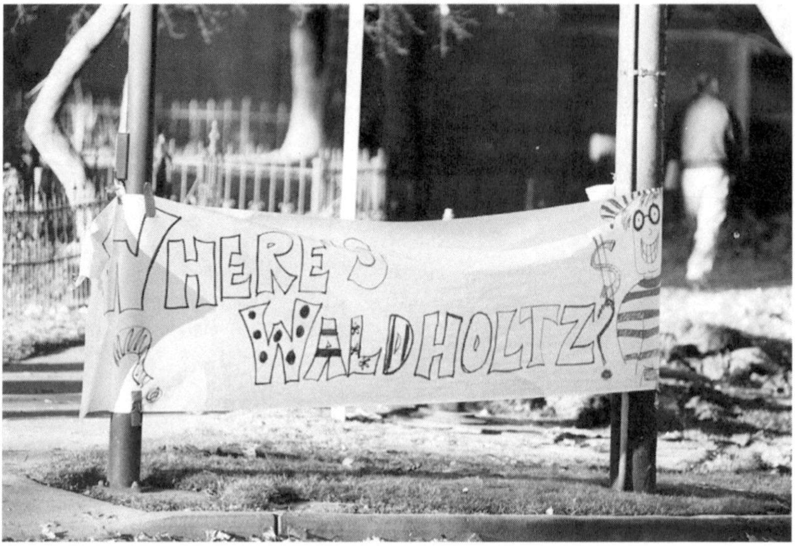

Nov. 17, 1995: A banner on the corner of 7th East and South Temple streets in Salt Lake asks the question that's sweeping the nation.
Photography by Tom Smart, Deseret News.

Enid's Washington D. C. based attorney, Chuck Roistacher.

The other side: Steven Slesinger, Joe's cousin, and Dr. Harvey Waldholtz, Joe's father, also got to entertain questions from the media.
AP Photograph.

An unhappy Utahn shows his view on Enid's place in the House at her press conference.
Photography by Carmen Troesser, Deseret News.

Enid and her attorney Charles Roistacher walk to U.S. District Court in Washington.
AP photograph.

Joe and his attorney Harvey Sernovitz leaving U.S. District Court in Washington.
AP photograph.

Flanked by her attorney, Charles Roistacher, and her accountant, Fred Miller, Congresswoman Enid Greene Waldholtz meets the press.
Photography by Carmen Troesser, Deseret News.

An intimidating row of cameras at Enid's press conference.

G. N. M. A. 36pt

CY56 12pt → Government National Mortgage Association [illegible] CY56 9pt

through

THE HILLMAN Company } CY[illegible]55 24pt

CY65 10pt
Received from Rebecca Levenson CY65 14pt

CY65 9pt

CY55 12pt The sum of — CY65 14pt $ 200,000 00 — CY55 12pt September 2, 1981 — September 2, 199

~~August 1989~~ — ~~August 1992~~

CY55 8pt AT RATE OF 11.35% (TAX FREE) — with a guaranteed rate of 8.5% (TAX FREE)

Contact CY56 12 — CY65 14pt Joseph Waldholtz — 422-8080 CY65 [illegible] 14pt — employee number CY65 9pt

These accounts can be extended at rates that prevail at the rollover ~~[illegible]~~ date.

CY55 12pt They are backed by the full faith and credit of the United States Government.

CY56 14pt Interest is payable at semi-annual intervals through the H.C. GNMA Disbursement Account

---

G N M A

Government National Mortgage Association

through

The Hillman Company

Received from Rebecce Levenson

The sum of $100,000.00 — July 26, 1989 — July 26, 1994

~~[illegible]~~ Variable-Interest Rate — adjusts every six months with a guaranteed rate of no less than 2% above prime

Contact: Joseph Waldholtz 422-8080 — Employee number

These accounts can be extended at rates that prevail at the rollover date. They are backed by the ~~full~~ faith and credit of the United States Government.

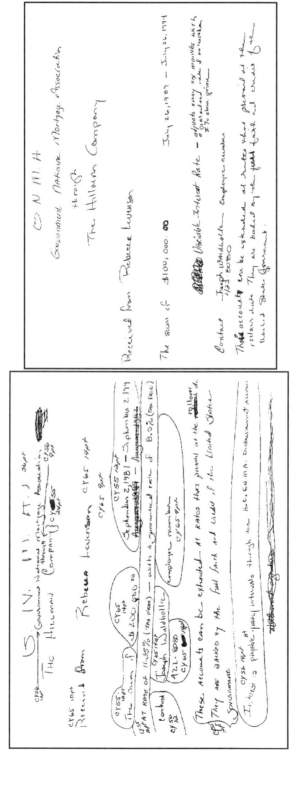

G. N. M. A.

Government National Mortgage Association

through

The Hillman Company

Received from **Rebecca Levenson**

The sum of **$100,000.00** **July 26, 1989 - July 26, 1994**

At Rate of 8.5% (Tax Free)

Contact: **Joseph Waldholtz** **Employee number**
422-8080

This account can be extended at rates that prevail at the rollover date. They are backed by the full faith and credit of the United States Government.

Interest is payable at yearly intervals through the H.C.G.N.M.A. Disbursement Accounts.

These three "G.N.M.A." documents show Joe's handwritten handiwork, which he presented to Kinko's copy center to produce the finished product.

"Team Enid" explaining the financial details at her press conference.
Photography by Tom Smart, Deseret News.

At her press conference Enid was on one side, the media on the other.
Photography by Tom Smart, Deseret News.

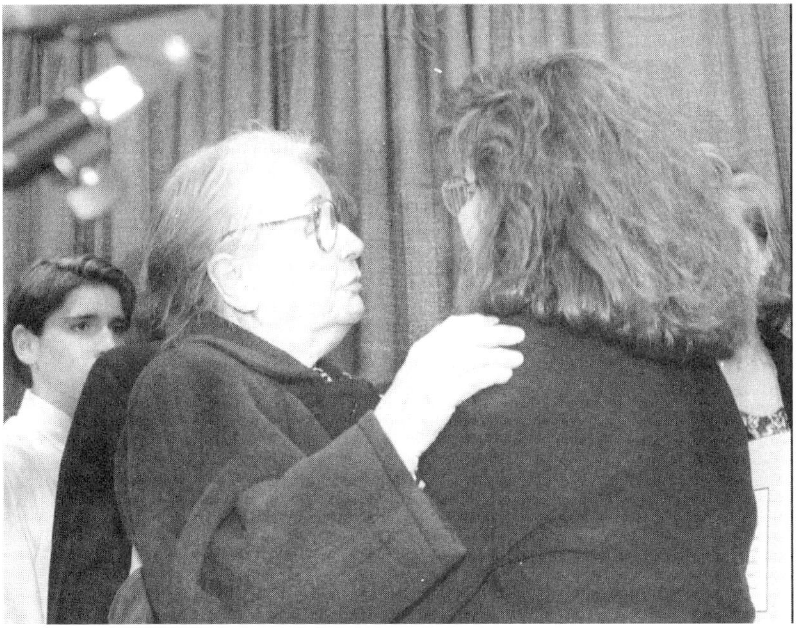

After her press conference, Enid is embraced by her mother, Gerda and her brother-in-law Jim Parkinson (top photo).
Photogaphy by Carmen Troesser, Deseret news.

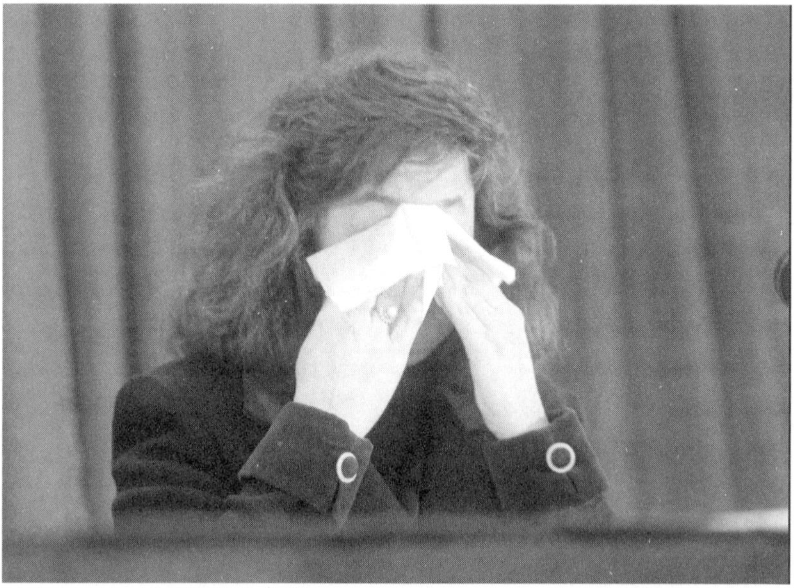

At her press conference, Enid's tears came unbidden.
Photography by Carmen Troesser, Deseret News.

CHAPTER VIII

Traditionally, a Mormon baby is blessed, or christened, on the first Sunday of the month shortly after the occasion of its birth. Elizabeth Greene Waldholtz's big day came on the fifth of November, nineteen hundred and ninety-five, when she was exactly sixty-six days old.

The blessing took place in the meetinghouse of the Federal Heights Ward (or parish) in Salt Lake City. It was Enid's childhood ward and she still knew most everyone in the congregation. There wasn't a lot of movement in Federal Heights, one of Salt Lake's few remaining bastions of old money, and for this occasion even some of those who had moved on had seen fit to return for the blessed event. Elizabeth was a famous baby already: Barely two months old and already the subject of a photo spread in *People* magazine.

Even before her blessing, the November 6, 1995 issue of *People* featuring Elizabeth–and her family–was on newsstands all across America. She hadn't made the cover; she had been nosed out by Princess Diana, Prince Charles and Camilla Parker Bowles (The headline: *"As Charles parties in public with his mistress, a stronger, sexier Diana returns to the royal spotlight to fight her homewrecker image"*). But the magazine gave Elizabeth plenty of play inside–three pages of text and two pages of photos. The article, entitled "Potty Politics," featured the infant children of two of Utah's members of the House of Representatives–namely, William Harvey Orton II, the seven-month-old son of Bill Orton, a Democrat from Utah's third Congressional district, and Elizabeth Greene Waldholtz, the six-week-old daughter of Enid Greene Waldholtz. There were photos of Elizabeth being held by her mother as she sat at her congressional desk, there was another shot on the couch in her mom's office, preparing for a bottle; and there was a shot of Elizabeth being held by Newt Gingrich as her mother looked on with an approving smile. Even if Democrats who had seen the magazine were already decrying Gingrich's "shameless baby politicking," how many other two-month-olds could say they had the undivided attention of the Speaker of the House?

D. Forrest Greene, a member in good standing of the Federal Heights Ward, a bearer of the holy Melchizedek priesthood, and Elizabeth's maternal grandfather, gave Elizabeth "a name and a blessing" by the power of that priesthood. He blessed his granddaughter with a long life, rich rewards, good health, the strength to overcome life's temptations, and the ability to be able to discern the good from the evil. After the blessing, Brother Greene rose to address the congregation. He looked directly at his family, which took up the better part of two long rows. He cleared his throat. "At the end of this life," he said, "I'm not sure what material possessions I'll have left. One never knows about the ups and downs of the business world. Whatever I do have, I will leave to my family. But even if all I have materially is gone, I know I'll still be able to leave them the most important possession I have, and that is my testimony of the gospel of Jesus Christ. No one will ever be able to take that from them or from me."

At the far end of the back row of the main chapel, Elizabeth's mother and father, Enid and Joe Waldholtz, sat in tears as the patriarch of the family spoke. Apparently, his words touched them deeply.

Although it was customary, and practically expected, for new Mormon mothers to do so, Enid Greene Waldholtz did not take the opportunity to follow her father and speak to the congregation on the occasion of her daughter's blessing. It was a day she had dreamed and hoped for all of her life. But she wasn't in a speech-making mood. Her life was too tangled for that. *People* magazine was one thing. Front page play in *The Hill*, Washington's own tabloid version of the National Enquirer, was another. The Waldholtz family finances were in the headlines again, and with yet another twist: Check kiting charges.

It had been just one year ago that she had been sent to the United States Congress by the constituents of Utah's second district.

By anyone's standard, it had been one whirl of a year. A veritable lifetime in twelve months. In almost dizzying succession the events had spilled out. Following the triumph on Election Day there had come the holiday in Hawaii, the orientation period in Washington, finding a place to live, swearing-in day, the Contract With America, The Hundred Days, office infighting, pregnancy, the flap over the financial disclosure and FEC reports, the month in bed, and the difficult birth of Elizabeth. And those were just the newsreel highlights. That didn't even get into the back-and-forths with Joe's family's money and the loans still outstanding to her father.

And now, there was this check kiting story–and while Enid was sure it was just more witch-hunting by the media or the Democrats, maybe both, she was beginning to seriously worry about what it was doing to Joe.

□□□

Joe had always been a big screen walking and talking through life. Nothing he did was small. His gestures were large. His tastes were large. His appetites were large. Heaven knew, his spending habits were large. *Everything* about him was large.

But lately, everything had grown even larger. After they returned to Washington, it didn't get better, it got worse. It was as if Joe had somehow plugged himself into the wrong voltage. His mood swings had become much more pronounced. Even the way he waved his arms, a kind of trademark gesture when he was exasperated, had increased. His temper was getting the better of him, more than Enid had ever seen. He didn't physically abuse her, or anyone or anything else, that she observed, but sometimes Enid thought it would help if he could chop some wood or swing a golf club or do *something* to let off some steam. He was too . . . too . . . churned up. All the time. And he was getting ill more often. He barely made it out of bed to make it to the church on time for the baby's blessing. They arrived in Utah Saturday at noontime and Enid hadn't even seen her family until just before the meeting, a day later. Joe had insisted she stay by his bedside at their home, across the valley from her family. To tell the truth, she didn't dare leave his side.

At the airport in Washington his behavior had truly frightened her. And that was the correct word: *frightened.* Joe had embarrassed her before, more than once, with his outbursts; and he had scared and shocked her multiple times with his talk of suicide. Those, however, had always been what she perceived as blips of irrational behavior across the screen of an otherwise rational man. But at the airport, Joe had displayed behavior that was one hundred percent irrational. It went beyond a blip. Enid seriously wondered if he might be losing his mind.

The problem involved a simple mixup with ticketing at the check-in counter. Joe said he'd been quoted a certain price; the agent said that price was incorrect and they'd have to charge a price that was significantly higher. As airport conflicts go, it was hardly out of the ordinary. But Joe's reaction *was* out of the ordinary, bordering on violent. He ranted and raved, ridiculed the ticketing agent with a voice that went beyond just *raised*, and, in general, caused a very public scene. Finally he'd thrown his arms up in the air (*way* up in the air) and announced to Enid (and everyone else) that he wasn't "going to pay that kind of money." And he was "going back home."

With Elizabeth in her arms, Enid had held her ground. "Fine," she said as levelly as possible. "But I'm going to Utah."

This was her baby's blessing, her family would all be in Salt Lake City, and she was not going to miss it.

Luckily, Joe did not call her bluff. If he had, she didn't know what she would have done. In truth, she didn't dare let him go back to the townhouse alone. But she did want to go to Salt Lake.

"I'll call Delta's government desk myself when we come back," she said, referring to the airline's liaison office that dealt with government-authorized flights. "Now come on, honey, let's board the plane."

To her relief, Joe, who had already started walking to the parking lot, relented and they were soon settled into their first class seats. Joe never flew anything but.

□□□

The waves of nausea overwhelmed Joe as soon as they landed at the Salt Lake airport. He simply didn't feel well enough to do anything except collect their luggage and go to their home. Enid's brother, David, and his wife had flown in from San Diego; her sister, Sue, had flown in with Jim and the kids from Palm Springs. They were at her parents' home along with her other two sisters who lived in the Salt Lake area, Gloria and Randi. Enid had hoped to see the whole family that night, and show off Elizabeth. But she didn't. She went home with Joe and stayed there.

It had been two months since they'd last been in Salt Lake City. Their departure just after the Labor Day Weekend had been a harbinger of better days, Enid was sure. She was certain that they had turned the corner on all their problems; they had all the documents they needed to solve the financial mess. She thought it was over.

She was wrong.

Those dozen mover's boxes of financial papers had made it to Washington, all right, but mostly they had served as a new style of interior decorating for Enid and Joe's bedroom. Enid was sure Michelangelo painted the ceiling of the Sistine Chapel faster than Joe was going through those boxes. He did work at it. That much was true. Every day it seemed he was sorting through papers. She couldn't fault him for no effort. But he never got anywhere. That was the problem. Every day, Keith Davis sat at his office at Huckaby & Associates waiting for the documentation that would allow him to amend Enid's FEC reports and forever clear her slate. And every day he'd get a trickle of documents, if that–certainly not enough to allow him to do much of anything, except continue to wait.

Enid had turned into a world-class meddler as a result. Throughout their married life she'd played it loose with Joe. If he was going to be super husband and show total support for her not only as she ran for office but as she held office, her philosophy was not to tell him how to do his job. Heaven knew the job description was unwritten. How many other men on the face of the earth were pulling the same kind of shifts as Joe Waldholtz, fulltime Congresswoman's husband?

But that was then and this was . . . ridiculous. Enid started to wonder about Joe's persistent excuse that he simply "didn't have enough time." He as a matter of fact *did* have enough time, now that Elizabeth was here and the office was running smoothly. He just didn't choose to use it to get the job done.

At least every other day throughout September and October Enid would say, "Have you gotten Huckaby everything they need?"

And Joe would reply, with increasing irritation, "I'm moving as fast as I can."

Enid volunteered to sort the boxes for him, but Joe insisted that he could do a better job since he had handled the paperwork up until then and knew what he was looking for. He didn't want Enid making the job worse by digging around and reshuffling the papers.

On one weekday morning in late September, when no votes were scheduled for several hours on the floor of the Congress, Enid decided to stay home and help Joe sort out the boxes. *This is a much better tack,* she thought, *if I just offer to help instead of suggesting I do his job for him.*

Joe said "OK" and as he sat in his underwear in front of the boxes, pulling out stacks of bills from campaign vendors, he said to Enid, "When I hand you these, straighten them out and put them in alphabetical order. Then I'll drop them off to Keith this afternoon."

For the next couple of hours they worked like that. Joe sorting, Enid filing. All the while, in between handing her invoices, Joe would toss great mounds of paper into a big green garbage bag at his feet. To Enid it was a heartwarming scene: a scene of progress. Or so it seemed.

Not that it wasn't a busy time. In many ways, it was busier than ever. Congress was back in session; in the absence of a true administrative assistant in her office, Joe was still a part of Enid's "management team"; and, of course, there was a new baby to take care of. To help on that score, the Waldholtzes had secured the services of a New York nanny named Marlene Bristol, a thirty-one-year-old native of Trinidad who, Joe's "connections" assured him, was the best in the business. Marlene moved into the bedroom next to the brightly painted nursery, where she and Elizabeth became fast friends. At least that was working out.

Every day, the four of them–Marlene, Elizabeth, Joe and Enid–would pile into their car and drive to Capitol Hill, where Elizabeth's second nursery doubled as Enid's office. In between votes and committee meetings, Enid would nurse Elizabeth.

For all of Enid's nagging–and she was getting more proficient with the passing of every non-productive day–Joe, if anything, seemed to be moving *slower.* Worse yet, half the time Enid didn't sense she was even registering with him any more when she talked. She had never seen Joe like this. Cajoling didn't work. Tantrums didn't work. Deadlines sure didn't work. Huckaby's threat to discontinue a working relationship if all documents hadn't been received by Sept. 30th had come and gone with no reaction by Joe other than an outburst about the insolence of "people who work for us telling us what to do!" For their part, the accountants had a heart and chose not to act on their threat. Despite his partner's considerable frustrations, Stan Huckaby asked Keith Davis to continue to stay on the case after Sept. 30. The firm was not anxious to abandon a client while rumors were swirling of an FEC investigation–even if it was receiving abominably slow responses by that client. Poor cooperation or not, they just didn't feel right about leaving the Waldholtzes high and dry.

□□□

To Enid, the more nothing worked, the more the thought that Joe might have serious mental problems became a genuine consideration. To what degree and what kind, Enid had no idea. Maybe he had some form of depression. Perhaps it was just too much stress. Maybe *he* had the baby blues. But he did seem to be cracking up. She got the number of a psychiatrist and suggested to Joe that he call "for some positive therapy." Joe agreed more than once to do just that, but never quite got around to making an appointment.

Not only were his moods exaggerated, so was his spending. As Enid's birthday–October 5th–approached, Joe talked of buying her a sable coat. Enid balked at that. He had already bought her two fur coats, which she rarely wore; she didn't want a sable coat. It wasn't a gift that, beyond the sheer grandiosity, made any sense. She had thought the same thing about the nearly inch-wide sapphire and diamond bracelet Joe had given her as a gift for having Elizabeth. It had overwhelmed her. Joe had given her jewelry ever since she'd known him, but that had been the grandest gesture yet.

"I don't want a sable coat," she told him flatly. "I don't want anything even *like* a sable coat. There's only one thing I want for my birthday."

"What's that?" asked Joe.

"I want you to finish sorting out those boxes," his wife said.

□□□

Another reason the extravagant gifts didn't make sense was the continuing problem with Joe's family trust. It had been over a year now and still the litigation generated by cousin Stevie lingered. The massive trust remained frozen. Joe continued to draw his monthly twenty-five thousand but that was all. It was more than enough for the Waldholtzes of Georgetown to live on, of course, even if they had added a fulltime nanny and an infant to feed. But Enid's father was still waiting for the money he had coming. Forrest was earning market-rate interest, Joe kept reminding Enid whenever the subject arose, and all the money would be repaid as soon as the trust was unfrozen. But, still, everybody's nerves had been fraying long enough. Enid knew how her father was about money. She worried that it was affecting his health.

There was a breakthrough with the trust, Joe had reported, early in October. He told Enid that the trust litigation was about to be settled and a large sum of money, a little over $25 million, was being held in an account at the Pittsburgh National Corporation in the name of . . . ta-da . . . Joseph P. Waldholtz.

Enid learned this bit of encouraging news in a round-about kind of way, however. Joe explained the situation to her only after she heard that he wanted to call her father for *more money*. On Oct. 12th he'd phoned Forrest Greene at his office in San Francisco and, explaining that it was good faith money the Pittsburgh National Corporation required to settle other debts of Joe and his mother before they could go ahead with the $25 million transfer, Joe asked for a "final" loan of $308,000.

Sitting alone in the modest office on Montgomery Street that he was about to close down for good, Forrest Greene balked. This time, Joe's pleas of "I don't think it would be a good idea to bother Enid with this at this busy time," fell on deaf ears.

"Let me talk to Enid," Forrest said.

When Enid got on the line, Forrest told her he would send the $308,000 only if she assured him it was all OK. He had heard vaguely about the questions regarding Enid's finances. The news was both troubling and disconcerting. He wanted to make absolutely sure that, if he made this loan, the bank would transfer the $25 million and all of these problems would be put to rest.

Enid told her father she would get back to him–as soon as she got through with Joe.

When Enid demanded an explanation as to what on earth was going on and why he wanted more money from her father, Joe patiently told her that it was "just a formality."

He said that the bank needed to be paid in full before it would release his funds. Because PNC was one of the banks involved in the earlier complications caused by Joe's mother, and because they had discovered yet more charges from those complications, they needed to have that taken care of before the $25 million could be transferred.

Enid said that sounded ridiculous. Even if she had almost flunked trusts in law school, this was nonsense. She asked Joe why the bank couldn't simply offset what they were owed by what they had on account. Joe assured her she was making perfect sense, but sometimes banks didn't function on perfect sense. He said the only way they could get the $25 million was if they first had the $308,000 in place.

Finally, Enid agreed to give her father the green light to transfer the money to their account at First Security Bank in Salt Lake City, but only on the stipulation that it would stay there until the officers at PNC signed a legal document that the entire $25 million would be released as soon as the $308,000 was put into the overdrawn account.

"Fine," said Joe.

Enid kept her word. She called her dad in San Francisco.

"Go ahead and transfer the money to our account," she said. "It won't go to Pittsburgh unless I have a signed settlement agreement that puts an end to all of this."

Forty-eight hours after that phone call to her father, as she waited for Joe to produce the legal document from the Pittsburgh bank, Joe excitedly rushed into her Congressional office. He had just finished talking on the phone with the bank. "They don't need the three hundred and eight thousand," he told her. "They don't need your dad's money. They'll release the rest of the money without it."

"Great," said Enid, looking up from her desk. "Wire it back to him–right now!"

"Already done it," said Joe, beaming.

□□□

If you know the right buttons to push, it isn't hard to get in touch with a congressperson. If they want to be, they are among the most accessible people on earth. Even when they're in session in the U.S. Capitol, going about the business of running the world's most powerful democratic government, any given member of congress is thirty seconds away from accessibility, tops. All it takes is a phone call from a congressional staffer to the Capitol cloak room, where pages are waiting like tennis ball boys, and girls, to sprint to the floor with messages. If he or she so chooses, a member of congress can then walk the few feet to the cloak room, enter one of the dozen phone booths lining the wall, and make contact with the outside world.

On Halloween Day, 1995, Enid Waldholtz chose to leave the floor of the House of Representatives after receiving a message from a House page. The message was from Kate, and it said "urgent." Kate Watson wasn't the kind to overuse that word.

Enid called Kate from the middle booth in the cloak room.

"It's me," she said. "What's going on?"

Kate told her a reporter had just called from *The Hill*, a biweekly newspaper publication that would be considered "tame" by supermarket checkout lane standards, but was nonetheless considered "radical" by Capitol Hill standards. It was the Washington publication that was constantly on the lookout for scandal, or, barring that, a hint of scandal. On a slow day, *The Hill* would settle for controversy.

"The reporter, Jennifer Senior, spelled just like it sounds, says they're running a story in tomorrow's edition that your finances are under federal investigation," said Kate.

"She wants you to respond."

Enid did just that. Inside of a minute she had Jennifer Senior on the line. The reporter said she had a source that confirmed that the finances of Enid and Joe Waldholtz were under investigation by the federal government. She didn't know just which part of the Justice Department was doing the probe, and she wouldn't reveal her source, but she told Enid that she understood the focus was on Joseph Waldholtz's handling of the couple's personal and campaign finances. She said there were suggestions of transferring money back and forth from account to account and writing checks that didn't reflect accurate balances. He had knowingly written worthless checks, in other words. A form of bank fraud called check kiting.

Jennifer Senior asked Enid if she cared to comment.

"This is the first I've heard of the investigation," Enid said, beginning a statement that would be accurately reproduced in the next morning's edition of *The Hill* underneath a banner, over-the-logo headline that said "Waldholtz overdrafts under scrutiny."

"I will tell you, most emphatically," she went on, "that there would be no truth to any allegation of wrongdoing by either my husband or me. I think it's disgusting that someone who would not identify themselves would create such a rumor and not give me the opportunity to clear my name. Any allegation of check-kiting by my husband or I is ludicrous and defamatory."

The Hill also quoted Joe.

"Good heavens, no," he said when he was asked if he or his wife were being investigated. "That's not true. We had transfer problems. There was a transfer that went awry; this was months ago, we thought it had taken place when it didn't. There's no investigation."

□□□

As soon as the story hit the streets—and it was learned that the financial institutions in question were the Wright Patman Congressional Federal Credit Union in Washington, D.C., and First Security Bank in Salt Lake City—Enid immediately called the president of the Congressional Credit Union, as it was known, and demanded to speak to Robert Hess, the president.

When Hess came on the line she got right to the point.

"I demand to know if any law enforcement agency has contacted you in any way about me or about my husband," she said as levelly as possible.

On Hess's end of the line, silence.

OK, fine, Enid thought, *I'll just outwait him!*

And she did.

Finally, after what must have been thirty seconds of dead air, Mr. Robert Hess said, "I will have to call you back," and hung up.

A couple of hours later, after Joe and Enid had gone to her office on Capitol Hill, Hess called back as promised. It was Joe who took the call. When Enid returned from a vote on the House floor he gave her this news:

"The inquiry is from the U.S. Attorney's office."

Enid froze in midstep.

"Then it's true?" she said, stunned.

But her mind was not frozen. Her mind was already in defense mode; already circling the wagons.

Before she took another step she looked at her husband and with complete composure said, "Joe, we're in serious trouble. I need to get us a lawyer."

□□□

She found their lawyer–better yet, an entire firm of lawyers–at 1001 Pennsylvania Avenue, on the sixth floor, in a conference room just to the left of a reception area that announced the law offices of Powell, Goldstein, Frazer and Murphy. The ink from *The Hill* had barely dried when Enid shook hands with Harry Huge, a Powell, Goldstein partner who had been referred by Ladonna Lee. A former client of Ladonna's had used Huge in particular, and the Powell, Goldstein firm in general, and found their work to be more than satisfactory. These lawyers came highly recommended.

The services of Powell, Goldstein, et al, did not come cheap, and Enid wanted them to know right up front that not only was she serious about retaining them, she was serious about paying. Before she left her offices she wrote out a personal check for $10,000 and made Joe promise "on their love" that he would make sure the account she was writing it on had sufficient funds. He said he would.

After hearing Enid's story, Harry Huge and two of his partners, Mike Chanin and Elliott Adler, told Enid they would be happy to represent her and do all they could to straighten out this problem. They further explained that another partner of theirs, a white-collar crime expert named Chuck Roistacher, was out of town but they would want him also to be involved in the case. They told Enid that since it appeared time was of the essence they better get started right away. The first thing they needed from her was access to the Waldholtz's financial records. To do that they had to have signed authorization by both Enid and Joe. If she could get them that, they could get the ball rolling.

The next day, Enid returned to the attorney's offices with Joe in tow. After they each signed forms that authorized the Powell, Goldstein lawyers to access their joint financial records, the attorneys asked to speak to each of them separately. By now, Chuck Roistacher, who had returned from a case in Florida, was heading up the legal team. He requested that Enid meet privately with the lawyers first. In that meeting Roistacher explained to the Congresswoman that since the firm was already representing her, the attorney-client privilege now applied to anything she told them, but it did not–and would not–apply with Joe unless he retained them as well. Further, he explained the potential for conflict if the firm did represent both of them–in case the course of their investigation turned up evidence against one of them but not the other. Chuck asked if Enid, understanding all that, might prefer to have the firm represent just her and not her husband. Enid did not hesitate. "Oh no, no," she quickly protested. "I want you to represent both of us."

Next the lawyers spoke privately with Joe, explaining his wife's wishes and offering their services to him as well. But Joe did not immediately accept their offer of representation. He said his family's trust already had lawyers, and he would have to think about it.

When Enid learned of Joe's reluctance to retain counsel she was perplexed.

"Joe," she said in front of her new team of attorneys, "We can't wait on this. We can't let this slide." Enid had seen how long Joe could string things out. She was trying to light a fire under her husband, trying desperately to get him to see the seriousness, and the immediacy, of their situation.

When Joe answered, he spoke calmly and almost meekly. "Still," he said to his wife, speaking almost as if he were in a trance, "I need some time."

□□□

Joe's lethargy was proving to be unshakable. Even an out-and-out threat of jail time didn't turn him into a man of action–or, at the very least, a man who squared up and defended himself.

Enid hadn't brought up the possibility of incarceration herself. That had come courtesy of none other than Utah's highest ranking national politician, the state's senior Senator and chairman of the Senate Judiciary Committee, Orrin Hatch.

After hearing persistent rumors for weeks of bouncing checks and tardy FEC amendments, and then seeing the article alleging check kiting in *The Hill,* the Senator had summoned Enid and her husband to his office in the Russell Building. The four-term Senator had known Enid since she was a teenager, when she began her involvement with the Young Republicans. He felt an affinity for her. He also felt he might be able to relate with Joe, since

Hatch had lived for many years in Pittsburgh before moving to Utah. He was concerned for both of them.

The Senator knew the intense scrutiny members of congress lived under; that in many ways, fair or not, they were held to a higher standard. If he could, he wanted to help the Waldholtzes from wading in too deep, only to discover there was no way out. He hoped they hadn't waded in too deep already. That was why he had convened this private hearing.

He went for the shock approach. Hatch was sitting on a couch on one side of his private office–Enid and Joe sat on the couch across from him. Avoiding Enid completely, the Senator fixed his gaze onto her husband, looking at Joe as intently as he'd ever looked at one of Clarence Thomas's accusers.

"If you don't get this straightened out right away, you're going to jail!" he said.

Joe got neither indignant nor upset.

"I know," he answered back. And that is all he said.

By the close of business Friday night, two days since the article in *The Hill*, Joe still hadn't made up his mind about legal counsel. The decision would have to wait at least until Tuesday–after he, Enid and Elizabeth had returned from the baby's blessing in Utah.

□□□

The Greene family wasn't terribly surprised about Enid's no-show at the family home the night before her daughter's blessing. She was front page news, as usual, in the *Salt Lake Tribune* and *Deseret News*. And not for some new freeway legislation or water project bill, either. It was her finances, again.

They'd read about the check-kiting investigation. They'd read about Joe's explanations that a box of checks had been stolen in the Cincinnati airport. Also, credit card receipts showing his signature had been with those checks. They'd read Enid's denials and assurances that it was all a big misunderstanding and would soon be cleared up. They were not at all shocked that the press reports had a negative tone. Enid had been under attack for so long now it was hard for them to remember her life when she wasn't in politics and under siege. The media could be, and usually was, by their view, brutal. It was the family's general feeling, and Gerda Greene's staunch belief, that these latest charges and attacks at Enid were part of a plot to get DeeDee Corradini off the front page of the Salt Lake newspapers. Corradini was the Mayor of Salt Lake and had been the subject of her own financial probe. With the mayoral election just a couple of days away, who better to deflect DeeDee's negative press than the first-term Republican Congresswoman?

As Enid did her best to nurse Joe back to health at their southeast valley home, that was the spin at the Greene home just east of downtown Salt Lake. *Democrats and the media. A lethal mix.*

□□□

Everyone agreed that Elizabeth looked beautiful on her blessing day. She was dressed all in white, wearing a velvet and lace gown that extended well beyond her tiny legs. Her father had chosen it for her before she was born. Joe and Enid had been on a "baby shopping spree" when it caught his eye. He'd marched to the cash register and paid for it. Didn't even look at the price tag.

After the meeting, Enid made her way across the foyer toward her brother-in-law Jim Parkinson. Along the way, she shook hands with old friends who were close to both herself and to her family, smiling and accepting their congratulations. But she moved briskly, and when she got to Jim the smile disappeared.

"Jimmy," she said. "I have to talk to you today."

"Sure," he said. "Let's talk back at the house."

□□□

Jim Parkinson was a lawyer married to Enid's older sister, Sue–it was fate, they always joked, an attorney with a wife named Sue. Jim and Sue lived with four kids, a hot tub, and a mortgage, in a house that flanked the fourth fairway of the Bermuda Dunes Country Club in Bermuda Dunes, California. Jim knew Enid and her husband were having some problems. He also knew he was the only lawyer in the family. He suspected a combination of those two factors were why Enid wanted to talk to him.

But, still, it took him by some surprise that Enid would want to consult with him at all. In the not-so-distant past they'd had their differences, and even though everything had technically been patched up, there were still feelings that lingered.

It had all started with Joe.

Not long after Joe and Enid were married in August of 1993, Jim had called Enid and his new brother-in-law had answered the phone. In the course of the conversation, Jim asked Joe if he and Enid were planning to eat Thanksgiving dinner at the Greene's home in Salt Lake City.

"I'd rather eat shit than go to my mother-in-law's for Thanksgiving," Joe said.

"What did you say?" Jim asked, taken aback.

"I said I'd rather eat shit than go to my mother-in-law's," Joe said again.

"If I were in Utah," said Jim, who had always adopted a certain protective posture when it came to his in-laws, "I'd kick your ass."

It was the beginning of a beautifully strained relationship.

Later, Jim told Gerda Greene what Joe said and, sure enough, the family communication network kicked into gear and before long Gerda told Enid and Enid was calling California to talk to Jim.

"This is all a big misunderstanding," she told him. "I talked to Joe and he didn't say he'd rather eat shit, he said he'd rather pound sand."

As if that makes a difference, Jim thought. Regardless, he wasn't buying.

"I'm from the desert," he said. "I know the difference between sand and shit."

From that point on, Jim and Joe–and, consequently, Jim and Enid–barely spoke. But the ice was finally broken the next spring, in June of '94, when the Greene family gathered in Salt Lake City to celebrate Forrest's seventy-fifth birthday. A restaurant in the Joseph Smith Memorial Building that overlooked the Mormon temple had been selected for the luncheon, which had gone extremely well until the guest of honor became so ill they had to take him home.

By the time they got Forrest home and into his bedroom he was pale and having a hard time finishing sentences. As they left him alone to rest, Jim, fearing that perhaps his father-in-law might be dying, asked Joe and Enid if he could talk to them. They went into a back bedroom where Jim told them he wanted to make peace and bury the hatchet. "We've had issues, but I want to drop them as of now," he said. "The past is the past. We're family. We need to get along." Then all three shook on it and hugged.

Now they were going back to the same house, and this time it was Enid asking Jim for a meeting.

After dinner, Enid and Jim repaired to the same bedroom where the group hug had taken place more than a year before. Enid started to cry, but composed herself enough to get right to the point. "I'm so scared," she said to Jim, who immediately assumed she was talking about the media. At dinner that had been the main point of contention–the media was the evil adversary. Jim thought that's why she and Joe had hired a lawyer in Washington, so they could sue for libel and slander.

Still, the three words Enid used–"I'm so scared"–shocked Jim Parkinson, and after years of doing trial work he did not shock easily. This was his sister-in-law, Enid Greene Waldholtz, talking. In the twenty-five years he had known her, he had never known her to be scared of anything. If something was in her way, she either shoved it aside or ran it over. That's the Enid he knew.

"What is it?" he asked. "What's got you so scared?"

"Joe," Enid said. "It's Joe. I think he's going to kill himself."

"Over what?" Jim was failing to absorb any of this. He had a trust fund brother-in-law worth about half-a-billion dollars and a congresswoman sister-in-law who, it seemed to him, no matter what the problem, always landed on her feet. What could be so wrong in their lives? If one of them was talking suicide, *maybe we should all get in line for Dr. Kevorkian.*

"He keeps threatening he'll do it," Enid persisted, not directly answering her brother-in-law's question.

"People who say they will, never do." Jim was doing his best to console her.

"I don't believe you," said Enid.

Never one to use subtlety when a sledgehammer might work, Jim opened the door to the bedroom and saw Joe at the end of the hall. He called him into the room.

Joe looked dumbfounded as he entered the bedroom. He threw both arms in the air and said, "Enid, what's the matter?"

Jim answered.

"Joe, she believes you're going to commit suicide," he said. "What's the matter with *you*? That's the question."

Joe thought a second before answering, "Oh, it's about the trust," and then, as he let the door shut, he, too, started to cry.

Amid a lot of tears, they thrashed it around for a while, the three of them. Both Enid and Joe were obviously upset, and Jim, as he heard their tales of financial woe, did his best to put those fears to rest. Although a personal injury lawyer, Jim had once handled a large fraud case in the San Francisco area and in that case he made several friends with expertise in accounting and bank fraud. He had a close friend in San Jose who was a top forensic accountant, just the kind of person, he told them, that they needed to sort out their paperwork, get to the bottom of it–make some sense of it all.

"I'll call him tomorrow and we'll arrange it so we can both fly back to Washington early this week," said Jim. "I guarantee you we can get this straightened out. This isn't anything to go killing yourself over."

"Thanks Jim," said Joe, dabbing at his eyes. "You don't really have to do it. But we really appreciate it."

Their meeting over, they discovered that the rest of the family was in the family room, waiting on them. They were getting ready to watch a slide show. Enid's brother, David, had put together the show in honor of his sister on the occasion of her baby's blessing. But Joe grabbed Enid's arm as they left the back bedroom and begged her to leave with him. He said he wasn't feeling well again.

Enid was torn. In one room sat her family that had barely seen her all weekend long and was waiting to watch slides of their growing up years. Outside the room stood her suicidal, half-crazed husband.

"Sorry I can't stay," she said to her family, as she scooped up Elizabeth and she and Joe walked out the door.

□□□

By late the next day, Jim, by now back in his office in Palm Desert, had arranged with his accountant friend in San Jose, Gary Madden, to leave for Washington by Wednesday, the day after tomorrow, at the latest. Madden had agreed to drop everything when Jim told him of the urgency involved. "Just pick up my expenses," he'd said. "If it's family, I'll do it on the house."

But on Tuesday, Joe had phoned from Washington–where he and Enid were trying to sort things out–and headed Jim off at the pass. He told his brother-in-law that the trust documents wouldn't be arriving from Pittsburgh in time and it wouldn't do any good if he came back before they got there. Jim should just sit tight, Joe said, and he'd call him later. When Jim didn't hear a word from Joe by Wednesday afternoon he grew frustrated. He'd gone to the effort to offer free accountant work to a multi-millionaire close to suicide, and he hadn't even gotten the courtesy of a call back.

By the time he'd driven home from work Wednesday night he'd had it. "Forget 'em," he said to Sue. "At this point I don't care. I went to the effort to get them help and nobody even lets me know what's happening. If they've got such big money problems, let them handle them themselves."

Very close to the same time that Jim was making his resignation speech in California, Joe Waldholtz was, in fact, on the telephone, and he *was* working on his money problems. But he was calling Salt Lake City, not California.

Sitting at the desk in his study, D. Forrest Greene answered the telephone. When he heard it was Joe, he motioned to his wife to go into the kitchen and pick up the extension.

"Yes, Joe, I'm here, and I've put Gerda on the phone too," said Forrest. "How are you? How's Enid? How's Elizabeth?"

Forrest had picked up on the emotion in Joe's voice as soon as he answered the phone. He had heard it often enough over the past two years. It was why he'd motioned his wife to the extension. Usually he was alone for these calls, tucked away in his San Francisco office, fielding them by himself. It felt better having company for what he knew was coming next.

"It's the trust," Joe began. He was sobbing. As Forrest could attest, Joe was always emotional during his calls, but this time he seemed more emotional than ever. At first, it was hard to understand him.

As Joe began to explain further complications with the trust litigation, Forrest knew it would mean Joe again needed help "just one more time." The lifelong financier suddenly felt very tired. He remembered all the calls over the course of the past two years, and he remembered all the broken promises. All the "One more times." On at least three occasions he'd gone to the lobby of his condominium complex in San Francisco waiting in vain for a Federal Express package Joe promised was coming, containing a check to pay back part of the loan. On more occasions than that he had checked his accounts at East/West Securities or Wells Fargo for wire transfers Joe promised he would send but never did.

It was always something. There was the time a Pittsburgh attorney delivering a check while on a case in California had dropped dead. Just died, Joe had told him, while on this business trip. Joe said that threw the trustees into a dither for a week. There was the time Joe himself was bringing the check to a family gathering at Jim and Sue's in the desert, and in the Denver airport he tripped. He hit the floor and his briefcase flew open, scattering his papers. Wouldn't you know it, the check had turned up missing. Enid saw the fall herself. She said Joe hit the ground hard enough to break his glasses.

Breaking out of his reverie, Forrest realized Joe was still talking about the trust, explaining that cousin Stevie, his evil cousin Stevie, was still causing untold troubles.

Gerda finally broke in.

"Joe," she said, "You're a big man. You have a strong back. You just take that strong back and stand up to your cousin Stevie."

Forrest actually managed a smile at that.

But the smile faded when Joe got to his punch line.

"To clear all of this up once and for all," he said. "I need six hundred thousand dollars."

Six hundred thousand. It was the most Joe had ever asked for. A new all-time high. He'd started out at $60,000 and stayed in that range for a long time, but now that seemed like peanuts. He'd gotten bolder during the height of the '94 campaign, when the money was covered by the real estate assignment of proceeds that Forrest still hadn't seen. He had asked for as high as $408,000 in one shot. In October he asked for $308,000–which Forrest knew still hadn't been returned as promised. Still, $600,000 was a new personal best for Joe Waldholtz, no question.

Suddenly D. Forrest Greene didn't care what the consequences might be, what public scandal might ensue, what embarrassment might befall Joe's mentally unbalanced mother or his family or the Waldholtz name. As Joe waited on the other end and with his wife as his witness, he put together a collection of words he had never before managed to say to his son-in-law.

"Oh no," he said. "No. I won't be able to do that."

On the other end, the line clicked dead.

After spending what was easily the most restless, anxious and combative night of their married life–and lately, that was saying something–Enid, completely oblivious to her husband's phone call to her father the night before, arose early on Thursday morning, November 9, 1994. Joe, she knew, was getting worse, not better.

She hadn't slept much. Neither had Joe. He'd been asleep, she assumed, about two in the morning but Enid had awakened him as she paced back and forth in their bedroom, stifling sobs the best she could. Somehow, the pacing helped. *For people who don't know which way to turn.*

Joe was angry when he sat up in bed and saw her out of bed pacing. "What are you doing?" he'd said, not hiding his displeasure.

"Joe, I can't take this anymore," said Enid. "You've got to tell me what's going on."

Joe threw his hands up in the air. "I can't live like this," he said.

"Neither can I," Enid, crying, wailed. She was kneeling by his bedside. "Whatever it is, we can work it out. But you've got to tell me. What is going on?!"

This was not new ground. Daily, if not hourly, since their return from Utah, Enid constantly peppered Joe with questions, and Joe constantly deflected them in one form or another, giving her everything but answers.

She tried every tactic she could think of: bullying, babying, shock effect, you name it.

She'd left him at home one day while she went to the office so he could relax and have no disturbances while he sorted out the financial papers. But that night the nanny told Enid that Joe stayed in bed all day watching TV and chomping on great mounds of hard candy he'd bought at the grocery store. Not only hadn't he looked at his boxes, he hadn't bothered to look in on Elizabeth even once.

So she'd shifted gears and tried to shock him into action. "Joe," she said on one occasion in her office, "Tell me the truth. Are we just living off my dad's money?" It was the wildest, most ridiculous accusation she could think of, one that was certain, she felt, to get a rise, and hopefully after that, a conversation. But from Joe all she got was indignance. "You're ruining our marriage," he'd said angrily. "How can I be married to someone who has no trust in me?"

She'd also resorted to the ever-effective married person's

bullying tactic of hitting your spouse's nerves head-on. Enid knew full well the remorse Joe had carried around for two full years because he felt, by his absence during the Pinocchio ad, that he had cost her the '92 congressional campaign. "Joe," she said one night in bed as they tossed and turned, "I don't think you could bear it if I lost the re-elect and you felt it was because you didn't clear up our finances in time."

But his only response had been, "What are you talking about?"

Nothing worked. Nothing even made headway. Enid just couldn't penetrate the mysterious veneer that surrounded Joe and kept him from opening up and dealing with their problems. *If he is crazy,* she would think, *he's making sure I wind up there too.*

But the fear that he would end it all was by far the worst.

After chastising her for pacing the bedroom floor in the middle of the night, Joe abruptly got out of bed and went to his closet. He quickly put on a short-sleeved shirt and a pair of shorts. Enid knew this routine. He was going to leave! Again! She ran to the dresser and grabbed his wallet. *He won't leave without his wallet,* she thought. *He won't leave to kill himself.*

But he was leaving anyway.

"I can't get any rest here. You won't leave me alone," he said. "And I need to get some rest." Joe was moving toward the stairs.

But Enid was quicker. She raced ahead of him down the stairs toward the front door, where she promptly sat down, her body wedged across the solid wood. Prior experience taught her that standing upright did no good if Joe really wanted to get past her. He was much bigger and stronger and he'd merely grab her wrists and pull her out of the way. Sitting was better.

"Where are you going?" asked Enid, fighting to buy time. "You can't leave, Joe. You just can't."

As he reached around her for the door handle, she played her last card, the one she'd played so many times before, the one that worked.

She surrendered.

"I'll shut up," she said. "I won't bother you. I won't ask you any more questions. I'll sleep on the couch. I'll do *anything*. But please don't leave. Please don't leave and hurt yourself."

As her husband sighed and finally turned back toward the bedroom, Enid sagged to the floor. Another crisis averted, but how many more were on the way? How much more begging did she have in her?

She had an awful feeling that emanated from somewhere deep inside, a feeling that something wasn't right. She didn't know what, exactly, and that was the maddening part, but something *was not right*. She had to talk to someone, she had to turn somewhere. She thought of calling her father but dismissed the notion. He didn't need this kind of stress. Not at his age. At 76, he should be out playing golf with his buddies, bragging about his grandkids. He shouldn't be sorting out why his daughter's husband is suicidal.

Early the next morning–with Joe upstairs, hopefully asleep–Enid stole her way up the stairs from the living room couch, where she'd spent the night, to the study. She picked up the phone next to the fax machine and punched out a number in California.

As she waited for the connection surrounded by the silent townhouse, she thought she heard a creak on the stairs.

PART II

AFTER

CHAPTER IX

Jim Parkinson was in the kitchen when the call came from Georgetown. Sue answered. She handed him the phone.

"What's up?" he said.

"Jimmy, it's Enid."

He knew that already. Outside of his wife and a few close friends, Enid was the only one who called him Jimmy. She'd called him that the first time they met–when she was twelve and Sue brought her college boyfriend home for dinner–and she'd called him that ever since.

At first, she did not have Jimmy's undivided attention. He was halfway through his usual breakfast–a bowl of mixed cereal, Grape Nuts, Frosted Flakes, Wheaties and Cheerios. As soon as he polished that off, chased by a Diet Coke, he would be out to the garage for an hour on the treadmill, then he'd fire up the Lexus and drive the ten minutes to the Palm Desert law offices of Regar & Parkinson, a personal injury firm not without an envied reputation in the Coachella Valley. Jim liked to get to the office reasonably early. He was an early riser. It was just before six in the morning, California time, when the call came from back East. In our nation's capital it was three hours beyond that, approaching mid-morning.

He idly wondered if they had a bad connection.

Then he realized Enid was whispering.

"Jimmy," she said, "You need to come back here . . . Now!"

Even when whispered, even when it's your wife's kid sister who insists on calling you Jimmy, even when you're halfway through breakfast, when someone says "Now!" it gets your attention. Jim put down the spoon.

Maybe it was his trial lawyer instincts, maybe it was his family instincts, maybe it was just instincts, period, but the next words out of Jimmy's mouth were these:

"Don't you want Joe to hear you?"

"Just come," she said.

"Please."

□□□

Enid hung up the phone and talked herself back into composure. This was new ground for her. She had never betrayed her husband before. Well, OK, betrayed might be a little harsh. All she had done was ask Jimmy to come to Washington without telling Joe. You didn't need to tell your husband your every move, did you? The vows didn't go that far. But the thing was, she always had. They were a partnership, a team. As hard as she'd been pushing him of late, still, she had never purposely kept anything from the man she married, never. There were no secrets between them. Not from her end, she could say that for sure.

But no matter how close their relationship *had* been, Enid had to talk to someone other than Joe. The more she talked with Joe, the more something that should have been simple only became more complicated. That's why she was calling in some help, why she was reaching out to family. That's why she picked up the phone and even though she knew Joe wouldn't be happy about it, she asked Jimmy to come to Washington. Now!

□□□

It took him a day to get there, which is how it is when you're bucking the headwind of the time zones. Jim left his home in the desert early Friday morning, drove west to the airport in Ontario on the outskirts of Los Angeles and caught an eastbound plane to

Dallas, where he connected to a flight that dropped him into National Airport a couple of hours after the sun had set on the Potomac. They charged him full fare for the flight, sixteen hundred dollars for first class, the only seat they had left. But even if just twenty-four hours earlier he had vowed to leave Enid and Joe to their own problems, there had been no mistaking the urgency in his sister-in-law's voice. Jim put it on his Visa.

At National he hustled outside the terminal and hailed a cab at the curb.

"Georgetown, 1671 34th Street," he told the driver.

Joe's going to be surprised to see me, Jim thought as he settled into the back seat. Beyond that, he had no idea either what to expect or just what he was wading into.

A drive that could take an hour at the height of rush hour took just fifteen minutes. Jim paid the driver and stepped out onto the sidewalk. The neighborhood was quiet, battened down for the night. *So this is where Kissinger lived,* Jim thought as he looked at the townhouse Enid and Joe had leased for her full two-year term. There was no yard to speak of, but townhouses aren't known for their landscaping. The exterior was brick, the trim was painted white and the doors green. There was a one-car garage, a rarity even in this tony part of town.

The Waldholtzes had selected the place more for its location than for its former resident. That's what they'd told the family. With the Capitol just a few miles away, few Washington residential locations are more convenient than Georgetown, or more storied. John Kennedy lived there when he was a senator. Bill Clinton lived there when he was a student. Originally called George Town, after George Washington, who used it as a base camp when he drew up the plans for America's capital city, it sits comfortably–and relatively safely–alongside America's corridors of power.

Jim rang the doorbell, bracing himself for what he thought would be a surprise on Joe. He was soon to discover he was wrong about his visit being unexpected, however. Despite Enid's efforts at stealth, she had been found out that morning. During the phone call that noise that sounded like a creak on the stairs had, in fact, been just that. When she walked upstairs to the bedroom the first words out of Joe's mouth, who by that time was back in bed, were, "Why is *he* coming?"

Startled as much by the realization that her husband had been spying on her as by the question, she began to cry and said simply, "Joe, we need help . . . I need help."

From Joe's body language as he personally answered the door, Jim immediately sensed his presence wasn't going to result in a call to kill the fatted calf.

"Jim!" said Joe, *trying* to act surprised. "What's going on?"

"Enid here?" Jim said as he slipped past his 300-pound brother-in-law and into the foyer. "She asked me to come."

□□□

The townhouse at 1671 34th street was much more impressive on the inside. It consisted of five roomy levels. There was a formal living room, an informal living room, a guest room (currently occupied by the nanny), a dining room, a den, two bathrooms, two bedrooms, a kitchen, and a room at the front of the house that, so legend had it, Kissinger had built for the Secret Service agents when they needed somewhere to cool their heels.

Jim, Joe and Enid, who soon made her appearance, met in the dining room, where they offered Jim some leftovers, which he did not refuse. Elizabeth, who had turned two months old on Halloween just ten days before, was upstairs in the nursery, fast asleep. Marlene, the nanny, was in her room, which adjoined the nursery. The evening news was about to come on television. There would be nothing on it about the Joe Waldholtzes. The purpose of the discussion they were about to have in the dining room was to make sure it stayed that way.

As is the hope for all family meetings, this one was going to have peace and calm. Absolutely. That was Jim's goal. He was determined to speak evenly and non-threateningly, to handle the situation with decorum and diplomacy. It must have been a full fifteen seconds before he was in Joe's face.

"Just what the hell is going on?!" he shouted.

Enid swiveled her head and looked at her husband. *Exactly*, she thought, *what I'd like to know.*

To Jim's lawyer mind, once you got past the emotion, the problem seemed relatively simple. Basically, the difficulties were with Joe's family trust. So he started there.

The cross-examination was on.

"Just how much is the trust worth?" Jim began.

"Well, it varies," Joe responded.

"Where are the trust documents located?

"They're all in an office in Pittsburgh."

"Who are the trustees?"

"I had to recently change trustees because the previous ones made a lot of mistakes and caused a lot of problems."

"What investments do they make?"

"I don't know, there are a lot of them. It changes all the time. Jim, you don't understand, we're into a lot of different things."

"What is the average return on investments?"

"It depends on the investment. I don't know. I don't keep track of that. Accountants do."

"You mean to tell me you have a four hundred million dollar trust and you don't have a clue how it's invested?"

"That's right."

"Who are the beneficiaries of the trust?"

"Myself, my brother Bruce, my cousin Steve, another cousin, my father, and my aunt."

"What is the average annual cash flow that goes to the beneficiaries?"

"It fluctuates."

"Well how much did you get last month?"

"I didn't get anything last month. That's what the problem is. If you'd been listening . . ."

"I have been listening," Jim answered, his face exclaiming his exasperation. "But Joe, everytime you've opened your mouth you haven't made sense."

On like that it went, Clarence Darrow versus Charles Keating. With the gloves off. Joe had an answer for everything, Jim had another question for every answer. Sitting between them, Enid watched their back and forth as if it were a tennis match. Until, finally, she'd heard enough.

"Joe!" she practically screamed, "this is not what you told me before! What is the truth? This is not making any sense!" This was the first time Enid had heard Joe give different answers to these questions. Always before, his answers had been the same. Now, as everything he said shocked her, Enid wondered if Joe was lying or slipping into dementia.

Joe threw his hands into the air.

"This *is* the truth," he said.

When Jim finished eating they took a break. Joe and Enid went upstairs, Jim went two flights downstairs to get some things out of his bag. After a moment he looked up as Enid walked into the room. She was alone. Her face was drawn. She was on the verge of tears.

"Enid," said Jim. "What's wrong?"

"Oh Jimmy," she answered. "There's something I haven't told you. There's something you don't know."

She broke down and sobbed.

He let her regain her breath and her composure, and she went on.

"What you don't know, is that we've borrowed money from dad . . ."

" . . . a lot of money."

She continued: "Whenever the trust had problems we used it to get money from him. Jimmy, we've gotten a lot. Around four million dollars. If we can't pay him back, I'm afraid what might happen."

This was hard for her to say. She was physically shaking, almost uncontrollably.

"What if I've bankrupted him? What if I've bankrupted my father?!"

Luckily, D. Forrest Greene's son-in-law was more aware of the extent of the Greene family fortune than his daughter.

Jim put his arm around Enid and gave her a reassuring hug.

"Four million?" he said. For the first time all night he allowed himself a smile. Jim didn't know exactly how much his father-in-law, D. Forrest Greene, was worth, but he knew it was a *lot* more than four million dollars.

"That's a major hit and I'm not saying it isn't," he said. "But trust me on this one, that's not going to put your mom and dad in a trailer park."

"Are you sure?" said Enid.

"I'm sure."

Now Jim had even more questions for his brother-in-law.

"Hey Joe," he shouted up the stairs, "Can you come down here for a minute?"

Joe descended the stairs with all the fight of a sickly poodle.

"I understand you owe my father-in-law a lot of money."

"We're paying it back." Joe turned and looked at Enid. "I wired him some more money just this week."

"Can I confirm that with a phone call?" asked Jim.

"I sent it. I can't confirm that it got there."

The interrogation resumed, Jim still on the offensive. He was not hemmed in by courtroom restraints so he let it fly. He asked open-ended questions, closed-ended questions, questions that called for hearsay, questions that were leading. Anything that might ferret out something that made *sense.* Who was going to object?

It was hard going. Getting a bead on Joe's family trust was proving to be slippery work.

"How much did the trust pay in taxes last year?" Jim asked Joe.

"Uh, well . . . the trustees would know that exactly. I think it was nine million."

"How much money did you make from the trust last year?"

"I'm not sure. The accountants take care of that."

Jim turned to his sister-in-law.

"Enid, you must have signed your joint tax return last year, how much did you pay in taxes?"

Enid looked at Joe and said, "Joe, you handled that, how much did we pay in taxes?"

Jim interrupted. "Wait a second, Enid," he said, "You had to sign your tax returns. Didn't you look at what you signed?"

"I didn't sign the tax return . . ." Enid looked at her husband. "Joe?"

"The accountant signed the tax return," Joe said. "That's how we've always done it."

Dumbfounded, Jim looked at the ceiling. "Joe," he said finally, "that's not how it's done. You have to sign your own tax returns. Everybody does. It's the law. Your accountant can't do it."

"Well, he did."

Jim reached for the phone. He got an accountant friend, Bill Thompson, on the line in Palm Springs. He told Bill he had a hypothetical for him: Could it be possible, under any circumstances, for an accountant to legally sign a client's tax returns? Bill responded quickly. "No," he said. "Everyone has to sign their own tax return. Why? Who's got that problem?"

"Bill, can I get back to you?" said Jim as he hung up the phone and looked at Joe.

"That was an accountant in Palm Springs. You can't have an accountant sign your tax return."

"Oh my God," said Joe, "maybe we have a problem."

Joe looked around the room for help. His face was soaked with sweat. His gaze fell on his wife. "Enid," he said plaintively. "You know there's a trust. You know this will all be worked out. Why are we going through this?"

Jim looked at his brother-in-law measuredly as Joe stared at Enid and Enid stared at the carpet. For his summation, Jim chose an old John Wayne line, the one he delivered to Richard Boone in *Big Jake*. "Your fault, my fault, nobody's fault," he said to Joe. "But if there isn't a wire by noon on Monday sending my father-in-law's money back to him, you're not going to be dealing with a nice old man in Salt Lake City, you're going to be dealing with a raging asshole, and that raging asshole is going to be me."

If a fistfight had broken out then and there, Jim wouldn't have been surprised. He half expected one. He had just completed a two-hour interrogation in which he continually demeaned and disparaged his brother-in-law, stopping just short of calling him a cheat and a liar. But Joe did not leap out of his seat. He just sat there. He was bowed but not, Jim realized, beaten. He'd given Joe his best shots, and yet, no matter how many times he had him up against the ropes, he could never get the ten-count on him. It was uncanny. There was always some substance, some sense, to his answers. Joe was always able to counter the blow. Maybe he did have all the answers.

"Look," Joe replied, "this is all my fault and my family's fault, I realize that." Tears welled up in his eyes. His shoulders sagged. His whole body was a white flag, fairly shouting resignation.

"The trustees will be here tomorrow," he said finally. "They'll have all the documents with them and we can clear all this up."

Two of the Waldholtz Family Trust trustees, Joe had informed them earlier, were flying to Washington the next day, due to arrive at 2:15 in the afternoon on a USAir flight from Pittsburgh. It wasn't the first time Joe had promised the appearance of the trustees. They had originally been scheduled in Washington on Wednesday, then Thursday, then Friday, and now, it would be on Saturday. Using past history as an indicator, it was not a mortal lock that they would be there.

But it was something they could sleep on.

A standoff secured, Joe turned to Jim. "Now," he said. "Let me drive you to your hotel."

Jim Parkinson was tired. He had crossed the country coast-to-coast. It was late. He was at his sister-in-law's house. And now his brother-in-law, for some reason, wanted to hustle him off to a hotel.

"See this couch?" Jim answered back. "It's got my name on it."

□□□

They turned to their left and walked west on Reservoir Road. Having squeezed all the sleep they could out of the night, which wasn't a lot, both Enid and Jim had decided to take a walk in the early morning chill, hoping they could make their heads as clear as the air. Joe wasn't happy when Enid told him she was going for a walk with Jim. But she promised to be back quickly-and she wanted to talk with Jim where Joe couldn't hear her. As they walked, Jim encouraged Enid to put her arm through his.

There were plenty of times when Enid and Jim hadn't been so united. As in most of their lives. A case in point was early in Jim and Sue's married life, when they were staying overnight at Sue's parents' house in Salt Lake City. They were just settling into dinner when Enid, who was fourteen years old at the time, had a complaint. She'd seen a can of Coca-Cola in the room Jim and Sue were staying in, and from her strict point of view, Coca-Cola was in contradiction of the Mormon health code, the Word of Wisdom. Right up there with wine and whiskey, the way she saw it. As a result, she wasn't very happy with Jim, and she told him so. Jim, who had only recently returned from two years voluntary service as a Mormon missionary in Argentina, thought to himself as he looked at Sue's precocious kid sister: *now that's interesting.*

When it came to the big picture, they believed the same things. But that's where the compatibility stopped. Where he was irreverent, she was reverent. Where she was conventional, he was unconventional. Where he was profane, she was proper. Ladies and gentlemen, in the same family, the yin and yang of Mormonism.

After that first dinner, they had been parrying ever since.

But of course wartime has a way of identifying your allies, and now they were just that, allies–and anxious ones at that. At the moment, both of them were wishing someone would tell them just what it was they were allied against.

They arrived at the entrance to Georgetown University, the oldest Catholic institution in the United States, the school that gave the world William Jefferson Clinton and Patrick Ewing. They were three blocks from the townhouse. Jim and Enid sat down on a bench.

It was Enid who broke the silence.

"So what do you think?"

Jim pulled his coat tighter. Maybe this was what passed for Indian Summer on the east coast, but his blood had just hours earlier taken leave of a Palm Springs summer.

He stopped shivering and waited to answer, as if he were weighing each word.

Finally he repeated essentially the same thing Enid had heard him say to Joe late the night before.

"My heart wants to believe him, but my head tells me he's full of shit."

"I keep adding two and two and I get five," Jim went on. "That's the part that bothers me. Something isn't adding up. It could be just a big confusing misunderstanding only an accountant could sort through. It could be that Joe and I will go to the airport today and the trustees will be there, armed to the teeth, and we'll have this all straightened out by tonight."

Then he paused.

"But I gotta' tell you Enid. I think you should brace yourself just in case. I think this could be the worst day of your life."

Enid didn't know what to think. She was trying to live through this one minute at a time. The Congresswoman from Utah knew her brother-in-law from California had a flair for the dramatic. *Well*, she thought, *I hope that's all this is.*

They walked some more before they went back to the townhouse, where Joe was finishing a phone call.

"Just talked to the trustees," he said as he hung up the phone. "They're coming to National on a USAir flight at 2:15."

To make sure the flight was on time, Enid called the airport. What she heard distressed her.

"Joe," she said. "There is no USAir Flight from Pittsburgh at 2:15."

"No, no," said Joe. "It doesn't *land* at 2:15. That's what time it leaves Pittsburgh."

Again Enid called the airport. Yes, she was told, USAir Flight 240 from Pittsburgh would be *leaving* on time at 2:15.

Not only would the trustees arrive, but they were bringing

documents they'd collected from Merrill Lynch in Pittsburgh. Joe had given Enid the name of the broker he said the trust worked with. Enid called the Pittsburgh number. "Merrill Lynch," said the voice on the other end. Enid asked for the broker. "She was here, but you've just missed her." Enid thanked him, hung up and looked at Joe, who said, "You see? She's driving to the airport."

Things were looking up.

Enid saw them off at the garage door. She wouldn't be accompanying them. With the two trustees, that would make four for the return trip in the passenger car, so there really wasn't room, and she felt she should be with Elizabeth anyway. She had hope as she sent Joe off. That morning Joe had done something he hadn't done in weeks. He'd moved to her side of the bed and thrown his arms around her. "Don't leave me!" he whispered plaintively, desperately, "Don't leave me!"

"I'm not going anywhere," Enid answered. "I love you, Joe."

As Joe passed Enid in the doorway and moved into the garage he turned to her with tears in his eyes and, with the same plaintiveness she heard in bed, he said, "Enid, just remember, these last few years have been the best."

□□□

At the wheel of the Cougar with Pennsylvania plates, Joe Waldholtz cut a full figure as he backed out of the driveway and headed south down 34th Street, in the direction of the airport. Jim was in the passenger seat. As usual, Joe was dressed *neo classical casual* for the occasion. When it came to dressing down on Saturday, this was it–tan slacks, tasseled Ferragamo loafers, a multi-colored sweater, the kind that go for hundreds of dollars in the shops that adjoin the casinos in Vegas. On his wrist was his $20,000 Rolex President. If he had walked into a Vegas casino right then they'd have given him a hundred grand credit just for looking the part.

Traffic was light on the second Saturday in November. Congress was out of session. Thanksgiving was less than two weeks away. But after they had been on the road fifteen minutes–enough time to get to the airport–they were still in the maze of the District of Columbia's downtown sector. Joe seemed to be short-circuiting. For one thing, he was sweating profusely in spite of the cool weather. For another, whenever Jim played tourist and asked him what this monument or that building was, he either didn't answer or didn't know. Finally, without a word to Jim, Joe picked up the cellular and called Enid at home.

"We're lost," he said.

Even by his brother-in-law's standards, Jim thought this was bizarre.

"How can you get lost in your own town?" he asked when Joe hung up the phone.

Joe didn't answer his question, but instead, as he negotiated a U-turn and aimed in the direction of the Washington Monument off in the distance, he began to proclaim his everlasting, undying love for his wife and daughter.

"I love them so much," he said as tears streamed down his face.

"I love Enid."

"I love Elizabeth."

"They mean everything to me. They're so sweet, so special. I love . . ."

Jim cut him off.

It was just the two of them. He did not need this.

"I don't give a flying fuck if you love her or not!" he said. "I just want to get to the airport and meet those trustees. Now do me a favor and shut the fuck up and drive!"

They were there in ten minutes. Joe pulled the Cougar into a parking lot next door to the terminal. It was legal. The license plate that said "Member, U.S. Congress" was in place in the upper lefthand corner of the windshield. There are some places you can't park with that plate in Washington, D.C., but there aren't many. This particular lot was reserved for members of Congress,

White House Staffers, pentagon officers, and a select few others with sufficiently high clearance. It was the first time all day Jim sensed that Joe was in anything remotely resembling a good mood, if but for the few seconds it took him to wheel into that "Members only" lot, get out, lock the doors, and nod arrogantly to the guard.

The monitors inside the airport entrance said USAir Flight 240 was on time, scheduled to arrive in twenty minutes. To the left of the monitors were the baggage claim carousals for both USAir and Delta. Beyond the carousals was a bank of phones and the restrooms. Directly ahead was an escalator leading up to the gates. To the left were the USAir gates, to the right, Delta's.

As Jim headed for the escalator he realized that Joe wasn't coming. He looked back at him.

"I'll stay here," said Joe.

"What the fuck is going on?" said Jim, trying to keep his voice down, his hostility out in the open.

"Look," said Joe, surprising Jim as he suddenly squared to the fight, "The documents coming off that plane represent everything I own. Those papers are all I have. I'm not about to let them come off that belt without me here to pick them up."

He told Jim what the lead trustee, Sally something, looked like, and told him to go on ahead. They would all meet back here at baggage claim.

Jim shrugged and left. He was glad to be rid of him. He figured he had just enough time to stop at *Frank & Stein*, a fastfood stand at the top of the stairs and pick up a hot dog. He hadn't eaten all day. He thought about getting Joe one, and then he let the thought pass. *That 300-pound cockroach could stand to miss a few meals*, Jim thought.

Twenty minutes later, that 300-pound cockroach was gone.

□□□

Jim Parkinson was on his hands and knees, checking under every stall, looking for a pair of black Ferragamo loafers, size 13. He knew he looked strange, of course he did. You could probably get arrested for this, he thought, crawling around on the floor of a public restroom in National Airport, but still he persisted, looking under every door. Because if he could find those shoes, he could find his brother-in-law.

Besides, he'd already made a fool of himself. It was getting easier. Just a few minutes before he'd been at Gate H-3, watching as the passengers disembarked from USAir flight 240 from Pittsburgh. He was looking for a blonde woman, about five foot four, fortyish, with blue eyes–Sally something, the trustee. He'd gone up to a woman who loosely fit the description, asked, "Are you Sally?" and got that "Go screw yourself" look Easterners have refined to an artform.

The funny feeling that *something is wrong here* started about then, and it built as Jim negotiated the escalator, two steps at a time, on his way back down to baggage claim, where he'd last seen Joe.

When he got back, Joe wasn't there.

He wasn't in the restroom, either.

Where the heck was Joe?

In a matter of hours, it was amazing how many more people were asking that same question.

Normally, a man can take off for a few unaccounted hours on a Saturday afternoon and not launch a nationwide manhunt, but there was now a problem of about four million missing dollars, and, more than that, the problem of a missing husband whose wife . . . was a member of the United States Congress.

□□□

Back at the townhouse, Enid was wondering what could be taking them so long.

It had been more than two hours now since she'd seen Jim and Joe off to the airport, and except for two calls from Joe–the first from the cellular right after they left, asking for directions, the second from the airport–nothing, no word.

The second call had not gone well. After the first call, Enid did something she had never done before. She opened Joe's briefcase, and started rifling through it. As usual, the briefcase bulged with a couple of inches of various papers. Just on top was a statement from Pittsburgh National Corporation Bank saying Joe Waldholtz owed them a payment of $99,999.99. *But he said he hadn't dealt with PNC for months!*

Joe's call from the airport had come just after Enid had found the PNC statement. She couldn't keep herself from asking about it. "Oh, Enid," Joe had sighed, "you don't understand what you are reading."

"Put Jim on," she'd said.

"He's forty yards down the concourse. I'll get him and we'll call you right back."

That had been an hour ago.

As they say about stakeouts, waiting is the hard part, and this was hard. She had not eaten. Some days you just aren't hungry; when you've got a big test coming up at school, or you're presenting a bill on the floor of the House, or you've sent your brother-in-law and your husband to the airport for four million dollars.

She mainly just sat there in the kitchen, a kitchen where, who knew?, Henry Kissinger may have done the same thing, waiting, hoping, that some pending crisis would blow over and everything would be fine again.

In truth, the Congresswoman had yet to see any overt threat to her person or her position. Both the Federal Election Commission and the Department of Justice were on her case, it was true, but no agents in bad-fitting dark suits had showed up at her office. Unlike in the movies or the Ludlum novels, the gumshoes never actually appeared. But their specter did. A rumor here, a story in the newspaper there, and not only did you know there was a fox hunt going on, you knew you were the fox. Enid's marriage was threatened. Her husband was threatened. Her job was threatened. And she knew no one would be saved till she got all the answers.

□□□

After he'd crawled around on the restroom floor, after he'd checked the phones, after he'd searched around the cinnamon roll stand next to the baggage claim, after he'd waited for the baggage claim area to empty, after he wished he hadn't eaten the hot dog, Jim Parkinson used his powers of deductive reasoning to arrive at two conclusions: The trustees from Pittsburgh weren't here, and neither was Joe.

Curiously, the Cougar was still in the parking lot. Wherever Joe was, he wasn't in his car. Jim knew what he had to do next. He had to tell Enid.

Her number was unlisted and he didn't have it with him, so he called home, across the country to Bermuda Dunes, California. Sue answered on the third ring.

"I need Enid's phone number." He blurted it out.

Sue heard him of course, but in the spirit of wives everywhere who realize husbands would be lost if not for them, she first needed to tell Jim that Doug Miller, a close friend of his who was going to be enrobed as a municipal court judge the coming Monday, had called that morning and he wanted to make sure Jim didn't forget that he was the keynote speaker at the ceremony; Jim needed to call Doug, right away.

"You're not listening Sue!" Jim shouted. "Give me Enid's number! Now!"

From Sue: "I don't have it."

Sensing that wasn't exactly the answer of choice, either, she quickly added, "Randi does," Randi being Sue's twin sister, who lived in Salt Lake City.

"Get it," said Jim. "I'll wait."

Sue put Jim on hold and called her sister. "Jim needs Enid's number," she told Randi. "He sounds upset."

"I thought Jim was *with* Enid," said Randi.

The twins were confused. And that was just the start of it.

"Thanks Sue, I'll call you later," Jim told his wife after she came back on the line and given him Enid's phone number. Before he hung up he added, "Sue, you're never going to believe what's happened."

"What's that?"

"Joe's disappeared."

□□□

Among the things Jim never dreamed he'd do in his life was call his wife's younger sister, who had grown up to become a sitting Congresswoman, and tell her that he'd lost her husband at the airport; but he'd just made that very call and now, for the second time in less than twenty-four hours, he was in the back seat of a Washington, D.C. taxi en route to 1671 34th Street, Georgetown. Talk about going around in circles. He felt like he was in that movie, *Groundhog Day*, where Bill Murray keeps living the same day.

Not your typical Californian in Washington, Jim thought. *Been here all of twenty-four hours and haven't visited a single monument.* He allowed himself a hint of a smile. After all, it wasn't the end of the world. He'd been kind of brusque with Sue. He decided he better try to lighten up. *But everything had happened so fast!* He allowed himself another hint of a smile as he thought about Joe, a man he had learned to tolerate but never liked. *Lard-ass sonofabitch* was his pet name for his brother-in-law, that and *cockroach. The Lard-ass cockroach sonofabitch has really screwed up this time,* he thought as he was driven past the Lincoln Memorial, again.

Around Enid, however, he'd never called his brother-in-law anything but Joe. Nobody did. Because as everyone in the family knew, Enid loved Joe. Worshipped the ground the *Lard-ass* walked on.

□□□

After the cab dropped him back at Enid's place, and after he did his best to comfort his sister-in-law and tell her everything was going to be all right, he was sure of it, just you see, Jim did not hesitate in making his next move. He knew what needed to be done. He needed to make a phone call.

They went upstairs to use the telephone in the master bedroom. Enid sat on the floor at the side of the bed as Jim picked up the telephone and carried it to the side of the room, where he sat on the floor, leaned against the wall, and began to tap out a number.

He called Harvey Waldholtz-Dr. Harvey Waldholtz, Joe's father, Pittsburgh dentist. Jim had met him just twice, at the wedding when Joe and Enid were married, and at the swearing-in ceremony eleven months earlier when Enid became a member of Congress.

The phone was picked up on the other end after just a couple of rings. It was Harvey himself.

Jim took a breath. He was going to do this in one take.

"Dr. Waldholtz, Jim Parkinson. I have one question and one question only. Joe's missing, a lot of money is unaccounted for. Is there a Waldholtz Family Trust worth in the neighborhood of three hundred million dollars?"

"I don't know what you're talking about," Harvey Waldholtz answered. "There is no Waldholtz Family Trust."

A chill ran through Jim. Six words that changed everything. He repeated them as a statement, not a question.

"There is no Waldholtz Family Trust."

On the floor, Enid tucked her feet underneath her and wrapped herself in her arms as her body began to rock back and forth uncontrollably.

□□□

The next few hours were a blur as Saturday afternoon turned into Saturday night–and still, no word from Joe and no sign of him either. Enid was sure the call would come any minute, informing her they found his body at the bottom of the Potomac, or maybe the C & O Canal that ran at the bottom of 34th Street. How many times had he said, "I'm better off to you dead?" How many times had he driven off in the car, announcing on his way out the door that this was it, he was going off to end it all, to "save" his family the only way he knew how? How many times, as he was out looking for a wall to run into or a bridge to drive off, had she talked him in off the ledge? *Too often*, she thought as she stared through the silence. And this time, she knew, there would be no call from Joe's car as it sat idle in a V.I.P. parking lot at National Airport.

The police arrived in force–a couple of detectives and several more patrolmen. This was a United States Congresswoman's "situation" and the officers were on their best behavior, taking care to display appropriate deference. They took care, too, to dot their i's and cross their t's. They knew there was potential for review on this one. Plenty of potential. Politics was politics, and make no mistake, this was a political town. The Vince Foster suicide hadn't happened all that long ago, when the White House lawyer ended it all at Fort Marcy Park, a Civil War bulwark not far from here, and the police had taken some bureaucratic heat for that one. Nothing stuck, but, still, you couldn't be too careful. At Enid's request, the police first searched the townhouse, looking for a suicide note.

On a practical level, Joe couldn't really be considered missing yet, and the police told this to the Congresswoman. Sometimes–in fact, most of the time–a person just needs some time alone, a cooling-off period, and then whatever it is that seemed so unmanageable seems manageable and the crisis passes. That was their experience. But in the case of Joe Waldholtz, because of the suicide potential (he had once told Enid he "knew" how Vince Foster did it), because of the unexplained finances, and because of who he was married to, they were willing to at least come to the house and hear her story.

But the truth was, there wasn't much the police could do. Their search failed to turn up a suicide note, so they had nothing to go on. Joe Waldholtz hadn't been charged with anything criminal. There was no probable cause–yet–that he had broken any law. And there was certainly nothing illegal about ditching your brother-in-law. Beyond assuring Mrs. Waldholtz that they would let her know immediately if they heard anything, the police were essentially powerless. They couldn't even file a missing persons report. Because Mr. Waldholtz was at National Airport when he disappeared, and because National Airport is across the border in Virginia, that meant the report needed to be filed by either the Virginia police or by airport security. Of the two, they weren't sure which, but the case was definitely outside of their jurisdiction.

There was nothing for the men in blue to do but pack up their clipboards, tip their caps, and leave.

□□□

The lights illuminating the United States Capitol were already shining brightly as Ladonna Lee pulled out of the parking lot of the Eddie Mahe Co. and swung her Nissan Pathfinder left, toward Georgetown. You could take the girl off the farm, but you couldn't take away her four-wheel drive.

The Waldholtz case was, as always, on her mind. Incredibly, it just kept getting more bizarre. As Joe's problems with "cash flow" mounted, so had his despair. He kept alternating between three plans of attack: One, Enid should resign her seat in Congress so they could work out their problems in private. Two, he himself should resign; just leave, vanish, drop out of the picture. And three, he should kill himself, because at this point he was better off to everyone dead than alive.

All week, Ladonna kept reminding Joe that none of those choices would do anyone, least of all him, any good. You didn't need to be a professional consultant to know that. All you needed was common sense. *How about balancing the ol' checkbook, Joe baby,* Ladonna thought as she drove. *Now there's a rational idea!* But rational wasn't a word anyone was using very often to describe Joe Waldholtz these days. This past week, Ladonna and Eddie, at Enid's request, had actually taken turns at Enid's office in the Cannon Building, watching over Joe while Enid was away at meetings, just to make sure he didn't do something stupid, like kill himself.

Now, after a full Saturday work day at the office, Ladonna was going to check on Enid and Joe, as she'd promised Enid she would. Her home–in Arlington, Va., not far from National Airport–was in the opposite direction from Georgetown, and to tell the truth, a nice glass of red wine on her deck sounded very good right now. But a promise was a promise, a case was a case, and on top of that, a friend was a friend. For Ladonna, this case had gone beyond professional and become personal. She and Enid were not that far apart in age; both were professional women negotiating their way inside the beltway; both were mothers; and, since she was just now emerging from the fog of a painful divorce herself, Ladonna knew full well the almost debilitating trauma that went along with chaotic interpersonal relationships. Ladonna Lee felt a good deal of empathy for Enid Greene Waldholtz, a woman trying to do her job as a Congresswoman, raise her newborn daughter, satisfy the media, head off an investigation by the Justice Department and the Federal Election Commission, and keep her husband alive.

Ladonna picked up the Nissan's cellular phone and hit Enid's number on speed dial.

"Hi, it's Ladonna," she said when Enid answered. "I'm on my way over."

She heard voices in the background. There seemed to be some kind of commotion.

"Brace yourself," said Enid. "The police are here."

□□□

Every time the phone rang, Enid would flinch. And the phone rang often. But never with Joe on the other end. Joe's father called back several times from Pittsburgh. He wanted more information. Jim dealt with him brusquely–there was really nothing more he could add, and he didn't want to talk to anyone named Waldholtz just now anyway.

Given the nature of the news he had to tell them, Jim wasn't exactly thrilled about talking to his in-laws, either. But some things you have to do, like it or not, and Jim knew this fit into that category. And it had to be done very quickly. The Greenes needed to be contacted before the news media got hold of the story.

Somebody had to tell Enid's dad.

Enid was in no shape to do it, so Jim got on the phone and punched out the number for the Greene's house in Salt Lake City. Gerda Greene answered the phone.

"Mormor," said Jim, using the term of endearment the family called Gerda. It meant "mother's mother" in Danish, and even though Mormor's husband wasn't Danish, to be consistent they called Forrest Greene "Morfar," or "mother's father."

"There's a problem," Jim said. "There is no family trust."

From Gerda: "There's no money? No money at all?"

"None," said Jim. "Can you tell Morfar?"

Mormor then reached Morfar in San Francisco, where that afternoon he had attended the funeral of a close friend. Forrest Greene was in the Sunset section of San Francisco at the home of another friend, halfway through dinner, when the call came from his wife. The conversation between two people who had observed their golden wedding anniversary a year before was a brief one.

"There is no money," said Gerda Greene succinctly, and–as was her way–stoically.

Then she added, "You better get back here."

Dunford Forrest Greene took the news pragmatically, which was his way. He didn't fly off the handle. He didn't panic. A man who had lived with the rise and the fall of the stock market and venture capital investments all his adult life–and who, at 76, was just now in the process of retiring–didn't tend to overreact to speculation and conjecture. For more than fifty years his conservative approach to investing had made a lot of people–himself included–a lot of money. All he knew right now was someone who owed him money was missing, and apparently couldn't pay him back.

He knew the amount of money was not inconsequential, of course. A man who grew up during the great depression, a man who never spent a reckless dime in his life, was well aware of the potential monetary loss. His face had gone slightly ashen at what was clearly bad news, but when his friend asked if he could drive him to his condominium in Pacific Heights, several blocks away, Forrest Greene politely declined. He went outside and caught the bus, like he always did. He paid the thirty-five cent fare and rode home; after taking the elevator to the sixteenth floor and opening the door to the one-bedroom condominium he'd owned since 1980, he pulled down his old suitcase and started to pack.

□□□

As Jim got off the phone with his mother-in-law, Ladonna, stepping around the departing police officers, walked into the townhouse. Jim introduced himself and the three of them–Ladonna, Jim and Enid–moved to the dining room, where shock and puzzlement took center stage.

Soon after that, Chuck Roistacher, Enid's attorney, joined the small group that was attempting to make sense out of something that made no sense. Not long after the police arrived, Jim had called the attorney at his home in nearby Bethesda. Chuck had barely come in the door when the call came–he'd been at the gym working out–and was about to change for a dinner appointment he and his wife, Susan, had scheduled that night with friends at a restaurant in Georgetown.

"I understand you're Enid's attorney," Jim said after introducing himself as Enid's brother-in-law.

"That's right," said Chuck.

"Well there's a lot happening over here. Joe's disappeared and the police are here . . ."

Jim cut to the point.

" . . . Can you get over here, right now?"

Chuck looked at his watch, then shouted to his wife, "Susan, call Kenny and Jeannie and tell them I can't make it. You go on ahead and maybe I can join you later."

He returned to the phone. "Where are you?" he asked.

"I don't know," Jim answered. "All I can tell you is somewhere east of California."

Chuck Roistacher did not stop to change or even grab a jacket. The day had turned unseasonably warm–one of those autumn gifts Mother Nature sometimes throws your way before bringing in the cold stuff. He was wearing NewBalance running shoes, jeans, and a gray sweatshirt that said "UVA" across the front as he made his way back out the door.

Chuck found the address easily. He knew the area well enough–Georgetown was just a few miles from Bethesda–and even if he hadn't known his way around, the police cars parked at all angles up and down the street in front of the townhouse at 1671 34th Street marked the spot like a beacon.

But if finding the place was easy, figuring out what to do after he got there was anything but. At this point, there wasn't much anyone could do–except wait and somehow try to find out what happened. Probably better than any of them, Chuck knew that was going to take some time.

In the dining room, Enid wandered aimlessly, sitting and standing alternately. One minute she would talk to Ladonna, Jim and Chuck, the next she'd go silent. She would cry on and off and her body frequently shook involuntarily. Her motor skills, the others noticed, were barely functioning. When she placed her hands on the table they shook and when she attempted to open a locked cabinet her fingers trembled so violently she could not put the key in the lock.

"Here, let me do that for you," said Chuck. He, Jim and Ladonna exchanged worried glances. None of them were doctors, but from all outward appearances they guessed Enid was clearly in the early stages of shock. If she had been in a car accident she'd no doubt have a blanket around her by now and would already be on her way to the hospital for observation.

Chuck called his wife at the restaurant and told her he wouldn't be able to make dinner. Susan Roistacher had a master's degree in psychology and ran a private psychotherapist practice in suburban Maryland. As Chuck explained to his wife the "situation" on 34th Street, she quickly grasped the gravity of the problem.

"You stay there as long as they need you there," she told her husband. "I'll catch a cab home."

Chuck stayed a while longer and then, after setting up a meeting with Enid, Ladonna and Jim late the next morning at the Powell, Goldstein offices, he made his departure. When he walked out the door he was hit by blasts of cold air and sideways-falling sleet. Just like that, the Indian Summer had given way to the first storm of the winter, bringing with it nearly gale force winds and plummeting temperatures that, by the next morning, would bring Washington it's first dusting of snow. In his now-inadequate sweatshirt and jeans, the attorney lowered his head and, as he considered the topsy-turvy events of the day, shivered as he double-timed it to his car.

Despite her condition, Enid knew Joe wasn't coming back. She didn't know if he was alive or dead, but she did know he was gone for good. The sure tipoff had come when she was searching the townhouse for a suicide note and discovered Joe's congressional spouse pin lying on the nightstand next to his side of the bed. The pin wasn't large, barely bigger than a quarter, but the thing was, Joe *always* wore that pin. It was his badge of honor, his ticket to the bigtime. He never went anywhere without it. Instinctively, deep down, Enid knew that pin was a signal. Its very presence, absent its owner, was like a neon sign announcing HE'S NOT COMING BACK!

Outside, it had started to rain. Enid went over to the window and looked down on the small courtyard that separated the townhouse from the street. She idly ran her finger across the window pane, tracing the tracks of the raindrops. "As much as I hate what he's done," she said aloud, "I hope he hasn't killed himself."

That thought hung in the air until Jim and Ladonna came to an almost simultaneous conclusion: This was no place to spend the night. It was uncomfortable at best, downright eerie beyond that. And in Ladonna's case, there wasn't any chance for that nice glass of red wine. There was too much they didn't know. Would Joe come back? Would there be a phone call that they'd found his body?

"Marlene," said Jim, shouting upstairs to the Nanny. "Get the baby ready. We're going over to Ladonna's."

Marlene did not argue.

Well past midnight, the five of them–Marlene, the baby, Enid, Jim, and Ladonna–piled into the Pathfinder and drove through empty, rainy streets to Arlington. Once inside Ladonna's house, with every light on, they dispersed quickly. As Marlene took care of Elizabeth and Ladonna went to her room, Jim and Enid remained in the main living room, where Enid lay prone on the couch. Jim was concerned about his sister-in-law. What they had gone through in the past twenty-four hours was enough to test the strongest of people. She looked pale and weary, stunned and frightened; and beyond that there was a wariness in her eyes Jim hadn't seen before. The look of someone who'd just seen a ghost, or was afraid she was about to.

To be honest, he felt the same way. As a trial lawyer, he thought he'd seen a lot in life; plenty of good guys and plenty of bad guys. *But today I found out I hadn't even scratched the surface,* he thought. *Tonight I got a glimpse of the big leagues.*

Jim shivered involuntarily as he turned to Enid and said, "I've never felt such evil as I felt these last twenty-four hours. It was like the doors of hell swung wide open and gave us a look inside."

Enid, her eyes full of tears, told him she'd felt the same thing.

"Look," he said, "I could give you a blessing."

"I wish you would," said Enid.

In the Mormon religion, it's believed that those who have been ordained to the priesthood have the power to bless others in times of unusual stress with added spiritual strength to combat adversity and the forces of evil. Jim held that priesthood. He placed his hands on his sister-in-law's head and gave her that blessing.

After Jim went to the rec room to sleep, Enid made her way to Ladonna's room, where Ladonna was still awake. The two women sat up in bed and talked; they talked all night long, until they looked out the window and it was light again.

□□□

They circled the wagons the next day, a Sunday, at the law offices of Powell, Goldstein, Frazer & Murphy.

At the head of the battery of attorneys lining up for this fight, dressed in a full suit and tie (Susan insisted) was Charles H. Roistacher–"Chuck" to anyone who'd known him longer than three seconds; an attorney whose specialty was the defense of criminal investigations and prosecutions.

Chuck had a background in dealing with bad guys. After four years of partying and receiving "gentleman C's" at the University of Virginia, he'd moved on to the University of Miami law school, where he discovered the library and managed to graduate in the top ten percent of his class. He then worked for a year as a public defender in Washington, D.C., followed by twenty years as an Assistant U.S. Attorney in the District of Columbia, specializing in the prosecution of white collar crime. First as a defense lawyer and then as a prosecutor, he had been on both sides of the courtroom.

He and his psychotherapist wife Susan lived in the Maryland suburbs where they'd raised two children: Lee, an attorney just getting started in San Diego, and Amy, fresh out of graduate school at the University of Chicago and now a clinical social worker just getting started in Maryland. Like father and mother, like son and daughter. In 1988, as he added up his credit card debt and anticipated the college bills that would soon be pouring in, prosecutor Roistacher had switched gears and entered the private sector. They had thrown him a nice going-away party at the U.S. Attorney's office, where he made about $80,000 a year–not a huge amount to combat the high cost of living in suburban D.C.–and he had gone down the street about six blocks to Powell, Goldstein, where the firm charged three hundred and ten dollars an hour for his services. Not so slowly and very surely, he was making up economic ground.

In years past, upper echelon law firms like Powell, Goldstein–with its roster of more than two hundred lawyers in Atlanta and Washington–would not have even considered anything to do with a criminal law practice. But as the 80's segued into the 90's and the government began more and more to prosecute criminally the country's top corporations and their officers and employees for matters that had been handled civilly in the past, most of the big law firms were looking for experienced white-collar crime types with prosecutorial experience. A mold Chuck Roistacher fit perfectly.

His background in the public sector along with his New York upbringing conspired to give Roistacher a view of the world that he considered realistic and others might consider cynical. That didn't bother Chuck. He knew that's what had made him attractive to a firm like Powell, Goldstein in the first place. He was a unique blend of corporate attorney and homicide cop; the kind of man who started every day with his hair moussed back nicely, a la Pat Riley, and ended every day with his hair on his forehead. He could deal with corporate CEOs, but he could also deal with people from the street. With his New York accent, he came across as a tough guy who could talk to tough guys. And it was no act. Nobody thought of Chuck Roistacher as anyone's fool. Least of all the criminal element. The week before, when Roistacher made Joe's acquaintance, they hadn't hit it off.

"Joseph Phillip Waldholtz," he called him; only when Chuck Roistacher said "Joseph Phillip Waldholtz" it sounded exactly like Jim Parkinson saying "cockroach."

As the little congregation gathered that Sunday morning in the Powell, Goldstein board room, it was Charles H. Roistacher who presided, plotting a legal strategy that was aimed at identifying the bad guys, and making sure the bad guys knew it.

□□□

As Ladonna Lee ferried Enid from the law offices back to her townhouse Sunday afternoon, Enid sized up her situation. She didn't have a husband at the moment, but she still had her daughter. Beyond that, she had managed to surround herself with what psychologists would call a strong support group. Jim, Ladonna and Chuck were already absorbing blows for her, and her father would be here soon. The only thing to do now was try to stay sane long enough to try to finally get to know the man she thought she knew better than anyone in the world–the man she married.

They started by searching the townhouse.

Jim took one closet, Enid another, Ladonna another. What they were looking for, who knew? Sometimes you can learn all you need to learn by the things a person leaves behind.

Jim had already made a cursory tour through Joe's walk-in closet the night before, when he accompanied the police on their search for a suicide note. He had been both astonished and disgusted at the sheer opulence of the contents. The closet was lined with dozens of tailored suits, another dozen or so pairs of shoes, expensive jackets, monogrammed shirts, assorted sweaters, silk ties, and expensive jewelry. When Jim factored in the newfound knowledge that Joe didn't have any family money to the fact that his father-in-law had advanced him *four million dollars*, he knew *exactly* what that meant.

It meant that everything Joe owned had been paid for by D. Forrest Greene.

The clothes in his closet accounted for fifty or sixty thousand dollars, easy. There must have been a hundred ties. *He's got more ties than Pat Dye,* Jim thought, remembering that old joke about the football coach at Auburn who kept playing for ties in the Sugar Bowl. Almost all of them were Hermés ties, made of the finest French silk and priced at $120 apiece. He knew that for a fact because several of them still had the price tags. *The cockroach hadn't even worn them!* The shoes were mainly Ferragamos. Jim owned one pair. He wore them on special occasions. He knew Ferragamos cost from three hundred to five hundred dollars a pair. There were at least ten pair.

Wall to wall and on and on the splendor stretched. There were enough designer suits–some size 54, others 56, 58 and 60, reflecting Joe's constant shifts in weight–to make you wonder if you hadn't stepped into the men's department at Barney's of New York. The suits were at least a thousand dollars plus, each. In the jewelry drawers there were solid gold cuff links, a money clip or two and two expensive looking rings. Joe was not one to scrimp on accessories.

The irony that it was his wife's father–the same D. Forrest Greene who, Jim knew, every year gave his daughter Sue a birthday present consisting of one dollar per year she'd been alive (forty-seven this past one!)–who had paid for all this *stuff* made Jim a little crazy. He didn't know whether to laugh or cry. And to make matters more hysterical yet, nobody he knew–and certainly not D. Forrest Greene–could fit into the cockroach's clothes.

An emotional type, Jim had to vent, either that or explode. He called out to Ladonna, who came to the closet. "Look at all this!" he shouted. "Do you know how much this cost my father-in-law?!" "Look at these shoes. They go for two hundred and fifty bucks. Per shoe!" He threw open the jewelry drawer. "This is the kind of shit he wore! If you melted the sonofabitch down you'd have enough gold to fill all the teeth in Washington, and enough whale oil to light up all of New England."

Ladonna laughed and managed a grin. Now Jim felt better.

While Enid and Ladonna were trying to make sense of the mass of boxes Joe had shipped from Utah, Jim moved to a closet on the side of the master bedroom, where several Federal Express envelopes caught his eye. He found that each package contained a single cigarette pack wrapped in black tape. Inside the cigarette packs were a variety of pills. One look at the pills and he picked up the telephone. He dialed the same number he'd called almost exactly twenty-four hours before, and said essentially the same thing.

"Chuck," he said when Charles H. Roistacher answered, "you better get over here."

The former prosecutor knew exactly what the cigarette packs inside the Federal Express envelopes meant.

"It's how drug dealers transport drugs and fake out the people who open the packages," he said. "They put the drugs–sometimes prescription pills–inside the cigarette packages. That way if someone suspicious opens it, they'll see what they think is cigarettes, and let it pass."

"It's an old trick," the attorney added. "From all these packages, and from the looks of the pills, I'd say what you've got here is a drugstore junkie."

"Come on," he said, looking around the room. "I'll help you search."

Just then, on the other side of the room, Jim made another discovery. Tucked well to the back of the bottom compartment of the end table at the far side of the king-sized bed–Joe's side–was a stack of magazines. Jim pulled them out and held them under the light. There was an assortment of Men's Fitness magazines, a catalog for men's clothing, specializing in provocative underwear, and an advertisement for transvestites someone had sent to Joe, with a vulgar comment attached. Since, as Jim well knew, Joe's idea of physical fitness was to turn on the treadmill, then sit beside it and eat a vat of Haagen-Daz, there was no ready explanation here. There was, however, an obvious and uneasy inference to be made–an inference that made Jim's blood run cold.

Since it had already been established that Joe was a fraud, that he spent thousands of dollars on ties *he hadn't even worn*, that he was in all likelihood hooked on prescription drugs, and that his bedside reading material featured male bikini underwear, well, it just didn't take that much of a leap to deduce that this man who wasn't anything that it appeared he was, was also probably gay or bi-sexual.

Jim thrust the magazines at Ladonna. "The sonofabitch," he said, and he wasn't referring to Joe's possible sexual preference, but to what might have been transmitted as a result.

"She might have AIDS!" he hissed.

Jim gathered up the magazines and moved toward the door.

"Where are you going?" asked Ladonna.

"To tell Enid," said Jim.

Ladonna jumped up and headed him off at the door.

"Look at what's happened here," she said. "Enid's already found out that her husband, the father of her child, is a fraud, a drug addict, and he's stolen from her father. And now you want to tell her he's also probably gay and she might have been exposed to AIDS, and so might have Elizabeth?"

Ladonna paused to let the weight of what she'd just said sink in.

"Don't you think we could wait on this one, Jimmy?"

Jim nodded, put the magazines in a box, and gave them to Roistacher.

□□□

It was Enid who carried the portable computer into the room.

"There might be something in here," she said.

It was Joe's personal computer, a state-of-the-art Toshiba that had been his constant companion. If he wasn't talking on the cellular phone, he was working on his computer. Another reason Enid suspected that suicide–and not mere larceny–was on her husband's mind was the fact that he left his Toshiba behind. If his exit had been calculated, he'd have taken his computer. But when she looked in the den, there it was, sitting on Joe's desk like a faithful hound on the porch.

"He did everything on this," she said as Jim took the machine and turned it on. After it booted up, they accessed windows and clicked onto Joe's personal files. Joe used the 6.0 version of WordPerfect for word processing. They scanned the files in the main directory. For the most part there was nothing that appeared out-of-the-ordinary, just basic political correspondence and reports. But at the bottom of the directory they ran into something that piqued their curiosity. A dozen documents wouldn't let them in. They had been password protected.

As far as anyone knew, only Joseph Phillip Waldholtz knew what those passwords were.

Roistacher took the computer to the office the next morning. Beyond the off and on switch, he didn't know much about computers himself. But Powell, Goldstein had a computer section at the end of the hall. There were hackers in that room who dreamed about challenges like this.

After transferring the material from Joe's hard drive onto the law firm's main computer–enabling several of them to work at once, and on bigger screens–the firm's computer aces first tried a few end-arounds, attempting to get into the locked documents without the passwords. When that didn't work they tried cracking the passwords in the conventional manner. They tried Joe's birthdate, his social security number, his and Enid's birthdays, a combination of the family's names. All the usual probables. But they came up empty. The documents didn't budge. The folders stayed closed. Their contents stayed protected.

Their next plan of attack was to secure a copy of a new software product called WRPASS. WRPASS boasted that it could recover passwords locking WordPerfect and Professional Write files. Coincidentally, the program had been developed by a company called AccessData Corporation, with headquarters in Orem, Utah.

Linda Murray and Jo Jo Rositch, two of Powell, Goldstein's crack computer experts, put WRPASS on the first locked document, named "asset.egw."

Not only did WRPASS work. It worked fast! Within three seconds the password for "asset.egw" flashed on the screen:

"*eatme.*"

In rapid succession, the technicians cracked the passwords of all the secreted documents. You can tell a lot about a person by the passwords they author. Quickly, the screen filled up, displaying first the document name, followed by its password.

These were Joseph Waldholtz's documents and passwords:

Document Name	**Password**
asset.egw	eatme
deed.egw	fuck
brent.mem	eat.me
elsie.let	dearie
dora.mem	eat.me
fg.let	help
hate.mem	eat.me

help.mem	fucked
roger.mem	eat.me
rose.let	fuck
slesinge.let	eatme

And finally, among all the profane deception, a password for the twelfth and final locked document that was so simple in its verity, so pinpoint in its accuracy, it defined all that preceded it.

The document name was "forrest.mem," identifying a letter to D. Forrest Greene from "The Waldholtz Family Trust."

When the password came on the screen, the hacker let out an involuntary gasp.

"lie"

is what it said.

CHAPTER X

As soon as Enid Waldholtz laid eyes on her father in Washington, she burst into tears.

He was wearing his favorite jacket, the lightweight kind London Fog made popular in the '70s, and just the sight of that jacket was enough to bring on the tears.

Enid had always seen her father as a strong man, and a disciplined man. From her childhood, she had countless examples. He once stopped eating between meals entirely, just to prove he could. But now he was seventy-six years old, and when she saw him sitting there in his jacket, surrounded by the lawyers in their dark suits, he looked so vulnerable, so out of place. She had an almost overwhelming desire to throw her arms around him and escort him out of this place where he did not belong.

They were in the conference room at the law offices of Powell, Goldstein, Frazer and Murphy. Forrest Greene had taken the early flight from Salt Lake City and they brought him here first, whisked him from Dulles Airport to Pennsylvania Avenue in the heart of the District of Columbia, to a boardroom filled with leather chairs, water pitchers, telephones, note pads, and high-priced attorneys. He looked as out of place as a nun in a night club.

He had packed light, carrying an overnight bag off the plane and that was it. He had come east for one reason and one reason only: To help his daughter. You don't need a lot of formal clothes for family.

It had been more than forty-eight hours now since Forrest Greene had gotten the news–two days to come to grips with the fact that the money he "loaned" his son-in-law might now more accurately be called a "donation." There was still some hope they would find some of it locked away in a file cabinet, perhaps, or maybe in a bank in Switzerland. But they were faint hopes, tied to a mysterious man whose whereabouts were as unknown as his agenda. A religious person all his life, Forrest consoled himself by remembering scripture in this time of worldly loss. His mantra the past two days had been from Matthew chapter six, verses nineteen and twenty: *"Lay not up for yourselves treasures upon earth, where moth and rust doth corrupt, and where thieves break through and steal. But lay up for yourselves treasures in heaven, where neither moth nor rust doth corrupt, and where thieves do not break through nor steal."*

If anyone cared to listen, Forrest Greene knew *exactly* how much this particular thief had broken through and stolen. During a 21-month span from January of 1994 through October of 1995, he had responded to Joe's solicitations and sent to his son-in-law a total of twenty-four payments via wire transfers or personal checks, all of it adding up to a grand total of $3,987,426 dollars. Before interest.

But as disgusted as he was over the loss–and to a man who valued a dollar as highly as D. Forrest Greene, disgusted was putting it mildly–he was not devastated. And for more reasons than Saint Matthew. Forrest Greene still slept like a rock because his conscience was clear. He was guilty of using poor judgment, perhaps, but that was all. He had done nothing wrong. He had aided and abetted no crime. He was the victim, not the victimizer.

Enid knew her father well enough to know that's how he would feel. When she walked into the boardroom and saw him sitting at the end of the table, she was certain he hadn't a clue that anybody would want to investigate *them.* It would be beyond his comprehension that the Department of Justice, whose fortress of buildings sat just kitty corner from Powell,

Goldstein's offices, and the Federal Bureau of Investigation, with headquarters just across the street, might be entertaining any ideas that the Greenes were the bad guys too. Forrest Greene, patriot, defender of these American shores in the Pacific Theatre in World War II, would never dream of his government thinking *that*.

She was right, of course.

About five minutes into the meeting, after a series of unsettling questions about government investigation, Forrest threw his hands in the air.

"Stop!" he said.

"What is this all about!? I've done nothing wrong! My daughter has done nothing wrong! We are the victims! We committed no crimes! Why is anyone investigating us?!"

The room went silent. Finally, Jim Parkinson walked over to where Mr. Greene was sitting, put his arm around his father-in-law's shoulders and, nodding toward Chuck Roistacher, asked if there was a room where they could talk privately. Jim and Enid and Forrest were ushered into an adjoining conference room. When the door was closed, Forrest got his second wind.

"I have done nothing wrong!" he again shouted out. "We don't need to be here. We don't need any lawyers!" He was looking at Enid, who was still sobbing, waiting for some help here.

"Dad," she somehow managed. "Please listen to Jimmy."

"Morfar," said Jim, adopting the familial approach, "I don't think you understand what's going on here. As a matter of fact you do need a lawyer. You might need a bunch of lawyers before this is through. There are major problems here. Joe's gone. We don't know where he is. He got four million dollars from you. We don't know where it is. We do know that a lot of that money went into Enid's campaign. And we do know that Enid is a Republican congresswoman. The FBI is looking into it and so is the United States Attorney, who was appointed by the President of the United States, who, I don't think I need to remind any of us, is a Democrat. We've got a real, live problem here."

For the second time in the space of five minutes, there was dead silence.

□□□

The good news was Joe hadn't killed himself. The bad news was Joe hadn't killed himself.

It was Monday morning, as her father was in the air, en route to Washington, that Enid had learned that Joe was still among the living. She found out, ironically enough, when she called First Security, their bank in Salt Lake City, to make sure their joint accounts had been frozen. Roger Dean, the manager of the downtown branch and a man who had become, over the course of the past couple of years, Enid and Joe's friendly–and most accommodating–neighborhood banker, told Enid that Joe had used his ATM Visa card twice over the weekend. Once late Saturday afternoon at the Baltimore-Washington International Airport & Train Station in Maryland and again early Sunday morning in West Springfield, Massachusetts. One of the lawyers at Powell, Goldstein familiar with train travel on the East coast knew that both ATMs were near Amtrak Depots. The deduction was elementary. After he fled the airport on Saturday, Joe had gone to Washington's Union Station and taken the train to points north.

He wasn't dead, he was running.

A chill ran through Enid as the news sank in, followed by a new hardening of resolve. Finding out Joe had been living a lie was one thing. Finding out he was running away from his wife and daughter was another. Hard as it was to imagine, Enid suddenly realized that the betrayal had been multiplied. He wasn't just a fraud, he was a fraud without a heart. *He wasn't out of his mind. He knew exactly what he was doing*. Enid had spent the weekend, despite her shock, still worrying for and about Joe, imagining that any minute she would get a phone call from the police reporting they'd found his dead body in some nearby hotel room because he just couldn't face her.

Turned out the hotel room wasn't nearby, the body wasn't dead, and Joe was still paying the bill with her dad's money.

He was the one who had taken the gloves off, not her. The man she had spoken with daily for practically the last five years, straight, the man who had pledged his undying love to her, the man she told everything to, the man she allowed into her bed–that same man had taken off without so much as a glance back.

"I want this man tracked down, arrested and punished for what he has done to me, my family and the people of Utah," Enid said in a statement released through the Eddie Mahe Company, who, it was decided, would now handle all of Enid's public relations pertaining to her personal life. "I can't begin to describe the anger and hurt over the incredible level of deception that we have uncovered."

A level of deception that, it was becoming obvious, wasn't about to die anytime soon.

□□□

By any normal standards, Tuesday and Wednesday, November 14th and 15th, were not banner days for Joseph Waldholtz, whereabouts unknown. On Tuesday, his wife filed for divorce and on Wednesday, the Justice Department filed a federal warrant for his arrest.

The arrest warrant was issued by the U.S. Attorney's office in Washington, but was in fact the product of behind-the-scenes maneuvering by Roistacher and his associate Ralph Caccia, who met in Washington with Assistant U.S. Attorney Bill Lawler and laid out the case against Joe as they knew it. Enid's attorneys wanted a federal arrest warrant based on Joe's alleged criminal activity. They didn't get that, but they did get Lawler to issue a warrant for Joe's arrest as a material witness.

As for the divorce papers, they were drawn up by a Utah attorney, Gary Paxton, and faxed to the Powell, Goldstein offices by midday Tuesday. Because of the baby, time was of the essence in the matter of divorce, Enid's advisers had decided. The theory was that if Enid didn't immediately petition for sole custody of their daughter and file for divorce from a man she had reason to believe was, among other things, a drug addict and sexual pervert, it was possible that down the road a custody judge would want to know why.

Enid was on her way out the door of the law offices to a Rules Committee meeting at the Capitol when the divorce papers were faxed from Salt Lake. There had been a question whether she should go to the Rules Committee meeting at all, considering the circumstances: Husband–soon to be ex–on the run, family in town, unanswered questions, and the media *everywhere*. Not to mention the fact that in nearly seventy-two hours Enid had barely slept, eaten, or stopped crying.

But she was determined to go to the meeting for a reason virtually everyone inside the beltway would understand: Politics. Already there were rumblings about whether this "situation" would prevent her from doing her job. Even a freshman knew the Democrats were poised to jump on this the way the Republicans had jumped on Bill Clinton's problems with the Whitewater scandal in Arkansas. As Orrin Hatch had put it to Joe and Enid just a week earlier, in Washington, perception is everything.

And now, the perception of the Congresswoman from Utah was that she was out there in the wind, swirling. Who knew where she would land? That very morning, commentator Howard Berkes of National Public Radio had said over the national airwaves: "Young and bright and passionately committed to the Contract with America, Waldholtz is considered an asset and ally by the house leadership. All of that is threatened now."

Not if Enid could help it. For one thing, she knew she was still considered an asset and ally by the house leadership. Newt Gingrich, the Speaker of the House, had telephoned her personally the night after Joe's disappearance to reaffirm his support. Newt reached Enid at Ladonna's home and the first thing Enid did when she picked up the phone was apologize. "I'm sorry," she said, beginning to sob, "for bringing dishonor on the House."

Newt had been quick to reply. "You didn't," he said sternly. "Take what time you need. Take care of yourself and Elizabeth. We know how to find you if we need you." Those few words had given Enid enormous relief as far as her job was concerned. Relief and resolve. She vowed to herself that she would not resign just because she had been victimized.

"I'm going to that meeting!" she said one last time as Chuck and Ladonna questioned the issue. "They're not going to get me to resign!"

But first she had to sign the divorce papers.

They took her to an empty conference room and handed her a pen and the faxed sheets. There were three of them. Enid was running late, but, still, she stopped to read the papers before signing them. She picked them up and began to read.

The first line nailed her.

Waldholtz v. Waldholtz.

She slumped in the chair as the tears started up again. She straightened the papers and tried to read on but her right hand was by now shaking so violently the papers shook loose and fell to the floor. Chuck gathered them up.

"Somebody call her office," he shouted. "She is not going to make that meeting."

And Enid did not protest.

□□□

For days the roller coaster ride continued with no real let-up. Enid would just be pulling it together when she realized she was at the top of the tracks, about to plummet back down again. *Keep your arms and legs inside the car at all times.* Simply hanging in there was no easy chore. Physically, there just wasn't any caretaking going on. She lost all interest in eating whatsoever. People kept shoving sandwiches and salads in front of her and she kept faking like she cared, but she didn't. She had so little in her stomach that every morning when she went through her new ritual–wake up, a thousandth of a second later realize it's *not* a nightmare, run to the bathroom, throw up–she never really threw up anything of substance. Dry heaves, they're called. But so be it. If she never ate again, fine by her. She had no energy. She walked slowly, she even talked slowly–and Enid Greene *never* talked slowly.

But her physical condition was downright robust–when compared to the emotional.

When she did stop crying it was just for a break. She tried her best to stop. *It's good to get it out,* she would think, *but this is ridiculous.* But she usually couldn't. She discovered the many forms of crying. Sometimes you can cry accompanied by shaking and sobbing. Sometimes you can just sit there, silent as a lamb, with the tears rolling nonstop down your cheeks.

The problem, of course, was that there was always something new to cry *about.* It seemed there was no let-up to the bad news. Every day it got worse. Every *hour* it got worse. There was one lawyer for Powell, Goldstein, an FEC specialist named Brett Kappel, who seemed to *always* have bad news. Kappel would walk into a room and Enid would flinch out of pure reflex. To his credit, Kappel was a diplomat and would habitually add as a postscript to whatever news he'd just delivered: "I hate this guy."

Well, so did Enid.

But that was a problem too. Because you can't work up a real world-class state of hate unless it's for something you once loved passionately. And crazy as it was, Enid actually found herself, that first week Joe was gone, lapsing into melancholy moods where she missed Joe terribly. They were her "My Joe" moods. She missed the Joe she knew, the Joe who liked her for who she was, who shared the same goals, the same dreams, even the same enemies. She missed her blanket, her shield, her best friend, her tireless defender. The craziest part was when sometimes, in the midst of all the horror he had caused, she would find herself wondering what Joe would think of this or that. She had always asked him for his opinions, his counsel. He was smart, he was well-read–the fastest reader she'd ever met. Even when examining bank records and other evidences of Joe's deceit, out of sheer reflex, she would sometime find herself thinking, "I should ask Joe about this." There were times, as she kept tripping over that fine line that borders love and hate, when Enid thought she just might go mad.

She dealt with her state of mind the only way she could: second by second. When her rational mind kicked in and told her she had to perform–at a congressional hearing, at a meeting with the lawyers–she would perform; otherwise she was content to just hold on.

When news of the divorce suit became public, one of the first reporters Enid ran into was Charles Sherrill, the Washington correspondent for KSL-TV, Salt Lake City's NBC affiliate. They were in a corridor in the Capitol when Enid agreed to a short interview.

Sherrill's opening question had to do with the divorce. He asked if there might be some possibility of reconciliation.

"No, there is no possibility," Enid said. "When we put it all together and I can tell you the whole story, you'll understand."

Although she was on camera and she didn't want them to, her eyes filled with tears.

"But you seemed so much in love," said Sherrill.

"I was," said Enid.

□□□

As soon as the Waldholtz story came to the attention of the media, it went to the top of the charts. How could it not? It had all the ingredients: money, power, suspense, betrayal, corruption, the FBI, the U.S. Attorney, the United States Congress, a broken marriage, and a 300-pound fugitive. It was every movie Harrison Ford ever played.

In Washington, D.C. and Salt Lake City and everywhere before and beyond, the story played out in the headlines and the airwaves. It was the topic of happy talk between anchors leading into newscasts, it was fodder for cartoonists, it was the subject of editorials.

The sketchiness of the media accounts, which created far more questions than answers, only heightened the mystery. "Where's Waldholtz?" became a national riddle. Joe became the "Missing Man" (*New York Times),* the "Money Man" (*Salt Lake Tribune)* and the "Mystery Man" (*USA Today).* If one of his fondest dreams was to make every newspaper in America, by the fourth day of his disappearance, he had reached it.

In Pittsburgh, the Waldholtz Watch particularly intensified, and not just because of the possibility that Joe would eventually wander back to his old hometown. As it turned out, Joe was supposed to have appeared in a Pittsburgh courtroom on Monday, two days after he disappeared. Acting on a petition filed by Joe's father, Harvey Waldholtz, and his cousin, Steven Slesinger, Joe had been ordered by a Pennsylvania judge to appear and answer charges about the disposition and whereabouts of more than six hundred thousand dollars his grandmother, Rebecca Levenson, had entrusted in his care over the past decade, beginning in 1986.

It was turning out that Enid and Forrest weren't the only relatives Joe skipped out on that week.

By Wednesday, the Waldholtz family joined in the search for Joe. A Pittsburgh press conference was quickly arranged, where both Harvey and Slesinger made appeals in the hopes they'd reach Joe. "Please contact me," urged Joe's father, the desperation clear in his voice. "There's nothing that can't be worked out somehow."

"C'mon home, Joe. Let's take care of this and get on with life," added his cousin, who the Greene's had known only as the villainous "cousin Stevie," the one Joe always blamed for the woes of the family trust. As with virtually everything Joe Waldholtz said, the information he had dispensed was based only on partial truths–just enough to turn the story one hundred and eighty degrees. It was true that cousin Stevie was bringing litigation against him, it was true that the dispute had to do with his grandmother's money–it was even true that Joe had gotten more of that money than anyone else. The part Joe had always conveniently left out was the part about how he stole the money.

□□□

Meanwhile, back at the townhouse, Jim Parkinson was having a hard time sleeping, and not because of emotional stress . . . but because he was freezing.

He was lying on the couch in the bottom level of the townhouse, shivering under the same quilt that had been more than adequate the night before. Then it struck him what was going on. His father-in-law, crusader against high energy bills, had arrived. Wherever D. Forrest Greene slept, the thermostat went down.

Forrest wasn't, in general, a take-charge guy. It was not his style to tell people how to run their lives. What *was* his style was conserving money. When he went to bed his first night in Georgetown–Enid gave him the top level bedroom while she settled in on the couch in the living room on the middle level–out of pure instinct he turned the heat down to a comfortable fifty-five degrees.

Jim got up, blew on his fingers, and turned it up to sixty-five.

"Gotta have some compromise here," he muttered as he went back to the couch.

You are what you are. Forrest Greene was a living testimonial to that. He couldn't do much about what he'd already loaned and probably lost, but he could do something about what he was spending. Turning down the thermostat was one way. Eating in was another. On his second night in town, after a long day of more meetings with the attorneys and long hours sifting through financial documents in the townhouse, Jim proposed a break for dinner. They were, after all, in Georgetown, within walking distance of some of the finest restaurants in America. Exceptional places to eat were minutes away along nearby Wisconsin Avenue and M Street.

But Forrest declined the invitation to go out to eat.

"We've spent too much money already," he said, digging in his heels.

"Morfar," Jim persisted, "I'm buying."

"No, no, we've spent too much money."

"But *I'm* buying!"

Forrest did not budge.

Jim shrugged. He was hungry, he wanted to eat. He grabbed

Ladonna and Enid, hoping he could talk her into eating something substantial, and they went out for a meal. Forrest stayed behind, went to the kitchen, and opened the refrigerator to see what he could find.

Eating was the least of anyone's worries that first week, however. Although Joe had stolen away quietly into the night, the chaos he left behind had the same effect as if he'd lit a fuse. The boxes he brought from Utah and had been "going through" for the past two months were stuffed full of papers, mounds of invoices and bank statements, bills, political records, and every other kind of financial document you could imagine. Enid and her "team" had a small forest to sift through.

In the study, Jim took the books off the lower shelves to create space for organizing at least some of the documents. Before long, his filing system spilled up the stairs into the master bedroom and down the stairs into the living room. There were stacks for campaign papers, stacks for personal bills, stacks for every separate financial institution, even a stack for Joe's forgeries.

There was at least a shock a minute.

The shocks had actually begun as soon as Joe had left, when the first document Enid discovered was the forged Ready Assets certificate he had used to answer the *Salt Lake Tribune*'s request for documentation of Enid's $5 million "wedding gift." Not only did Enid find the "original," she also found the hand-written rough draft Joe had submitted to a print shop. After that she found separate copies of her financial disclosure statements–the originals with X's in boxes showing a blind trust, exactly as she and Joe had checked them, and, alongside the originals, the forgeries with different X's, showing no blind trust, that had been filed with the House Ethics Committee. Joe himself had changed the boxes in order to avoid any scrutiny of his family's trust–a trust that did not exist, a trust so "blind" it was visible only in the confines of the mind where it had been fabricated.

Evidence of that fabrication–of Joe's fraud–was everywhere. Evidence of more than four years of lies and deception. Enid opened one box and there, sitting on top, was a statement from the mortgage company that had carried the second mortgage she had once taken out on the Penrose house in Salt Lake City to help a friend–the second mortgage Joe had assured her he had paid off with his own money. The date on the statement was from the summer of 1994, over a year ago, and a year since the mortgage had supposedly been "paid."

She called the mortgage company's offices in Utah. Her mortgage had not been paid off, she was told, although her friend had continued to make his required payments.

Forrest Greene set up a makeshift office at the kitchen table, where, using a butter knife for a letter opener, he would open unopened bill after unopened bill. All the while a dull ache spread through his body as an incredible realization increasingly dawned on him: Joe had borrowed $4 million and *hadn't paid the bills!*

Outstanding debts were everywhere. Some for fifty dollars. Some for five hundred dollars. Some for fifteen thousand dollars. And all points in between. Virtually all of the bills were *over 90 days* past due. For Forrest Greene, it was like walking into a sewer. It was beyond his comprehension that anyone could live like this. It seemed that Joe (and Enid) owed everybody. Federal Express, the water company, the landlord, this Visa card, that Visa card, the cellular phone company, the clothing store, the butcher, the baker, the candlestick maker. They owed them all. Each new bill brought new horror for Forrest Greene, a man not just reared, but tempered and shaped, by the Great Depression. "Ohhhh," he would groan when he would see "amount due." "Ohhh noooo," he would groan when he would see "late fee." They were loud, audible groans, completely unfeigned, that came from somewhere deep and long ago, when fortunes were lost overnight and men jumped from buildings. The groans of a person who had worked for every dime he ever made.

Forrest Greene had been around money all his life. He could add and subtract. He knew they wouldn't be finding any of his money in Switzerland or under a brick in the backyard. The fact was, Joe Waldholtz had taken his money and spent it so recklessly, showing so little prudence, that in less than two years he had blown it all and, incredibly, then some. At a rate of just under two hundred thousand dollars a month he had exhausted well over four million dollars. In addition to Forrest's "loans," he had also managed to go through the money Joe made during his short term with the Utah Republican Party, plus whatever Enid had made as a corporate lawyer and U.S. Congresswoman.

Joe Waldholtz possessed a consumption appetite Forrest couldn't begin to relate to. Much of the evidence of that appetite was right there in front of them. Joe had spent the money on cellular phones, big screen TV's, first-class air fare, four-hundred-dollar-a-night hotel rooms, western art, diamond watches, ruby cufflinks, solid gold chokers, mink coats, cars, caterers, limousines, manicures, hair stylists, gardeners, cooks, maids, nannies, nurses, linen dresses, silk suits, the home shopping network, bottled water, separate residences in two states, rented furniture, baby furniture, stereo systems, security systems, a full-time drug habit, restaurants, Federal Express, gourmet candy . . . and the most expensive House of Representatives freshman campaign in the country in 1994.

This man gave new meaning to the term *spendthrift.* In sifting through Joe's bank accounts after he left–there were nearly a dozen of them, many of which Enid never knew existed–they discovered that all of the balances were either below deficit level or close to it. Incredibly, when Joe Waldholtz and his $20,000 Rolex hit the streets, headed for the train, he was broke; a fact he verified silently when, after less than three hours on the street, he ponied up to his first ATM, rattled off the personal identification number, and punched out numbers for the daily limit: three hundred bucks. Just hours later, when Saturday sequed into Sunday, he hit the ATM again, for another three hundred. And even at that, he was behind his usual pace. Way behind. With Forrest Greene as his bank, Joe had spent, on the average, nearly $7,000 every single day the past four years. To keep up that kind of outgo, he'd have to draw three hundred dollars from an ATM every hour of every day.

It got worse before it got better. The more bills he sorted through, and the more lawyers' meetings he attended, the more Forrest realized he had actually underestimated his son-in-law's caper. Not only did he understand that he would have to stay in Washington for the long haul, but he realized the money drain was far from over. It would require more of his money to get to the bottom of the mess Joe had left and thereby exonerate his daughter–and himself. But Forrest, make no mistake, was willing to spend it.

"We want to clear my daughter's good name," he emphatically told both Chuck Roistacher and Ladonna Lee, "It's all we can do, it's what we have to do; because she did nothing wrong."

His extended stay also left Forrest with a wardrobe problem. When Thursday came along and he was getting ready to accompany Enid and Ladonna to the Capitol, he discovered that he needed a tie.

With Ladonna showing him the way, he opened the door to the stash of ties Joe had left behind–more ties than you could count in a lunch hour. All of them pure silk. All of them very expensive. Many of them never worn.

Forrest reached in and selected one of the new ties, a red one with blue stripes.

"I suppose it's OK if I wear these," he said.

"Since I paid for them."

□□□

On Thursday–Day Six of Joe's disappearance–Enid Waldholtz's gift ban bill, prohibiting members of the House from accepting "freebies"–passed by an overwhelming majority on the House floor, 422 yeas to six nays. Who says irony doesn't have a sense of humor?

Although the bill had been her baby from the beginning, Enid didn't manage it to its conclusion. For reasons the Republican leadership deemed "prudent," she yielded that privilege to her colleague from Connecticut, Chris Shays. As Tom DeLay, the majority whip, had explained, it just wouldn't do for the bill to get lost amid the controversy concerning its founder's current personal problems.

That was a political decision. The House was still the House and no one wanted to lose sight of that. Without question, there was more than a little concern that the person introducing a bill designed to improve the "tarnished image of elected representatives" was involved in a federal investigation of her own finances.

But it was also a Republican House, and Enid's plight met with a good deal of sympathy and support from within those conservative walls. Her most heartwarming moment of the week had come courtesy of her colleagues. In a Republican-only conference held the day before the vote on her gift ban bill, Enid stood to address her peers and go over the particulars of a bill that was not, considering the heavy restrictions it would place on accepting perquisites, without controversy.

As she approached the speaker's rostrum, fighting for composure, she looked into the crowd and saw Charlie Bass of New Hampshire, like her a freshman, stand up and begin applauding. Within seconds everyone in the room had joined him–more than two hundred Republican members of congress, on their feet, showing support for one of their own.

For Enid, in both the early days of the ordeal as well as later on, Congress became her only real sanctuary, a genuinely kinder and gentler place. Newt Gingrich was one of the first to come to her public defense, releasing a statement from his office that said, "Enid is widely loved and has our total support . . . You do not blame another human being for falling in love with a scoundrel."

□□□

Late Thursday afternoon, about the same time Enid's bill was turning into a law, that scoundrel was turning himself in.

Joe called the U.S. Attorney's office in Washington, D.C. from Philadelphia, where he was staying at a friend's home. He had already hired an attorney, a Philadelphia lawyer named Harvey Sernovitz. He told the federal agents in Washington that he was not aware there was a warrant for his arrest until that morning when he picked up a copy of *USA Today.* The news was hard to miss. The story ran at the top of the front page, just under the logo, "No. 1 in the USA . . . First in Daily Readers."

WARRANT OUT FOR JOE WALDHOLTZ shouted the headline.

The newspaper story, written by Mimi Hall in the just-the-facts-ma'am style of "The Nation's Newspaper," got right to the point:

"A federal arrest warrant was issued Wednesday for Joe Waldholtz, the missing husband of Rep. Enid Waldholtz, R-Utah, as part of an investigation into the couple's finances.

"The warrant seeks Joe Waldholtz as a material witness in a grand jury investigation into:

** Her campaign finances.*

** Their personal accounts.*

** A suspected $1.6 million check-kiting scheme at the federal credit union.*

"'We . . . will be looking at all the irregularities,' said Kevin Ohlson of the U.S. Attorney's office in Washington."

After reading the article, Joe told the authorities in Washington, he quickly secured legal counsel and made contact. They could expect his full cooperation, he told them, and arrangements were immediately made for him to turn himself in. He was instructed to report to the U.S. Attorney's office in the federal courthouse in Washington the next day at 11:45 a.m.

Joe did just that, appearing at a hearing before U.S. District Court Judge Emmet G. Sullivan wearing the same clothes–khaki pants, multicolored sweater and tasseled Ferragamo loafers–he'd been wearing when he'd given Jim Parkinson the slip nearly a week previous.

Joe spoke only briefly to the judge, leaving the explaining to his attorney, who told the judge Joe had left town to get away from personal and media pressures and to "get his thoughts together." There was no explanation forthcoming–nor was it demanded by the judge–about the fictitious trustees Joe had said were flying to Washington, about the court hearing regarding his grandmother's estate he had dodged in Pittsburgh on Monday, or, for that matter, about the fictitious Waldholtz Family Trust itself.

Nor was there any elaboration by Joe or his lawyer as to where he had been or what he had done. All that was revealed was that during his six day disappearance, he spent two days in Springfield, Massachusetts, and the remaining four days in Philadelphia, on the other side of the state from where his family waited.

Judge Sullivan released Joe to the custody of an attorney friend in Philadelphia, Jeffrey Liebmann, on the condition that he surrender his passport, report daily to the FBI in Philadelphia, limit his travel between Philadelphia, Pittsburgh and Washington, and return to Sullivan's court the next Wednesday for a hearing to determine whether Joe would be required to testify before a federal grand jury that was looking into his and Enid's finances.

Beyond that, the man whose disappearance had captivated the country, who owed his father-in-law four million dollars, and who was wanted by his own family for questioning about his grandmother's money, was free to go and do as he pleased.

□□□

Joe sent a note to Enid by way of his lawyers. He needed clothes for his next court appearance, he said, specifying his blue suit, a shirt, a tie, cufflinks, suspenders, and some underwear. So quickly it had all changed. A week ago they had driven to the office together, had eaten lunch together, had driven home together; as inseparable as they'd ever been. *Just a week ago!* Now they were adversaries, their lines drawn in the sand, their communication through their lawyers. *How long can he keep this up?* Enid wondered. *How long can Joe keep running from the truth?* And then she went upstairs to look for a garment bag.

It was Friday, Congress was out of session for the weekend, and Enid and her father were at home in Georgetown, still shuffling papers, still sorting, forever sorting. Earlier, Jim had bid them so long and left for the airport. He was flying back to California, to his family and his law practice. His weekend in D.C. had turned into a full week and that full week had turned into something he was still having a hard time putting a handle on.

I never did like that cockroach, Jim thought to himself as his cab raced through town, backtracking his steps to the airport where it all began. His thoughts took him back to a time more than two years earlier, when he'd been on the telephone speaking long distance with his in-laws, first with Gerda in Salt Lake, then with Forrest in San Francisco. Jim was close to Mormor and Morfar, always had been. For years, he called Mormor once a week in Salt Lake without fail. He talked to her more than his wife Sue, her own daughter, did. He remembered how the subject during that particular phone conversation had turned to Joseph Waldholtz, the young man to whom Enid was then engaged. More specifically, the subject had turned to his mysterious wealth. Supposedly it was unlimited, but Gerda Greene confided to Jim she wasn't so sure. "He doesn't do things like a rich person," she said. "Why would someone that rich want to have a mortgage on a house?"

"Well," Jim had cut in matter-of-factly, which was his style, "we can have him investigated. Give me the word and it will take one phone call to Pittsburgh. I'll tell you how much he's worth down to the dime."

Jim then called Forrest in San Francisco and asked him if he wanted him to "check out Joe." There was a slight pause; then Forrest answered, "Oh no, Jim, we don't do that . . . The Greenes don't do that."

Might not have been such a bad idea, thought Jim in the back of his cab, but the smugness soon left him because he knew, as everyone in the family knew, that they all could have asked more questions, they all could have been more skeptical. In hindsight there were signs any of them could have picked up on. Jim remembered when one of his closest friends, Dr. Steve Lake, a dentist, met Joe at a campaign fund-raiser for Enid that Jim had organized and held at his country club in Bermuda Dunes. Jim had mentioned that Joe's father was a dentist, like Dr. Lake. Jim had also mentioned that Joe's family was in the possession of a trust fund worth in the neighborhood of four hundred million dollars. To which Dr. Lake had replied, "I'm not buying it. If the trust is worth *a million dollars*, there's no way that guy ever drills another tooth."

Joe's fraud was always there, just below the surface, and no one had dipped underneath to see what lurked below. But why should they? They weren't private investigators. They weren't accountants. They were family. *Amazingly enough,* thought Jim, *Joe was one of us.*

It was hard for Jim to quantify the week he'd just spent. It was going to take a while. In many respects, it all still seemed more surreal than real. For most of the week his name had been in every newspaper in the country. People from all over, Sue told him, had been calling their home in California, reporters, friends, old school classmates, golfing buddies, the list went on. His best friend, Neil Dimick, read the story in the *New York Times* while flying back to California from New York on a business trip and immediately called the Parkinson's home on the airphone. Dimick was somewhere over Iowa when Jim's youngest son, Matthew, who had been instructed to simply tell all callers he didn't know anything, answered. Matthew did as he was told. After Dimick asked for Jim, his son said, "My dad's not here, I don't know anything," and then he hung up.

The biggest story since the O. J. Simpson trial and Jim Parkinson, personal injury attorney-at-law, had landed smack in the middle of it. Imagine that. Jim felt a kind of empathy for the lead lawyers in the O. J. case. *Now I know how Johnny Cochran and Marcia Clark feel.* To see the media at the height of a feeding frenzy had truly been something to behold. Reporters had staked out their positions at Enid's office, at the Powell, Goldstein law offices, at the Georgetown townhouse. At the townhouse they parked their satellite trucks on the sidewalk and set up their minicams in the driveway, the lenses pointing at the door, just in case. They rang the doorbell day and night, to the point that Enid finally tacked a note on the door, asking the media to stop ringing the bell because there was a three-month old trying to sleep inside.

The media was not easily dissuaded, Jim had discovered that personally. He was constantly taking cab rides between Georgetown and the Powell, Goldstein offices downtown. During one ride, at the height of Joe's disappearance, Jim, being a natural talker, struck up a conversation with the driver, who he noted from his license was from The Sudan. The cabbie spoke only broken English, but after opening pleasantries he looked in the rearview mirror and, as if reading the question off a piece of paper, asked in his best English, "So where is Mr. Waldholtz now?"

"Just drive the cab," said Jim.

Now he was in another cab, racing for the airport, with the whereabouts of Mr. Waldholtz already yesterday's news.

In eight days, he had done the best he could do, Jim realized. He'd lost his brother-in-law, protected his sister-in-law, briefed his father-in-law (*and* offered to buy him dinner), joined Chuck Roistacher's legal team (pro bono), and, just before he left, interviewed two accountants from Big Six firms, finally recommending that Enid should hire Frederic Miller, a top-rated forensic accountant from Coopers & Lybrand. It would be Miller's job to probe the ledgers and the balance sheets and sort out exactly what Joe had done and how he managed to do it.

At the airport, Jim paid the driver and walked into the terminal. To his left was baggage claim where, six days ago, Joe had told him he'd wait for the boxes of documents; to the right and up the escalator was *Frank & Stein's,* where Jim had stopped for a hot dog.

This is where it all began, or, to be more accurate, where it all ended. The week had forever changed Jim Parkinson, the way eye witnesses to explosions are forever changed. A psychological bomb had gone off in front of his eyes, and in full glare of the national media spotlight, and he sure hadn't managed to dodge all the shrapnel. It wasn't just seeing the disintegration that changed him, it was the man whose fingerprints were on the bomb. Jim thought he knew a lot about human distress. In his personal injury practice he dealt with pain and suffering on a daily basis.

But that pain and suffering involved accidents, for the most part, and what he'd seen in Washington had been no accident. What he'd seen in Washington had been perpetrated by the baddest man he'd ever met–and he hadn't met him in a biker bar or a crack house, he'd met him in his sister-in-law's home, and he was wearing glasses, he had a huge stomach, and he was a Republican.

Through the week, especially after his father-in-law arrived on the scene, a thought that settled in Jim's mind and would not leave was the alarming contrast between the two men he had seen, in succession, sleeping in the upstairs bedroom of 1671 34th Street, Georgetown. Jim knew them both, and he knew they were as extreme and diametrically opposed as any two men he'd ever known: Joe Waldholtz and Forrest Greene. Joe talked about who he knew and what he knew, Forrest talked about who you knew and what you knew; Joe wore shoes that hadn't been out of the box more than two weeks, Forrest wore wingtips he bought twenty years ago; and Joe always talked about his fortune when he didn't have one, while Forrest never talked about his fortune and it was vast. The two most prominent men in his sister-in-law's life, he realized, were on the absolute opposite ends of the scale. Polar opposites. Enid sure hadn't married her father.

Jim was no prude. He cut other men their slack. He cut *himself* slack. Heaven knew he wasn't perfect. *Yeah,* he thought, *for one thing, I swear too much*. But that was just it. Everybody who knew him knew he swore too much. He didn't hide it. He did try to watch his mouth in front of his mother- and father-in-law–out of respect for them and because, hell, he didn't want to offend anyone. But he was who he was and everybody knew who he was. Joe Waldholtz couldn't say that. Joe Waldholtz was nothing what you thought he was. He was a chameleon. A parasite. A mole. A wolf in sheep's clothing. A traitor. A fraud.

And a cockroach sonofabitch, thought Jim as he headed for his gate and a five hour flight that would return him to his wife and family in California.

□□□

As her father continued to open bills and groan at the kitchen table, Enid found what she was looking for: Joe's hangup suit bag. She pulled it out of the closet and laid it on the bed. This wasn't the first time she'd packed for Joe. He often told her he never packed anything as a kid–the servants always did that–and as a result he wasn't any good at it. When he did try to pack, his shirts were always wrinkled, his suits always slipped off the hangers. So Enid would do it for him. Just as she was doing now.

She'd heard about Joe's "surrender" the day before from Chuck, who'd heard about it from someone who was watching CNN. It hadn't surprised her that Joe hadn't called her, not like it would have surprised her three or four days earlier. The old Joe still had a grip on her, but it was lessening.

Still, she was constantly getting reminders that you couldn't turn love off like a spigot, you just couldn't. She found she had to constantly remind herself of *what has happened* so she wouldn't lapse into unwarranted sympathy or melancholy. Sometimes her thoughts were so stupid. Like today, when she heard that Joe had turned himself in wearing the same clothes he'd had on for six days. Her first reaction was sympathy. She felt sorry for him. She wiped out the thought as soon as she could, but it wasn't as easy as anyone might think. And it wasn't easy now, as she laid out the clothes he had asked for in his note, and she kept lapsing back to the old days, again and again. She had done this so many times. She knew what Joe liked. She knew what Joe needed. She knew he had to have extra underwear because a guy his size couldn't just walk into any store and buy it off the rack. She mentally slapped herself at that one. *He should rot naked in the town square,* she thought. But then she packed extra underwear anyway.

She went ahead and packed the blue suit he asked for and some ties and suspenders she knew he liked, but then she caught herself again and by the time she got to the cufflinks she was determined to make him suffer. She sorted through the drawer to find the cheapest pair in there. The irony was, there were no cheap cufflinks. But she sure wasn't going to pack the ones she had given him for their wedding, or his favorite pair, the ones lined with rubies; finally she threw in a pair of gold ones she once gave him for Christmas, with his initials, JW, engraved on the sides. She could think of no reason why she would ever want those around again.

She zipped up the bag and stood to take it downstairs to the front door. She dabbed at her eyes. She had been crying again. She chastised herself for that, too, but the trouble was, she usually didn't even realize she'd begun. It was strange, this mourning business, especially when you were mourning something that had never been.

CHAPTER XI

Chuck Roistacher slid the piles of paper off his desk and, with his foot, deftly arranged them on the floor–his horizontal filing cabinet. He was eating in today. Somebody had gone across the street to the Pavilion Shops, the shopping mall in the historic Old Post Office building, and brought him a turkey sandwich. It wasn't that there weren't a lot of lunch options in the area. *Planet Hollywood* was across from one corner of the building that headquartered the law offices of Powell, Goldstein, Frazer & Murphy. *The Hard Rock Cafe* was across from the other. And if those tourist hot spots weren't to your liking, there were gourmet delis, regular delis, hotdog stands and four-star restaurants all within range. But today, like a lot of days lately, he just didn't have the time.

As Washington locations go, you couldn't get much more central than 1001 Pennsylvania Avenue. The White House was just up the street, the Capitol was just down the street, a few blocks past the federal courthouse. The headquarters for the Federal Election Commission sat kitty-corner across the intersection of 10th and E Streets in the old Pepco building, co-tenants, as it turned out, with the *Hard Rock Cafe.* Two buildings, and a couple hundred years, down from that was Ford's Theatre, where President Lincoln was shot.

Although not a native, Roistacher, who grew up in Long Island, knew Washington well. He arrived in 1968, on the threshold of Watergate, fresh out of the University of Miami law school. He first signed on with the District of Columbia's public defender's office and for eleven months he'd worked there–at ground zero, as they say, defending bank robbers, drug dealers, con men, you name it. His colleagues tended to be anti-war ideologues, liberals straight out of central casting who worked with pictures of Woodstock and Fidel Castro on their desks. It was not a dull life, but it wasn't for him, mainly because when he looked at the scum that's what he saw: scum. When Chuck Roistacher saw a bank robber, he saw a bank robber; when he saw a rapist, he saw a rapist–he didn't see victims of society, sad byproducts of the system, people powerless to stop their crimes. For him, sociology and the law did not overlap. Before the year was up, he reversed his field. He joined the other side.

The United States Attorney for the District of Columbia took him on board as an Assistant United States Attorney in 1969. Now, instead of defending them, he joined the team that was chasing the bad guys. Richard Nixon and his henchmen were among those the team wound up chasing. The Watergate case originally landed on a desk in the Washington, D.C. U.S. Attorney's office.

He wound up working as a federal prosecutor for two months short of twenty years. He spent time in several sections of the office but white collar prosecution became his specialty. He had an intuition, a kind of sixth sense, for rooting out the bad guys when they looked like good guys. His most high profile case was *The United States of America v. Paul Thayer.* Thayer had been Ronald Reagan's Deputy Secretary of Defense, a man of considerable reputation, a one-time Navy ace pilot and respectable family man with a wife and a daughter who sat on the boards of Allied and Anheuser Busch and was chairman of LTV. That was his public life. But Paul Thayer had another life, one that included a mistress–an LTV receptionist–and an extensive network of illicit insider stock trading. In concert with a number of brokers and others, Thayer leaked news of company acquisitions and other secrets, stock was transferred as a result, and small fortunes were realized by everyone involved. Small *illegal* fortunes. Paul Thayer helped popularize the phrase "insider trading."

Thayer and his gang were exposed when Roistacher got the girlfriend to talk. Reagan's one-time aide went down hard. He was almost sixty-five years old at the time, but a federal judge, wanting to make an example out of Paul Thayer that would send a message to other men of power, sentenced him to four years in prison, an unprecedented sentence for a white-collar criminal in the mid 1980's. Roistacher actually felt sorry for the guy.

At Powell, Goldstein, Frazer & Murphy, where he moved in 1989, Chuck still worked the white collar side of the street. But now, armed with over twenty years of education as to the intricacies of fraud in all its many facets, he was back on the defense, still chasing bad guys, but from a different perch. He'd worked on more health care fraud cases than he cared to count. He'd seen insurance scams and pyramid scams and pension scams. He'd dealt–and still dealt–in the world of lies and liars, surrounded by people who weren't who or what they said they were. It was sad but nonetheless a fact of life: some people just didn't tell the truth. Sadder yet, it seemed some people *couldn't.*

The first time Chuck Roistacher met Joseph Phillip Waldholtz his antennae went straight up. It had been at the firm's offices a little more than a week before Joe disappeared–when Joe first balked about using the law firm's services. "It's my family's money that has caused all this mess," Joe had said, almost resignedly, and right then, as soon as he'd offered that flimsy explanation, Chuck Roistacher began to wonder about Joe. Because what Joe was saying was true–it was his family's money that had caused their mess, at least the way he was presenting it through what proved to be pure fantasies–but the point was, SO WHAT? Why did that preclude him securing the same legal services as his wife?

It was a pattern, Chuck Roistacher knew, that was common to all con men: Always tell the truth, just don't tell the whole truth. Tell just enough, five percent, ten percent at most, to wedge your foot in the door and deflect the issue, but no more. Tell just enough to establish a front of credibility and keep up your facade. Live to lie another day.

In the next couple of days after first meeting Joe, Chuck's

suspicions rose exponentially. The Congresswoman's husband had too many excuses, too many reasons, too many alibis. Both he and Enid had given the law firm authorization to access their various joint bank records, but many of the phone numbers Joe gave them always rang busy, a large percentage of the records he promised were being faxed didn't arrive, and neither did Federal Express packages. On Friday afternoon, the day before Joe's disappearance, Chuck had personally gone to Enid's office on Capitol Hill, asked Joe to get the hell out of the office, and proceeded to tell the Congresswoman that he had serious doubts about the guy she had married.

When Joe disappeared the next afternoon, the attorney was in prime position to say, "I Told You So." And he might have allowed himself that indulgence if not for the devastation Joe's exit had wrought on his client. As a prosecutor, Chuck had been around a lot of victims, and when he saw Enid Waldholtz the night of Saturday, November 11th–a Congresswoman fully capable of taking the gavel and commanding the House of Representatives without missing a beat, now reduced to a barely functioning human being–he knew he was seeing a victim. Enid was no perpetrator. Her behavior in the hours immediately following Joe's disappearance proved that to Chuck beyond a doubt. She was the oppressed, all right, and Joseph Phillip Waldholtz was, as the guys down at the precinct would say, *the perp*. This was no Bonnie & Clyde act. Chuck Roistacher would bet his reputation on it.

So he was right. *The guy was a scumbag. Congratulations.* But that didn't stop anything, or make anyone feel any better, or, worst of all, solve anything. Charles Roistacher, attorney at law, knew that better than anyone. He knew the federal prosecutors–the guys in his old office, where you assumed that everyone was lying because much of the time, they were–weren't going to believe Enid just on the strength of her word. He knew the Federal Election Commission wasn't just going to close its books either, content to write "Husband was a fraud" on the phony campaign reports. He knew the government had already started to prepare for a grand jury investigation–that's why the warrant had been issued for Joe's whereabouts–and he knew that grand jury would hear testimony from every man, woman, cat, dog and nanny who had been even peripherally associated with Enid and Joe.

Most foreboding of all, he knew this: Joe wasn't going to start telling the truth.

Those kind of guys never did, and Joseph Phillip Waldholtz was one of the most extreme of *those kind of guys* Roistacher had ever come across. The very worst of the breed: a predator who didn't just stalk and steal, but who stalked and stole from people who were kind to him.

This was no Paul Thayer, a man who made a fortune from inside tips and led a double life. Thayer broke the law to get rich and he led his double life so his wife wouldn't find out about his mistress. Although well off the moral high ground, his motives were nonetheless clear: money and sex. You could understand a crook like that. Any man on the street could imagine, but for the grace of God, going the same place on a bad day. But Joseph Phillip Waldholtz had no such lofty motives. Joseph Phillip Waldholtz lied and stole from those who loved him, who empathized with him, who championed him and took care of him–he was no better than a vagrant sitting on the sidewalk who would mug the compassionate soul who'd just given him a twenty.

It hadn't taken them long to plumb the depths of the deceitful man they were dealing with. It was on Sunday, the night after Joe's exit, that Chuck had gotten his first clear perception of Joseph Phillip Waldholtz.

He arrived in a businesslike manner, ready to do his job as a lawyer and make sure evidence was properly collected and catalogued. "I've seen lots of bad guys, I've seen their tricks," he cavalierly said to Ladonna as she first showed him the prescription pills Joe had hidden in the cigarette boxes. After that he moved on through the house. He looked at the men's magazines, the forged documents, the phony certificates, the mountains of unpaid bills, and, finally, he walked into Joe's closet, where, despite the jadeness he'd developed after nearly twenty years of tracking down parasites and frauds, he was stopped in his tracks. It was a small and simple thing that froze him: a price tag that said "$120" still hanging from a Hermés tie made of pure French silk. *The asshole didn't even use what he stole*, thought the lawyer.

Chuck Roistacher turned to Ladonna.

"Can you believe how bad this guy was?" he said.

"I thought you'd seen lots of bad guys," Ladonna shot back.

"Not this bad," said Chuck.

□□□

They could beat this bad guy, Roistacher knew that; and not only could they beat him, it would be easy. A first-year law student could take Joseph Phillip Waldholtz down. That wasn't the problem.

The problem was preventing him from taking his client, Congresswoman Enid Greene Waldholtz, down with him.

Chuck sized up the situation. He'd spent two decades in the U.S. Attorney's office and he knew they would look at Joe Waldholtz as small potatoes. Con men were as common as rats. Congresswomen, on the other hand, were not so common. If they could prove Enid culpable, not only would it add to the Justice Department's image as the public's watchdog, but the prosecutor who brought her down would have the kind of trophy that could launch a career. Chuck's hunch–and it would prove to be right–was that the prosecutors would be inclined to listen to whatever Joe, his fraudulent past notwithstanding, had to say. They'd listen in the hopes it might move them on to bigger game, to the very halls of the U.S. Congress.

To keep that from happening, Chuck's legal strategy from the very beginning was centered around keeping a step ahead of the government prosecutors. The idea was to investigate quicker, interview witnesses faster, and then spoon-feed the findings to the FBI and the U.S. Attorneys. Do their case for them, in other words, but do it faster and in greater detail. That way, the truth would come out, and it was the truth that was going to set the Congresswoman free.

The key was to find out as much as possible about what Joe had done, and how he had done it, in as little time as possible. Chuck knew the feds would want to hear from Enid sooner rather than later (she would in fact be subpoenaed to testify in front of a federal grand jury barely a month after Joe left) and he knew why. He'd used the same tactic as a prosecutor: get testimony from any possible subjects on the record as soon as possible, "lock them in," thereby increasing the chances that later developments, evidence, and testimony, will contradict that testimony in some way. If they're lying, they'll eventually expose themselves.

He also knew that, unlike the vast majority of the general public, it would not be realistic for Enid to invoke her Fifth Amendment rights and refuse to testify on the grounds it might incriminate her. While it's true that the very purpose for the Fifth Amendment is so it can act as a safeguard against rushes to judgment, it's also true that in the case of public figures it usually doesn't work very well. High profile defendants who "take the fifth," no matter how innocent they might be, are liable to run into a kind of boomerang effect. When the news comes out in the press, which it invariably will, the public's natural tendency is to assume guilt. Otherwise, why wouldn't the person just go ahead and testify? From a public relations standpoint, that can spell disaster.

Chuck Roistacher's client–a sitting member of the United States House of Representatives–certainly qualified as high-profile. From the start, not only did he determine that he would not advise Enid to invoke her Fifth Amendment rights, but he would spearhead an effort so aggressive and thorough that it would beat the other side to the punch and make it so she wouldn't even *want to*. In locker room vernacular, he was adopting the time-honored game plan strategy: the best defense is a good offense.

Not that his client, per se, would be the initial object of the government's scrutiny. Their investigation would first be into the *finances* of Joe and Enid Waldholtz, both campaign and personal. Any indictments handed down by the grand jury would be based on what was discovered after examining those finances.

In official prosecutorial terms, those who are subpoenaed to testify in front of grand juries fit into three categories: witnesses, subjects, and targets. A witness is one who has facts that are relevant to the case–he or she has simply "witnessed" events and occurrences relevant to the case and is subpoenaed to deliver that testimony. A subject is one whose involvement in the case in question goes beyond the bystander status of a witness–he or she actually participated in events that transpired. A target, of course, is one who is not only suspected of wrongdoing but a person who will likely be indicted by the grand jury.

Going in, Joe quickly became a target and his wife Enid, along with her father, became subjects.

Chuck's job was obvious: make sure Enid Waldholtz and her father, D. Forrest Greene, did not become targets.

Besides Chuck Roistacher, Enid's legal "team" involved three other Powell, Goldstein attorneys. Brett Kappel and Michael Chanin specialized in federal election laws and they headed up the FEC defense while Ralph Caccia assisted Chuck with the criminal investigation. Caccia was a younger version of Roistacher–a fellow New Yorker (he grew up in Brooklyn, the son of a cop) who had also first worked as an Assistant U.S. Attorney before joining the private sector.

Roistacher and Caccia wasted no time in jumping on the case. Ralph was immediately dispatched to Salt Lake City, where he checked in at the downtown Marriott Hotel and began the task of interviewing dozens of potential witnesses. He also organized systematic searches through bank records as well as a search of Enid and Joe's home. The search of the home proved to be particularly helpful. It was there that, among other things, Ralph found a bogus Ginnie Mae certificate that purported to be collateral for money Joe had withdrawn from his Grandmother Levenson's estate. The evidence showed that Joe had printed the certificate at a local Kinko's. It was a valuable piece of evidence, particularly when laid alongside the bogus "Ready Assets" securities deposit Enid had found in the Georgetown house. Not only did the two certificates demonstrate that Joe's duplicity stretched from Pittsburgh to Utah to Washington, but that he wasn't just a buffoon who pathologically lied about a family fortune. He was a con artist with enough sophistication to premeditatedly prepare fake documents to help camouflage his trail–a trail that clearly extended well before he ever met Enid Greene Waldholtz or her wealthy father.

When Ralph telephoned Roistacher to tell him of the Ginnie Mae "find," it was nearly midnight on the east coast. But Chuck's head soon cleared. "The fucking asshole," the attorney cursed into the phone. "He stole from his senile grandmother."

By early the next morning, information regarding the bogus Ginnie Mae certificate was forwarded to the feds–a pattern that would be followed throughout Chuck's and Ralph's investigations. The goal of Enid's lawyers, through the evidence, was to posture Joe as a cold-blooded, calculating liar, allowing their client to emerge as the unwitting victim that she was.

The good news was that Joe left so many clues just waiting to be uncovered it was as if he wanted to be caught. The bad news–as Ralph and Chuck became increasingly aware–was that in spite of those clues, the prosecutors were not eager to exonerate Joe's wife. Even though, on paper, the case looked to be an open and shut fraud case, in reality, it became obvious very early on that it was going to take some time. The feds weren't going to let a member of Congress off the hook that easily.

Luckily, the defense had the resources to, as Forrest Greene put it, "Do what they had to do." For all his turning down thermostats and eating meals at home, Forrest Greene was a wealthy man–worth well more than the $4 million he had loaned to Joe–and a patently decent man. He had both enough money and motivation for him to clear his daughter's name, and his. He might not enjoy paying the bills, and he might, as Powell, Goldstein would come to discover, take his sweet time scrutinizing them, to the point of arguing over every single billable item, but in the end, he'd pay what he thought he owed, and he'd buy what he had to buy.

Fully funded by Forrest–just as Joe had been–the law firm was thus able to not only spare no expense in its legal work, but was also able to retain the services of Ladonna Lee and the Eddie Mahe Company to handle public relations, and Fred Miller and the accounting firm of Coopers & Lybrand to sort out the books.

□□□

One floor up from where Chuck sat, in a room someone had decided would be perfect for the accountants, sat Frederic Miller.

They'd given Miller and his staff a windowless conference room on the seventh floor, overlooking nothing but an amazingly large and unorganized collection of financial books, records, papers, documents, filings and floppy discs. It was, by anyone's definition, a mess. But Frederic Miller wasn't anyone. He was a forensic accountant, "One who applies accounting methods to questions of law."

To Frederic Miller, the mess was a case.

Fred knew he was one of the lucky ones, not just because he was good at what he did–finding financial fingerprints–but because he enjoyed his work. Chasing down people in ledgers, his second love, had largely taken over from his first love, chasing down people in footraces, and how many people could honestly say they'd been doing what they wanted to do practically their whole life? In earlier times–"a lot of years and fifty pounds ago," he liked to say–Fred had run the middle distances for Rutgers University. He once ran 5,000 meters–3.1 miles–in fourteen minutes and three seconds, which isn't exactly dawdling, and the fastest mile of his life, a seriously quick four minutes and twelve seconds, came in the 1975 Championship of America four-mile relay, where Rutgers put a scare into heavily favored Villanova before fading at the tape and finishing third. At Rutgers, Fred ran cross-country, indoor track and outdoor track, carried a full class load, lived with ten guys in a house off campus, and never got in trouble because, well, who had the time.

He graduated Phi Beta Kappa from Rutgers, and that got him accepted at three Ivy League graduate schools; he chose Cornell over Dartmouth and Penn because he was (still) broke and Cornell gave him an academic scholarship. Three years later he graduated with a masters in business administration and an emphasis on accounting that helped get him a summer internship with the New York City division of the General Accounting Office–the investigatory arm for the United States Congress. After that he branched out on his own. First he paid his dues working at a branch office of the Arthur Anderson Company in Washington, and then he moved to Coopers & Lybrand, where he became a partner. He lived in suburban Virginia with his wife, Mary Anne, and three children, two girls and a boy, ages twelve, eleven, and nine.

He discovered his affinity for what his industry called "special projects" early in his career, and he supposed it had something to do with his roots. He came from a close-knit Irish family from Jersey City, New Jersey, that, at least until him, had contributed firemen and priests to the world. His grandparents had emigrated from Ireland during the potato famine and, after processing at New York's Ellis Island, traveled five miles due east and settled on the banks of the East River, under the watchful gaze of the Statue of Liberty. From one generation and into the next, the Millers stayed put. As far as his family was concerned, when Fred went forty-five miles away to Rutgers for college, he might as well have gone to China. Then, when he became an accountant and moved to Washington, he was without dispute the oddest and farthest-removed duck in the family.

But if he'd proved you could take the Irishman out of Jersey City, he'd also proved you couldn't take Jersey City out of the Irishman. He'd grown up in the greater New York City urban sprawl–that gave him his street smarts. And he'd grown up in the moral structure of a loving Catholic family–that gave him his principles. No matter where he went, he took his hometown with him.

To be effective at the kind of work he was involved in, you needed to be able to understand people and you needed to be able to use your wits. Forensic accounting was much more than mere numbers. Tracking white collar criminals entailed a lot more than adding two and two. These were criminals who generally thought of themselves as smarter than anybody else, and who used that intelligence to get what they wanted. To catch them you had to understand what it was they were after; you had to know human nature. As Fred said, "at the base of most of our cases lies sex, drugs and rock-and-roll."

He had worked on dozens of big-money cases. One of the biggest was when he headed the investigation that exposed William Aramony, the director of the United Way. Aramony had built the United Way into the country's leading charitable umbrella organization. But then his leading charity became himself. He formed a phony company that he used to siphon off millions of dollars of United Way contributions, all for his personal pleasure. When he was finally busted he had condos in New York and Florida, a twenty-four hour limousine at his private disposal, and he'd just recently dumped a 19-year-old girlfriend for her 17-year-old sister. Bad move. When the 19-year-old talked, Fred Miller got to see the books.

It was when Joe Waldholtz walked that Fred Miller got to see *his* books. He piled them on a large desk in a small room on Pennsylvania Avenue and went to work. He had a trail to track, and fingerprints to find.

□□□

Like Chuck Roistacher and Fred Miller, Ladonna Lee, who made up the third key prong of "Team Enid," was a child of the streets. Only hers weren't paved.

She grew up driving a tractor and attending an honest-to-goodness one-room school in the upper northeast reaches of Colorado. The second of eight brothers and sisters raised on a sprawling ranch, she became a second "mom" from the age of ten, when her older sister left home to attend high school.

She went to college at the University of Northern Colorado

in Greeley, double majoring in business and home economics. She thought she'd be a high school teacher until she realized she didn't even have the patience to help her little sisters with their homework. She had too much energy to stand still very long. Her father had been a member of the Colorado House of Representatives for eighteen years and that had always intrigued her, so she tried politics, going to work for John Vanderhoof, Colorado's Republican Governor. The choice was good–she found she loved politics–but the timing wasn't. The year was 1974, and in the wake of Watergate, Vanderhoof lost his bid for re-election. Out of work, Ladonna heard of an opening at the Republican National Committee, where a man named Eddie Mahe was the executive director, so on New Years Day, 1974, alone, free and curious, she got in her car and drove due east, to Washington. It turned out to be a one-way trip.

Ladonna settled in Washington, D.C., and soon fell in love with and married a former Army Special Forces officer, and they had a daughter they named Jessie. Although there were days she longed for a pickup truck and a prairie, the East suited her fine. She liked working with the RNC and found that she got along famously with her boss; so well that she and Eddie went in partnership together and formed the enormously successful Eddie Mahe Company.

If Ladonna learned anything during her many campaigns it was the topsy-turvyness of it all. There were no guarantees, in politics or in life. One day you could be on top of the charts, the next at the bottom of them, and sometimes it all crested or fell on a fluke. Her education began early. When her father, after eighteen years of public service and nine straight wins, finally lost an election for the Colorado legislature, it had a lot to do with an article that appeared in the *Rocky Mountain News* during the height of the campaign. The headline read, "Candidate Picked Up For Drunk Driving." Next to the story was a picture of Ladonna's dad. The story was about his opponent.

She knew, too, that her father's defeat also had something to do with his wife leaving him. Ladonna's mother had divorced her father after nearly forty years of marriage.

If Ladonna had seen too much of anything, it was leaving. Her mother left her dad; and then her husband left her and Jessie. She liked to think that it hadn't turned her into a defeatist as much as it had turned her pragmatic. It also made her more compassionate. She knew that was why she had been willing to step over the line from professional advice-giver to friend for Enid Greene. Her empathy was genuine. She'd been there, in her own way. She really wanted to help if she could.

In retrospect, Ladonna had to smile at her attempts at "marriage counseling" just before it all blew up for Enid and Joe. A few evenings before Joe's disappearance she got a call from Enid, who sounded close to hysteria, asking her to please come over. Ladonna was at home in her sweats and her glasses, not her usual out-in-public dress, but Enid sounded so distressed she feared Joe might be hurting her, so, without changing, she told her daughter Jessie where she was going, jumped in the Pathfinder, and set out for Georgetown. As she was crossing the Key Bridge, leaving Virginia for the District, she realized how foolhardy this might be. She hadn't brought her handgun–by point of fact she couldn't legally bring her handgun into the District, anyway–and she had no idea what state Joe, who'd been acting more than a little crazy the last few days, was in. What if he were physically dangerous?

So she'd reached for the cellular and phoned Eddie at his home. She explained to him where she was going, finishing as she pulled up in front of Enid and Joe's townhouse. "I'm going in Eddie," she'd said. "But stay on the line. I'll come right back to tell you if it looks dangerous." With the motor running and the phone off the hook, she trotted to the door and rang the bell. When Enid answered, Ladonna saw that Joe was at the opposite end of the hall, coming toward them.

"Is he hurting you?" Ladonna whispered.

"Oh no, I'm OK," answered Enid. By then, Joe was at the door.

"What's this about, Enid?" he asked.

As Enid began to explain, Ladonna trotted back to her car,

told Eddie, "Everything's under control," shut off the ignition, returned to the house and escorted the warring couple into the living room. Once they were seated she proceeded to give them a speech about hanging in there through the tough times and staying together. That's the important thing, she told them: Stay together. You can work out anything if you'll just communicate and work with each other.

But, of course, there were always exceptions.

Given the almost unbelievable revelations following Joe's departure, Ladonna knew Enid not only needed damage control on many fronts, and that included the media, but she also needed a support system to help her get back up from Joe's bodyslams. She needed to realize that she wasn't less of a person because she'd been taken in by Joe. By point of fact, she'd joined a rather large and, if she did say so herself, sometimes prestigious club. He'd certainly fooled her. In reality, hadn't Joe fooled them all? Hadn't he done a number on everyone he'd touched?

That "number" definitely included the Eddie Mahe Company. When Ladonna and Eddie first got involved with Enid's campaign in the fall of '94 they'd made routine inquiries with their political contacts in Pittsburgh about Joe Waldholtz. "Spoiled, arrogant rich guy," they'd been told, and they'd let it go at that. When someone idly remarked that they'd heard he had a few problems paying his bills, they let that go too. They had never run a credit check on a client before, and they didn't see any reason to start now.

In fact, Ladonna realized, the last time Joe had pulled the wool over her eyes was just a week before he disappeared. After speaking with him about the "Waldholtz Family Trust" and the impending visit of the trustees from Pittsburgh, Ladonna had turned detective and asked Joe for the phone number to the trustee's office. She wanted to speak to those trustees herself. Joe gave her a phone number in Pittsburgh. She called it twice on Friday, November third (she'd given the FBI her phone records). Both times she got a recording, announcing she had reached the offices of the Waldholtz Family Trust, no one could come to the phone right then, and please leave a message so someone could return her call.

She'd left a message, but no one ever called her back. The FBI subsequently discovered that the number was to a phone in Joe's father's home. Joe had talked a friend into making the recording on the answering machine, explaining that it was "a joke" he was playing on some people.

That would be her.

Each in their own way, they had all been hoodwinked, just as they had all unwittingly facilitated Joe's con. They had all dealt with Joe as honest people–thinking he was honest as well. Ladonna understood that. But she knew Enid didn't. At least not yet. Ladonna saw her "consultant" job as twofold: personal and professional. On one level, she needed to be Enid's friend and help her retain her emotional stability; on another level, she needed to help her set the public record straight.

In concert with Eddie, Enid, the accountants and the lawyers, Ladonna coordinated a P.R. game plan that called for Enid not to say anything until they had a chance to piece together the whole story.

It just didn't make much sense, they all agreed, to give out the information prematurely, when they still weren't sure of all the facts. Enid was a wanted newsmaker. All the major morning network shows wanted to speak with her, as well as a majority of the TV talk shows, and newspapers from all over the country were begging for interviews. But until they got to the bottom of everything, she wouldn't say anything. Once they were confident they knew what they were talking about, they'd talk, but not until.

Ladonna checked with the accountants and the attorneys to determine how quickly they could piece together what happened. Working as fast as humanly possibly, they told her they needed about a month to lay a coherent foundation and be in a position to tell an accurate story. Ladonna gave them their month. She called the Doubletree Hotel in Salt Lake City and reserved their biggest ballroom for a press conference to be held on Monday, December 11th. On the one-month anniversary of the disappearance of the Joe Waldholtz they'd all once known and, if not loved, at least trusted, the story of his greatest con would become public.

□□□

It was a busy month. Joe had been a busy boy. At the height of the investigation, Fred Miller supervised a staff of ten accountants in Washington alone, working six days a week and long into the night, along with an adjunct staff working out of the Coopers & Lybrand office in Salt Lake City. Chuck Roistacher's legal team, also expanded to Utah to include divorce lawyers there, was just as sizeable. A small army, hot on Joe's old trail–a trail they were to discover didn't begin a mere four years ago, when Joe met Enid, but many years before that. Daily, almost hourly, the evidence presented itself. Forgeries, lies, misrepresentations, a veritable avalanche of revelations of a long-hidden life of thievery and deception. Through bits and pieces from the boxes Joe had personally escorted onto the airplane in Salt Lake in September, the accountants discovered another dozen bank accounts Enid never knew existed; in addition to that they uncovered more than twenty credit card accounts–Visa, Discover and Mastercard–that Joe had either maxed out to their ten thousand or seventy-five hundred dollar limits, or were overdrawn. They discovered wire transfers going from Salt Lake City to Pittsburgh to Washington and back again. They discovered proof of at least two small check kiting scams and one very large one, involving nearly two million dollars.

The gist of their findings was this: everybody Joe could steal from, he did . . . including Enid herself.

She was sitting in the conference room when Brett Kappel brought in the news.

"What now?" Enid said, bracing herself.

"Well, we now know he stole from your campaign fund in

'92 as well."

Enid's face froze into an apoplectic stare as Kappel went on to explain that in the process of going through Joe's checks dating back to 1992 they were able to determine that after Enid had turned her campaign books over to Joe, he had written checks to himself from Enid's campaign account, and then deposited them in his own personal account. So far they had uncovered an embezzlement of more than $35,000, and they were still counting.

"What months were those?" she asked.

"November and December," said Kappel.

Working faster than any calculator, Enid's brain processed the data immediately. She began crying, realizing that at the same time Joe had professed undying love and had asked her to marry him, and in the wake of her crushing defeat to Karen Shepherd–he had been robbing her blind.

At least that news softened the blow a few days later, when the accountants uncovered a check Joe wrote to himself from Enid's '92 campaign for $25,000–just a day or two before buying Enid's engagement ring, which cost $22,500.

On top of everything else, Enid now also was convinced that she had bought her own ring.

□□□

In truth, Forrest and Enid Greene joined a sizeable roster of victims, the exact scope of which, Fred Miller soon deduced, would probably never be measured. Joe's larceny knew no bounds, it was as all-encompassing as it was impossible to completely quantify. The truth of the matter was, some records had simply been destroyed, others had been lost, and some, they knew, were hidden from view. A couple of the banks Joe had dealt with were no longer in business, and who could know how many he'd used in complete secrecy?

Still, what they did have was enough to satisfy anyone even remotely familiar with arithmetic that Joe Waldholtz had spent a lot of money, almost none of which was his own. Methodically but indubitably, the data fed into the computer on the seventh floor at 1001 Pennsylvania Avenue built a case against Joseph Phillip Waldholtz that was irrefutable, exposing a bookkeeping system that had just one ultimate recipient: himself.

He stole from little old ladies who sent ten dollars to Enid For Congress, he stole from wealthy benefactors who sent a thousand dollars to Enid For Congress, he even put checks made out to the Utah Republican Party into his own checking account at First Security Bank in Salt Lake City–where the evidence showed that the bank gave Joe Waldholtz uncommon red carpet treatment that trampled on accepted banking checks and balances. Little details such as the fact that checks he deposited were not made out to him, or that he might be tens of thousands of dollars overdrawn, were somehow routinely overlooked for Joe.

There was also plenty of evidence that Joe hadn't turned into a thief only after he became acquainted with the Greenes of Salt Lake City. The fact of the matter was, his grandmother *did* once have a substantial amount of money, and she had entrusted a sizeable portion of it over to Joe for safekeeping. But Grandmother Rebecca Levenson's estate, at its height, was worth around a million dollars, not four hundred million, when Joe first got his hands on it in 1986. It was Joe's suspected mishandling of that money–as his grandmother slipped into dementia–that brought about the lawsuits filed by his cousin, Steven Slesinger, and Joe's father, Dr. Harvey Waldholtz, demanding a full accounting of the whereabouts of at least six hundred thousand dollars of that money. Money that, they would eventually discover, had long since disappeared, evaporating out of Joe's bank account into the same thin air of consumerism as Forrest Greene's.

On top of that, they found forged checks from Joe's mother's Pittsburgh bank account, signed by Joe; and they found evidence of a hundred thousand dollars Joe had squandered after his stepmother, Marilyn, had entrusted it to him for the purpose of investing. Not only had Joe stolen from his own wife and grandmother, but from his own stepmother and mother as well.

To add to his list of female targets, Joe had also apparently stolen from Elsie Hillman, his former employer in Pittsburgh. Shortly after Joe's initial disappearance, an aide for Ms. Hillman, John Denny, told Ladonna Lee that the reason Elsie had "let Joe go" was because she had reason to believe he was embezzling from her–to the tune of close to two hundred thousand dollars. When subsequent inquiries were made to expose that embezzlement, however, Elsie Hillman declined to cooperate. She would neither allow her books to be examined nor would she comment on Denny's allegations.

The thought would plague Enid–that a wealthy political activist, a relative (by marriage) of a former president, the wife of a billionaire, had in her own way facilitated a con man and a thief. For it was Elsie Hillman, after all, who gave Joe his most compelling calling card. Of all the names he dropped, hers was the weightiest. On one of their trips to Pittsburgh before they were married, Joe took Enid to a party at the Hillman's, where she met Elsie and watched as Joe's former boss gave him a big hug and warmly welcomed him–and his fiancee–into her home. To anyone on the outside, it was all smiles and warmth, all good feelings and good faith. Joe always insisted that he left Pennsylvania politics on his own terms. He in fact expressed reluctance to leave Elsie because she counted on him so; and there had certainly been nothing in their embrace to suggest otherwise.

□□□

Incredibly, for all of Joe's income, he never did satisfy the demands of the outgo. He kept bringing in fresh millions, but kept spending even more than that. The more he got, the faster he got rid of it. Amazing but true: a millionaire deficit spender. The various account "histories" uncovered by Fred Miller clearly showed that if he wasn't buying clothes or furniture or jewelry or art he was using his money to cover his tracks, or presumably to fund a rather large and consistent drug habit.

Among Joe's regular transactions were cash advances from credit cards sent at fairly regular intervals via Western Union to Pittsburgh. Who picked up that money at the Western Union office, and what it was for, remained officially speculative, but in light of the numerous suspicious "drug-type" Federal Express packages found addressed to Joe in Georgetown, Chuck Roistacher felt comfortable in presenting the case that at least some of that money financed Joe's prescription drug habit. After getting the money via the Western Union wires, Joe's supplier in Pittsburgh would mail him the drugs.

Fred also found that Joe, to confound and confuse, would send his money around in circles. He regularly wired money to Pittsburgh to his mother's bank account, for example–money that was used to pay the mortgage on his mother's home. Such were the strange trails Joe's money led the accountants along. First he'd embezzle money out of his mother's account, and then, in turn, he'd use some of that to pay her mortgage.

Joe's occasional forays into check kiting further complicated his trail. Check kiting refers to the releasing of checks that have strings attached–hence the name. Joe's biggest check kite scheme involved First Security Bank in Salt Lake City and the Congressional Credit Union in Washington, D.C. He would first write a number of large checks from First Security and deposit them into his account at the Congressional Credit Union, then he would write checks from the Congressional Credit Union to whatever creditors he wanted to pay off, and the credit union, thinking it had a huge supply of available funds, would honor those checks. Next, Joe would write a number of large checks from the Congressional Credit Union and deposit them into his account at First Security, and use that infusion of funds to write checks drawn on First Security Bank to even more creditors. Then he would start the process over again. By keeping the deposit checks swirling between the two accounts, he was able to create the illusion that he had twice as much money as he actually had. It can take time to spot a check kiter, and even more time to catch him. By the time the Congressional Credit Union noticed the discrepancies–First Security was still in the dark–the kite had reached $1.7 million dollars and each bank had overdrafts in the neighborhood of a quarter of a million dollars.

From a professional standpoint, Fred Miller was actually disappointed. He'd seen more sophisticated frauds on the sidewalk in front of his office. He expected a better run for Joe's money. Joe essentially created a lot of smoke, but once you looked at the records, catching him was like shooting fish in a barrel. Everyone was very careful in the beginning. The FBI and U.S. Attorney's office insisted that Fred and all the members of his staff use rubber gloves while working with any of the bank statements and other documents Joe and any possible accomplices might have touched. If there were usable fingerprints, they didn't want them smudged. It made for sweaty, smelly, and–in the end–unnecessary discomfort. They had all the fingerprints they needed from the money trail Joe left behind–a money trail so obvious any amateur could have followed it.

□□□

If the accountants were fishing in a hatchery, so were the lawyers. Joe didn't leave them a signed confession but he might as well have. In his hasty departure he left behind enough incriminating evidence to blur past anything resembling a reasonable doubt. Stone-cold irrefutable proof of fraud was everywhere–in forgeries, in computer documents, in copies of letters and memos; all of them in the very closets he left behind.

In many cases, they didn't just find the final product, they found the fraud in all its stages. In the case of the Ready Assets certificate, for example, right next to the completed forgery were Joe's rough, pencil-written drafts of how he wanted the forgery to look; the same was true with the federal mortgage, or "Ginnie Mae," certificate, that Joe had forged in an effort to show that he had collateral for money he'd taken from his grandmother. In both cases, the documents did not come from the purported financial institutions, but from copy companies on the corner. (The Ready Assets came from either a mystery man or a mystery copy shop referred to in Joe's computer only as "Andreas," the Ginnie Mae certificates were printed by a Kinko's copy center in Salt Lake City).

It was easier yet to produce copies of the 1991 and 1992 federal income tax returns Joe had submitted to First Security Mortgage to qualify for the home loan on the Benecia Drive house. They were still on file with the mortgage company–tax forms that clearly declared an annual income in excess of $250,000 from the completely fictitious "Waldholtz Family Trust."

Over time, Chuck Roistacher commandeered an entire filing cabinet in the Powell, Goldstein evidence room just for materials that linked Joseph Phillip Waldholtz to his phony existence. There he cataloged long lists of names of supposed donors to Enid's campaigns–fictitious names to provide a cover for the money Joe stole; he catalogued copies of the numerous erroneous FEC reports; he filed away evidence that Joe had contacted real estate attorneys in Washington, D.C. and briefed himself on how to write up an assignment of real estate proceeds, just in case his father-in-law decided to push for written evidence.

The most damning evidence against Joe had come out of his own computer–from the personal files he had password protected. Once the Powell, Goldstein computer experts cracked the codes, if there was any doubt they had their man, it evaporated with the appearance of those files. From those dozen documents, Joe's voice of deception and deceit rang out without argument or distortion.

The letters, notes and memos in those files covered the range of Joe's voices, from profane and insulting, to plaintive and gushing, to conciliatory and supplicating. In some his language was lewd and offensive, sprinkled with "bitch" and "whore" and "fuck." In others his language was sophisticated and complimentary, full of praise and grace. In yet others it was full of pleading and humility. Added together, those files produced a chilling profile of a full-blown, full-time master of deceit.

Among the dozen password-protected files were two letters and a memo addressed to Forrest Greene–three documents that, by themselves, were enough to effectively expose Joe and all his lies. The letters, written in April and August of 1994, carried the passwords "help" and "fucked" and reflected a similar theme: Joe didn't deserve it, but he and Enid desperately needed Forrest's help.

The first letter, which carried no exact date but was shown by the computer to have been written in April, was addressed during the '94 campaign to D. Forrest Greene at the D. F. Greene Company, 235 Montgomery Street, San Francisco, CA 94104. It read:

Dear Mr. Greene:

Please excuse this typed note, but I fear if I hand wrote it, it would be illegible! I wanted to give you an update on what is going on with the financial matters we have been dealing with. I have not discussed all of this with Enid because I don't want to upset her any more than she has to be. The days have been very hard on her–they are so long and the people are demanding, as always. There is good news, though! Things are going very well for the campaign. Enid will clear convention and become the Republican nominee on May 7th.

There are several large problems that I have been dealing with. Things with my mother have not been well at all. She has ransacked other accounts that I didn't know she had access to. She has put me in a very precarious financial situation again. While you have heard it before, I have taken the necessary steps to remove myself from this situation. We are going to get a guardian and I will be relieved of day to day responsibility.

She has overdrawn two accounts in Pittsburgh that I transfer money through. The total is about $114,000. What an incredible sum. The problem is this–it involves Utah banks now because that is where we transfer the money to. While they have tried to be understanding, we are out of time. In fact, because of the American Express fiasco, I think they are very nervous and would consider legal action if I can't resolve this.

Mr. Greene, I have never felt like a bigger failure in my life. I have tried, as a good son should, to help my mother. Her life hasn't been easy–this illness isn't her fault. It has been my duty to deal with this, and ordinarily this wouldn't be a problem. As you know, my family is in an uproar. My grandmother is failing, and there is going to be legal action over her will. I cannot stop that. But, I cannot access those funds, either.

I have tried to get a loan, but it cannot be done in time. I don't feel that I can ask you to help again, but I really don't know where else to turn. I have never been at a lower point in my life. Enid has all that she can deal with–her job is so hard. I haven't talked with Mrs. Greene because she hasn't felt well, and she is dealing with her own problems and I know she is very concerned about her health.

If you are wondering why I can't access the money that was to be returned to you, it is because she accessed it on jewelry and the house. The items cannot be returned and even if they could, their value is much less than she spent on them. She was really taken advantage of. But that's another matter.

Mr. Greene, I would pay you any interest rate, sign any legal document, give you a mortgage on our home, or whatever you wanted, if you could help us. I say us, because this will bring her campaign and all of her dreams down. I feel as if I am ruining her life, and her chances for success. I realize what I am asking, yet I have tried for weeks to come up with alternatives. I have none. The loan will not make it in time.

If you can help, I would like to sign a legal document detailing the interest rate, terms of repayment, etc.

Mr. Greene, I am so afraid of scandal, I am just a wreck. I think we need to keep this between us. I cannot cause more pain for Enid or Mrs. Greene. She has been so kind to us; our relationship is really such a positive force in my life.

No matter what your decision, please know how much I appreciate your advice, your concern, and your love.

The second letter, written four months later on August 24, 1994, at the height of the '94 campaign, was addressed to Mr. and Mrs. D. Forrest Greene, 1456 Penrose Drive, Salt Lake City, UT 84103. It read:

Dear Mr. and Mrs. Greene:

I have spent the past four hours on the phone with Pittsburgh, the attorneys, First Security, and other investigators. I made Enid a promise that I would never "give up" or say that I should leave her for her own good. That was my anniversary present to her. Yet, once again, because of my failure as a husband, son, son-in-law, and I guess even a person, we are in a horrible position.

The money was transferred to us and ready for wire. Do you remember two weeks ago when First Security had to take money out of my account because I deposited a check of my mother's and she signed a statement that she never received it? . . . Well, it appears that all of the checks that I have deposited she has done this with. We re-invested four large CDs for her through this account, and in banks back in Pittsburgh. Part of the money was used to pay her incredible overdrafts, part for her to live on, and part was stolen.

The worst part is that we are in a minus position again because of my family.

I would not and could not tell Enid this today, as they are filming. We couldn't cancel it even if we wanted to. I had money in the account to pay for the production today. It's gone, with the check reversals.

I know we have said to you the last two times that it is over, and it hasn't been. I am sorry for that. I feel this entire episode is taking place because I am being punished for something. I had to do something to deserve this. Enid and you have not. And yet, because I am being punished, and am married to your daughter, we had to involve you.

I will return to Pittsburgh during the Labor Day weekend and sell two million dollars of real estate to cover this. I dealt with that this morning. There is a buyer; I have no choice.

Every penny you loaned us will be repaid at market rates–just like we were borrowing from a bank. It is my obligation to you.

The problem is this: We can't wire you money today, and we are in a desperate situation because of the reversals. The total is staggering, over $200,000.00. I really am at a loss here; I will *not upset Enid any more. I have failed her as a husband. My mother is ruining her campaign's chances . . .*

. . . I want you to know that I have offered to leave Enid to stop hurting her and both of you. Whatever I did to cause this ruin and heartache, I am not aware of, but things like this don't happen without some cause!

If you still want me in the family after all that has happened, we can talk about you and Enid becoming more active with the trust and charitable responsibilities that I have. At this point in my life, after all that has happened, I have no desire to participate in these matters. My family's money has become such a negative in my life I wish we never had it and I weren't involved. It is only because my grandmother wanted me to do this that I have done so. I always tried to fulfill her wishes.

This money has been a source of great aggravation; Enid and I have shed too many tears over it. I have lost all confidence in myself as a person, husband, son and son-in-law. We have come to you so many times I am literally sickened. I used to be a person who helped people, now I am a leech.

My plan to repay you stands. It is just set back two weeks. Again. As for our current fiasco, if you could help, you will save the campaign. Enid never should have run this year. She is the right person for Utah with the wrong husband. I am the problem, not Enid. If you can't help, I understand completely. I have put everyone through enough.

I would have delivered this letter in person, and called you both, but campaign activities today prevent me from doing so. I feel that this, too, is a cowardly thing to do and yet I have responsibility here, and need to protect Enid from further harm. I will be in and out of the office and can be reached there.

I am including the wire information, not on the assumption or presumption that you will help, but if you do, you will need the information and I might not be available because of the filming day and the campaign has me everywhere anyway today.

1. Wilson Communications
First Union Bank of Virginia
Acct # 200 000 514 586 1

ABA # 051 400 549
They are owed $30,000.
2. Joseph P. Waldholtz
First Security Bank
Acc. # 051-10075-51
ABA # 124 0000 12

This is the account that is overdrawn because of my mother. They still don't have a total figure (I just called as I was typing this) but they need at least $25,000 now.

Quite an incredible sum and that isn't the end of it. The total is over $200,000.

Again, I will close on the real estate when I go back to Pittsburgh. We will have the money that we recover from the fraud (around $935,000), plus the two million dollars in cash from selling property . . .

. . . I would again offer to leave Enid but I promised her not to. If you think that I should, I think we should talk about that this weekend. I never have loved any woman in my life other than my wife; the pain that I am causing is too unbearable to live with. She deserves better. She really does. In my wildest dreams, I never imagined that this could happen to us. I am supposed to protect her and I have failed.

Well, I guess I will close now. I am sorry for wrecking your day, for imposing on you–emotionally and financially, and for letting everyone down. You are good people, you have always been there for us, and you don't deserve this.

I have to fight every impulse in my body not to be on the next flight out of here so Enid can remake her life. Enid has begged me not to do that. I have prayed for the answer to why is this happening. It hasn't come. Maybe I don't deserve even that. I don't know.

In both letters, Joe displayed his subtle powers of suggestion and his knack for appealing to–and preying on–human feelings and emotions. While none of these communications were actually delivered—a simple phone call always worked—they reflected the depth and tone of his plotting. His requests for money were always based on what could be saved, and it was always Mr. and Mrs. Greene's daughter, Enid.

Finally, there was the memorandum, dated September 21st, 1994, with the protected password of "lie." Sent from "The Waldholtz Family Trust," it purported to serve as a cover letter for documents concerning the assignation of the Pittsburgh real estate. To the best of Forrest Greene's knowledge, he never actually received the memo, but its very existence in Joe Waldholtz's computer revealed clearly its author's intent: to make a fictitious family trust appear to be alive and well.

MEMORANDUM

To: Mr. D.F. Greene c/o East-West Co.
CC: Mr. and Mrs. Joseph P. Waldholtz
From: The Waldholtz Family Trust
Date: September 21, 1994
Subject: Assignment Letter and US Attorney Information

Mr. Greene, we apologize for the delay in sending the materials to you. Joe and Enid asked that we send you the assignment of the real estate and the letter from the U.S. Attorney. We apologize for the delay and the confusion.

If we can be of further assistance, please give us a call.

Thank you.

Wiith this memo alone–a note written to Forrest Greene from the Waldholtz Family Trust on Joe's own computer, with a CC to

Joe himself–Chuck Roistacher had his smoking gun. Like most crooks, Joe Waldholtz wound up incriminating himself.

□□□

Team Enid took a Thanksgiving break, but it wasn't much of one. Ladonna had Enid, Elizabeth and Forrest over for dinner, along with Jim, who had flown back for another four days to help organize the paperwork and assist Chuck in the legal effort. For her part, Enid was glad when Thanksgiving Day was over and they were back to work. The investigation of Joe, despite all of its revelations, was a blessing because, along with the Congressional sessions, it kept her occupied. Every minute of every day was filled. When you're just trying to stay upright, having every minute scheduled can be a very good thing.

It wasn't just the deception, it was the scope of it all. It was as if Joe's duplicity had no end. He was the black hole of deceit. His whole life was a lie. Virtually everything he did, everywhere he'd been, he had lied to get there and he had lied to stay there.

Sometimes she couldn't help reflecting on it. She'd be sitting at her desk, working as intently as she could on something, and her mind would wander. She'd remember Joe flipping his hands back and saying, "Oh Enid," impatient at her nagging him about money, making her feel the fool for bringing it up in the first place. She'd remember his eyes filling with tears when he'd talk to her father about money. She'd remember his threats of suicide.

All of it a facade, a giant false front.

Joe Waldholtz was a big, fat, living lie.

The clarity of hindsight showed just how adept Joe had been at the partial truth, at wrapping a lie in just enough fact that the whole package seemed genuine. With that tactic, he'd taken Enid–and everyone around her–on a very expensive four-year ride.

It began when he'd gotten out of that stretch limo in Newport Beach. The limo was real. So was the suite Joe rented–and paid for–for the Pittsburgh Young Republican delegation. The lie was where the money that paid for the suite and the limo came from. It did not come from an unlimited family trust. In 1990 the money either came from what Joe had remaining from the money his grandmother had entrusted him to invest, or–more likely–from money he embezzled from Elsie Hillman.

From the start, it was a given that he had unlimited funds. That made it easy for Joe to set the hook on Enid. He was a natural to become her campaign treasurer when she ran for national chairman of the Young Republicans, and it made perfect sense when he came to her at the end of that campaign and told Enid that her campaign manager, Audrey Merkin, had overspent the budget by some $30,000. Audrey had indeed gone all-out on the campaign. That was the modicum of truth. What wasn't true is that Audrey had overspent anything without Joe's approval beforehand, or that she had spent anywhere close to $30,000 beyond budget. Joe's magnanimous offer to square the books was pure fabrication, a subtle way of further cementing his reputation as not just a rich man, but a benevolent rich man who picked up the check.

It worked so well that a year later, when Joe took over Enid's books after she lost the 1992 Utah congressional campaign, the groundwork had already been laid for Joe to play the "campaign manager did it" card yet again. This time it was Peter Valcarce, Enid's departed campaign chief, who got the blame. Using Valcarce as his scapegoat, Joe was able to embezzle well over a hundred thousand dollars from the woman who had sold her house to fund her campaign–the woman he intended to marry.

You name it, Joe lied about it. The all-expenses-paid beach trip in New Jersey he invited Enid and Audrey to on Memorial Day in 1991? Three years later Forrest Greene wired money to a bank in New Jersey, thinking he was helping Joe take care of his family financial entanglements. He wasn't. He was paying the back bill on that beach house rental, unwittingly saving Joe before the owner of the property took legal action to get his money.

On their Hawaiian honeymoon in '93, Joe had run into problems at both of their hotels. After his credit card was rejected at the Four Seasons Hotel on Maui he had phoned a friend back in Salt Lake and asked him to wire money to the hotel to cover the bill–and not to tell Enid. The reason the Waldholtzes didn't stay at the Four Seasons when they returned to Maui a year later was because the hotel management, after what had happened the year before, wouldn't let Joe register. At the second hotel on their honeymoon, the Royal Hawaiian, the police report was filed because Joe had flat out stiffed the bill. His American Express card, maxed well beyond its limit, had bought the newlyweds enough time to get out of town, but that was it. The card was maxed out. As a matter of fact, Joe *did* owe $47,000 to American Express. His ability to repeatedly tap dance his way around that fact with Amex operators is only further testimony to his skills of duplicity.

When Joe finally settled with American Express in the summer of '94, he had no choice but to pay the $47,000. When he told Enid he'd only had to pay about a thousand dollars and the rest had been dismissed, it was a lie. He also lied about not being served any legal papers.

He lied to virtually everyone about virtually everything, and always for his advantage. He said he knew the prominent Washington accountant Stan Huckaby personally. He didn't. Huckaby had never personally laid eyes on Joseph Phillip Waldholtz (and still hasn't). And when Joe continually insisted to Enid and others that he'd checked with the Huckaby accountants on numerous occasions to make sure of FEC rules, he in fact had never picked up the phone.

What a web he weaved. And not just with Enid, but with everyone on the periphery. Who could even begin to fathom the full extent of Joe's deception? Would the conflicts Enid had with Kaylin Loveland and Steve Taggart and David Harmer, for instance, have even occurred, or escalated beyond resolve, without Joe's meddling? Did he set all of them up? Did he create chaotic staff problems just so he could clear them up and come off as the good guy?

It was unsettling to realize that when Joe's anxiety was at its most intense, it had been spurred not by genuine feelings, but by the possibility of getting caught. His pensiveness at the real estate closing of their new home? His agitation prior to his entire family coming to Utah for the wedding? It was all because the possibility of being exposed was so high.

It was downright chilling to consider how far his duplicity stretched. Was it Joe who called Carol Nixon with the unsettling midnight phone calls that prompted her to get out of the '94 congressional race? Was it Joe who stirred up the myriad conflicts with Karen Shepherd? Maybe, maybe not; but in the aftermath, it certainly wouldn't have been surprising.

Much of what Joe Waldholtz said about his family was true. Yes, his mother did have mental health problems, and yes, she was being ripped off by a scoundrel. But the scoundrel was her own son. And yes, Joe had been his grandmother Levenson's favorite growing up, and yes, she had entrusted him with a good portion of her estate to invest for her safe-keeping. But Joe invested it for his own safe-keeping, leaving a thrifty old lady penniless as her mind went and her health failed.

As for his cousin Stevie, it was true that he was causing problems and threatening a lawsuit over family money, but it wasn't true that cousin Stevie was the problem. The truth was, Joe was the problem.

It turned out Joe even lied about his religion. He wasn't Episcopalian, and as far as anyone in his staunch Jewish family knew, he had never showed any interest in becoming one. In his boyhood neighborhood of Squirrel Hill, a bastion of Judaism where synagogues abound and the shops on Murray Street sell kosher food–and where Christmas is just another day–they had no idea at all what to make of that.

With his partial truths and tales of grandeur mixed with outright lies, Joe capably reeled in an amazing succession of unwitting accomplices. He was the man walking through the casino waving a roll of bills, his lone hundred stacked on top of a thousand ones. People flocked to him as if he were the real deal.

Through it all there was the Big Lie–the trust, and the trustees. They were the core and the constant. The trustees were always at the ready in Pittsburgh, always poised to correct all of the problems and right the ship. Joe talked constantly of their personalities, of their personal lives, how many children they had, even what their hobbies were. The Trustees, his fantasy family. Sometimes Enid would come home when Joe was on the phone and after he'd hang up he'd say, casually, "Just talking to the trustees." On the last day she saw Joe, when he went to meet the trustees and they didn't show up at the airport, Enid actually had to catch herself when she began to worry that something had happened to them.

The bottom line was, the trustees weren't real and neither was Joe. The real Joe was somewhere underneath the veneer, somewhere Enid wasn't sure she ever even wanted to look. The breadth and scope of what he did was too overwhelming to completely absorb. Everything was suspect, including his sexual habits. Beyond the underwear catalogue and men's fitness magazines Jim found in the Georgetown house, when the FBI, in cooperation with Enid's attorneys, searched their Salt Lake house, they discovered a hard core gay male pornographic video stuck high in a corner shelf above Joe's closet. *Young Hustlers*. Well, *Young Hustlers* was a part of Joe Enid knew nothing about, and a part she hoped neither she, nor the daughter he'd fathered, ever would.

Still, it *was* somehow ironic. She knew so much more about her husband after he was gone than she ever knew before he left.

□□□

They sat motionless as she made her appeal, a rapt audience hanging on her every word, practically transfixed. Enid was so full of information she was about to burst and it showed. She knew her stuff. She was a walking, talking encyclopedia on the subject of her former husband, Joe Waldholtz. She started at the start and she didn't miss a step. She left nothing out. He'd duped her at every turn, conned her at every corner, charmed his way into her heart and her father's checkbook and then stolen away as a thief in the night. It was a sordid, compelling, convincing tale of a heartless homewrecker. She cried some, but quickly found her handkerchief, and her composure. It was a heart-wrenching story and she told it well, as if her good name depended on it, which it did.

When she was finished, she thought she'd talked for maybe twenty minutes, twenty-five tops. But it had been just over an hour. A nonstop confession with hardly an "uh" or a "you know" in the whole discourse.

The best part was at the end when her audience applauded. They loved her. More important, they believed her.

"I don't know if I can tell it any better than that," said Enid, exhausted by her delivery.

"You don't have to," said Eddie Mahe, who had set up this informal dress rehearsal so Enid could practice giving the opening statement she would deliver for real the next Monday at her press conference in Salt Lake City.

Posing as her "audience" in the living room of her townhouse in Georgetown were Enid's staunchest allies–including Chuck Roistacher and Brett Kappel from Powell, Goldstein; Ladonna Lee and Eddie Mahe, her public relations consultants; and her father. In four weeks they had all worked to put these words together, the words their "client" had just spoken so eloquently. Their investigations weren't finished, not by a long shot. But enough of the framework was in place, they were convinced, that it was obvious what had happened: a world-class con had gone down, and even if she was a Congresswoman and a lot of people were looking for a scapegoat, Enid Greene Waldholtz had been the target of Joe's fraud, nothing more, nothing less, and they had the proof to back it up.

If anything, they had too much proof. Joe's con had been so widespread and so devious that it touched virtually everything he did. The result was a mountain of evidence–and an hour-long opening statement–but practically no frame of reference. As any fisherman knows, when you catch a lunker, you need something relative to place alongside the prize–a ruler, say, or the fisherman's hand–to give perspective to the size of the fish. If Team Enid was short on anything, it was perspective. There just wasn't much to compare Joe Waldholtz to and put him in perspective. He was that far beyond anyone's norm of experience.

All they could do on Monday was go with what they had, and hope that would paint him as black as they knew he really was.

□□□

The dress rehearsal was better. A lot better.

But, then, who expected otherwise. The media wasn't exactly into a Barbara Walters mode; Jerry Springer was more like it. A month had been a long time to invent any number of conspiracy theories and other rumors. Such is the product of a free market media. "Sources" were everywhere, the majority of them unnamed, suggesting that the Congresswomen–the "razor-sharp, corporate attorney"–knew more than she was letting on. The most annoying source, however, was named, that being Joseph Phillip Waldholtz himself. While Joe had said virtually nothing to the media in the month since his celebrated flight from justice, it was his silence, and total lack of either a confession or an apology, that was unsettling. In just one statement, he could have absolved Enid of any conspiracy in the mis-filed FEC reports and allegations of financial impropriety. But from Joe, that statement never came.

A sizeable ballroom was reserved at the Doubletree Hotel in the heart of downtown Salt Lake City, a block from the new $90 million Delta Center, home to the Utah Jazz, and across the street from the Salt Palace Convention Center. To say Enid and her team had come prepared would be to make a sizeable understatement. Enid was as prepped as any witness could be; Chuck Roistacher and Fred Miller had poster-sized exhibits to put on display, along with well-polished summations; and Ladonna Lee and Eddie Mahe had taken care to ensure that the press arrangements went well beyond adequate. More than seventy media credentials had been given out, a number that included all the major television networks and most of the country's major newspapers.

As an added bonus, C-Span was there to televise the coverage from start to finish.

But you can only plan so much. The wild card in the show was the media, and the media had whipped itself into an anticipation frenzy, poised to pounce on anything that had the scent of scandal. Enid had first sensed the mood when she, Chuck and Fred had arrived at the Salt Lake airport Saturday morning, two days before the scheduled press conference. They'd stepped off the plane into a flood of television lights and microphones. It was as if Madonna had walked into the concourse. "I already said I wouldn't say anything until the press conference," Enid told the reporters, waving them away like pesky schoolchildren. "You're just going to have to wait till Monday."

The battle lines were already forming.

Enid turned and saw her twin sisters, Randi and Sue. They both had tears in their eyes as they hugged their kid sister, but Enid whispered and said, "Don't cry. If you cry, I'll cry, and that's what these people want. But I'm not going to give them the satisfaction."

They would just have to wait till Monday.

The tears, unbidden, came about a third of the way into her opening statement. Enid was talking about Joe and his betrayal and suddenly there they were, rolling down her cheeks. Just as suddenly, every camera in the ballroom went off virtually simultaneously. On the stage all she heard was one huge "Click."

She'd been determined not to show a loss of composure, and she'd actually gotten off to a good start. Jim–who had flown up from California with Sue–had helped her elbow her way through the media in the hotel lobby. It had not been easy. Several reporters had tried to get Enid to talk, but she had ignored them and just pushed on. The press was in a snarling mood. As they broke free, Jim had leaned close to Enid.

"Fuck 'em," he said.

In spite of herself, Enid smiled at that.

But the longer she went on with her opening statement, the longer she could sense they were moving in for a kill. There were supporters in the crowd, people wearing warm smiles and carrying signs that said "I Love Enid." But overall this wasn't a friendly audience sitting around her Georgetown living room. These were people who would not shed a tear if Enid was guilty of doing something wrong. Some in the crowd carried "Enid, It's Time to Resign" signs. Enid looked out on the front row and saw Merrill Cook, the man who just a little more than a year before she'd raced for Congress. He had a radio talk show on KALL, a local AM radio station, and thereby qualified as "media."

In the end, no one could say Enid and her entourage didn't expertly and completely lay it all out. Chuck and Fred answered every question put to them; as did Enid. She was determined not to leave until no more hands were raised, and even though it took nearly five hours to wear down the media, she pulled it off. "Any more questions?" she finally asked at a quarter to three–four hours and forty-two minutes since the press conference began–and when there were no takers she sighed, said, "Thank you for coming," and sagged back on the stage. She hadn't even taken a bathroom break. And neither had C-Span.

She barely had time to drive to her parent's house, pack up Elizabeth, and make it to the airport for the 5:30 flight to Dulles. There was a vote scheduled on the floor the next day, and she was determined to make it. A part of her didn't care any more what anyone thought. So what if she'd cried? That didn't change anything. The facts were the facts. She'd told her story from start to finish, exposing her personal life as well as her professional life in the process. She didn't see that there was really anything more that she could say or do. She'd told the whole truth and nothing but. Laid it all out. Now, the way she saw it, she still had a job to do, and she was flying back to Washington to do it.

CHAPTER XII

She was sixteen when she first saw the girl who blew her brains out. They were in the autopsy lab at the University of Utah medical center when a medical student threw the cover off the corpse of the twenty-year-old girl who had stuck a gun in her mouth and pulled the trigger. It was the kind of image you never really lose, just put in the far reaches of your memory and try to keep it there.

But now, twenty years later, sitting in an office with her attorney and her father, it was all Enid Greene Waldholtz could think about.

She was amazed that she remembered the scene in such great detail. They had been on a high school field trip to the med center when their guide had decided to give his group a scare. He said it was an object lesson in suicide; but he probably just wanted to see how much of a rise he could get out of a bunch of teenage girls. Well, he got a big one. Enid remembered that her first impulse was to turn away, and she did, but finally she just stared, like they all did. She saw a girl with long shoulder-length blond hair and gray, contorted features; across her scalp was a fracture line from ear to ear. When she'd pulled the trigger the explosion literally cracked her skull. There was a huge exit wound out the back of her skull about three inches in diameter, where everything had just disintegrated. The end had come violently, but quickly.

At the time, Enid Greene, an honor student at East High School, couldn't imagine why anyone would want to stick a gun in her mouth and pull the trigger. But now, as she only vaguely listened to a discussion going on between Chuck and her father, she understood. She couldn't get that image out of her mind. *If there was a gun right here on the table,* she found herself thinking, *I could do it now. It could all be over.* It unnerved her to realize that if there were indeed a gun in front of her, she honestly doubted she'd be able to resist.

She didn't tell anyone about what she was thinking, a reaction she somehow knew the psychiatrists would say meant she wasn't in the crying-for-help stage, but had moved into the fast current. It scared her, this fixation she had with blowing her head off. *Just like that girl.* She could feel the cold steel of the barrel in her mouth. She could feel her skull fracturing evenly along the top. But more than that, she could imagine the peace and quiet after it was over. *Just like that girl.*

It was a couple of days after the press conference in Salt Lake City and suddenly everything was crashing down. The lull after the storm, or something like that. It had been a crazy and traumatic month getting ready, the pressure had been ridiculous, and they'd all talked about how glad they'd be when it was over. But there was therapy, Enid realized now more than ever, in being busy, in having a focus, in concentrating on something other than *what just happened to you!*

Which is what she was doing now. And so, it seemed, was everyone else.

From a strictly practical, objective standpoint, the press conference was a roaring success. If anything, it was overkill. Team Enid had systematically laid out a case against Joe, and for Enid, that was backed completely, and irrefutably, by black-and-white, undeniable totally objective evidence. They had left no room for doubt. It was no contest. Enid stood there and straightforwardly answered every question. She didn't hold back a thing. She told it all.

But she was, after all, a politician, a representative of the people, and the people's reaction, in general, was neither objective, nor positive. Slamdunk case or not, her presentation, which was initially well received, in an academic kind of way, was thereafter met with a severe public backlash. The prevailing sentiment cried out for the congresswoman to take, if not the blame, the responsibility. Maybe if she had been in Congress in, say, the Eisenhower administration, it would have been different. Or maybe if she had pre-dated Richard Nixon. But in the wake of Watergate, Iran Contra and Whitewater, with the periodic Abscam and Paula Jones thrown in for good measure, it just wasn't good fashion for a politician to be blameless, or to cry about anything.

If the press conference had been a Broadway show, they'd have cancelled it. By and large, it got panned the next day in the papers. The story wasn't Joe being a liar, a cheat, a crook, a con man, and a scumbag. The story was that Enid called Joe a liar, a cheat, a crook, a con man, and a scumbag. Instead of looking at Enid as a victim, she was looked at more as someone who had bought the Brooklyn Bridge . . . and then explained away the purchase with a slick legal team and even slicker Big Six accountants.

Headlines around the country reflected this mood. "Rep. Waldholtz Says Her Husband Duped her" was the headline in the next morning's Washington Post. Others followed suit. "Blaming It On Her Husband"–in the New York Times; "Congresswoman says husband duped her"–in the Denver Rocky Mountain News; "I believe I was tricked"–in the Pittsburgh Post-Gazette; "Lawmaker Blames Husband For Campaign's Financial Troubles"–in the St. Louis Post-Dispatch; "Waldholtz depicts long pattern of betrayal"–in USA Today.

Other newspapers picked up on Enid's tears, which had been plentiful, and, in addition to taking the "blame" angle, added an emotional dimension: "Tearful Lawmaker Says Husband Duped Her"–in the Orlando Sentinel; "Tearful Waldholtz Says She's A Victim of Love"–in the Los Angeles Times; "Utah congresswoman: I was blinded by love"–in the Houston Chronicle; "Teary-eyed congresswoman says husband conned her"–in the Detroit

News; "Sniffling Pol: I Was Snookered"–in the New York Daily News.

The television sound bites continued the cry-and-blame theme. ABC's Peter Jennings said, "Mrs. Waldholtz blamed it all on her husband." CBS's Paula Zahn called the press conference "A marathon session of talk and tears." NBC called it a "tearful public confession." On CNN, they said, "Her story: He did it all, she was gullible, she was misled, but she was not a participant in all this. The question now, of course, is whether the voters will believe her."

The public debate settled mainly on trying to square Enid's myriad roles as wife, woman, trained lawyer, and Congresswoman. She posed an unusual combination. She was hard to draw a bead on. Questions abounded. Was it OK for a leader to cry in public if she was a woman? Was it OK for a leader to pass the blame under any circumstances? How did it square that a one-time corporate lawyer could be so slickly swindled? Should a congresswoman be so unaware of her own finances?

Material for radio talk shows and newspaper editorials abounded. One story in the *Salt Lake Tribune* turned the tables and imagined a male Congressman holding a press conference in which he behaved like Enid, blaming all on the wife he loved and trusted. The article written by Jim Wright, was headlined "What If A Man Told Enid's Sob Story?"

The public's fascination with the Waldholtzes did not escape the nation's talk show comedians. The Salt Lake press conference provided both Jay Leno on NBC and David Letterman on CBS with enough material for the week.

"Who wouldn't be taken in by this Redford clone?" wisecracked Leno the night after the press conference. Letterman answered the next night with an observation on Enid's complaints that Joe stole from her: "I'm thinking to myself, clearly they elected the wrong person to Congress." Leno followed with a comment on Enid's contention that she was "stupid, blind and trusting." "Not good attributes," he said, "if you want to be a member of congress . . . but she could be a member of an L.A. jury."

In Utah, one joke making the rounds was that Enid had renamed the well-known Wasatch Fault, the continuous earthquake-prone fissure in the Rocky Mountains of northern Utah. It was now "Joe's Fault." Another joke said that Joe had not even left Washington, D.C. during his disappearance; he had actually stayed in the basement of the Georgetown townhouse; to which Enid, when she heard the news, replied, "A basement? Joe never told me we had a basement."

Back in Congress, where Enid had always before counted on sanctuary, she found more criticism. On the day after the press conference, Pat Schroeder, the twelve-term Democratic Congresswoman from Colorado, wasted no time in calling for Enid's resignation. The call was, of course, quickly countered by the Republicans. "I don't think there's any one of us that can look at Enid's story and not say, 'That couldn't happen to me,'" said Susan Molinari, a New York Republican and Enid's contemporary.

Beyond partisan politics, Schroeder's call for resignation was a sobering and substantive point–one not lost on either the Congress or the voters back home in Utah.

If Enid had indeed won her election by improper means, should she not give it back? Was ignorance a defense for breaking the rules?

Those who clamored for her resignation–and for a new election to determine her successor–suggested that it was irrelevant whether Enid knew about the illegalities that had pumped the $1.7 million into her campaign. The comparison was made to a car race: if a race car driver won at, say, the Indy 500 and standard postrace mechanical inspection revealed an illegal power booster in the engine, the title would of course be taken away from the driver–no matter if the driver knew the power booster was there or not. If the driver's mechanic had slipped the booster in there without telling him–and even if the driver hadn't used it during the race–it wouldn't matter. By breaking the rules they would be disqualified. No questions asked.

Well, Enid had won her race that way. She had used her father's money, which was clearly against the federal campaign rules, no one was arguing that. Just because she didn't know she was using her father's money didn't change the rules and did not exempt her from having to follow them.

Enid and her supporters saw it differently. Her contention was that the voters had elected her because of her views, not because of her money–a point from which the Congresswoman refused to budge. Intent, she maintained, was what mattered, and she did not intend to break the rules. But her critics–and they weren't all Democrats, not by a long shot–didn't budge either. They countered by pointing out that the voters wouldn't have known what her views were if she hadn't spent the $1.7 million in the first place.

Beyond the substantive debating, even more to the point was the perception that this representative was under siege, a perception that deepened with every new headline and Tonight Show monologue. Nobody was calling Enid Waldholtz the "Mormon Maggie Thatcher" any more.

But it wasn't the criticism in Congress and among the Utah constituents that made her think about ending it all, and it certainly wasn't the media (for one thing, she would never give them the satisfaction). And it wasn't the money, either. In the end, money is, well, money. Great if you have it, bad if you don't. But the fact was, even if she had blown an enormous amount of her father's money, and even if she was embarrassed and mortified and downright sick because of it, that wasn't a reason to kill yourself. On the contrary. It was reason to get back on the horse and make some money and pay the man back.

The real reason she had those moments when she didn't want to go on was because she was running out of hope. She was running short on something to hold onto. Something to believe in. Joe's betrayal had emptied her of hope.

Even in her most lucid moments, Enid honestly wondered whether she would ever return to anything resembling a reality she could hold onto and count on. She questioned if there would ever be an end to the madness. Joe was still out there, escaping responsibility, and she was still very much a captive of his inability to square up and tell the truth. She feared that would never let up. Not only would she have to live her life in the shadow of Joe's facade, but so–and for Enid, this was the ugliest thought of all–would Elizabeth.

Enid felt at times as if she'd fallen into another dimension, where she could talk and people didn't hear her, where she could walk and not make a sound. She began to question her own sanity, she began to question everyone's sanity. Not only had Joe been able to get away with his lies before he, quote, got caught, unquote, but it appeared to her he was able to do pretty well afterward as well. He had told her up was down and down was up and she had believed him; now he was telling others–the media, especially, and in due course the United States Attorneys and the grand jury–the same thing and, incredibly, he was making headway there too. Enid questioned the very existence of reality. She took nothing for granted. *I used to know 1 plus 1 is 2,* she thought, *now I'm not sure. Now I have to question where I learned that, and who taught me; now I'm thinking, hey, maybe 1 plus 1 is 97. Who's to say it isn't?*

It was as if the rules had been changed overnight. After everything Joe had done, his voice was given more consideration than ever. The media still listened intently. They still gave Joe full voice. Why? Enid grew up rooting for truth and justice and Perry Mason. The good guys got off and the bad guys did time. But this real-life episode she was living sure wasn't turning out that way.

Most chilling of all was Joe. He was no longer in her life, but his specter still lingered, as did a thousand new questions every day. Why had he victimized her so? Why would he want to say or do anything untoward to her father, a man who had accommodated him every step of the way, believing with all his heart that it was to help Joe's mother and to help his daughter and son-in-law? When there was nothing left to steal, why would Joe want to lie and keep lying?

With all her might, Enid struggled to keep her wits about her, to cling onto her sanity like a life raft. It wasn't easy. She'd been adrift for what seemed like a very long time.

□□□

Through it all, however, there was always one reason above all the rest that not only kept her breathing, but kept her wanting to breathe. Elizabeth Greene Waldholtz, the epitome of an innocent victim, was barely three months old and already fatherless.

Elizabeth desperately needed her mother; and her mother desperately needed Elizabeth.

The discovery of Joe's hidden life had thrown both of them into a precarious position. Not only did they have cause to be insecure about the future, but the past as well. Joe Waldholtz had been neither the doting, dedicated husband, nor father, he said he was, and that created one concern that was almost too awful to think about: had he given Elizabeth AIDS?

There were good reasons to believe that he had not, of course, not the least of which was no evidence that Joe was suffering from a collapse of his immune system. Even if Joe's extracurricular activities had involved homosexual activity, he could have practiced safe sex. But given all his other deceptions, who could be sure? The fact was, there was reason to be concerned. He might have exposed his daughter, and his wife, to a disease with no known cure. Certainly it was the first thought Enid had after she found out about Joe's "sex stuff."

Jim and Ladonna had told her about it several days after discovering the gay-oriented magazines at the back of Joe's nightstand. They'd first consulted with Chuck Roistacher's therapist wife, Susan, who had advised them that they should take care not to sound any alarms. Maybe all Joe did was look at the pictures of men wearing slinky briefs. Who could say what was in Joe's mind? Maybe he was planning to buy himself a pair. Maybe he was a voyeur. The point was, there was no absolute evidence that Joe had ever physically engaged in homosexual behavior and thereby put his family in any kind of

AIDS danger.

Still, the only way to know for sure was to have Enid and Elizabeth undergo blood tests.

For Enid's tests to be conclusive, she was advised to wait until six months after the last sexual contact; Elizabeth, on the other hand, could be tested right away. Enid waited until her daughter was just past three months old—she couldn't face it until then. Elizabeth still wasn't very big for a blood test, but the more evidence they found about Joe's sexual inclinations, the more imperative the test became. He obviously had appetites Enid never knew about. They not only found the *Young Hustlers* gay porno video among Joe's things, but Ruthie, their former housekeeper in Utah, came forward to confess that she had seen "boxes" of pornography in Joe's closet, and Joe's friend from Pittsburgh, Greg Hughes, mentioned that he'd seen pornographic material among Joe's possessions. On top of that, there was the postcard advertising a transvestite show in Las Vegas they'd found in the Georgetown house. Pictured on the front was an obese transvestite performing on a stage. On the back was a note, unsigned, that said, in part, "I didn't know you had a second job." The card was addressed to Joe and it had a postmark from West Springfield, Massachusetts–the same city Joe had run off to and spent the first two days of his disappearance.

Elizabeth was in a happy mood the day in mid-December that Enid and her grandfather carried her into the pediatric ward of the Georgetown Hospital not far from their home. She was smiling and gurgling, without a care in the world. But the winds of life can change abruptly, even for a three-month old.

The test for the HIV virus that causes AIDS requires a substantial amount of blood. The normal heel pricks done on babies would not suffice, so the nurse had to probe for a vein large enough to accommodate the needle. Elizabeth was soon crying uncontrollably but there was nothing her mother, or any of them, could do, except try to hurry. Finally the nurse hit a vein and the tube began to fill. But when it was full and she carried it to the tray, the nurse started to cry too. "I got the wrong tube," she groaned, realizing that in her haste she hadn't used a vial already coated with the necessary chemicals for an HIV test. They would have to start all over. But with another nurse. "I just can't do it again," said the nurse, who walked away in tears.

A pediatrician took over and finally got the proper vial filled with Elizabeth's blood. The ordeal took twenty minutes. They told Enid the results would be back in five or six days. She could call back on Tuesday.

When she called back on Tuesday, they were out to lunch.

When she called an hour later, they said they'd give the doctor the message.

When she called an hour after that, they said the doctor still wasn't available.

"Look," cried out Enid. "This is an AIDS test for my three-month old daughter. This is making me crazy. Could you please go back and tell someone that they were supposed to call me back two hours ago, I haven't heard anything, and I'm really frightened." She was crying on the phone.

The woman on the other end took pity on her.

"You stay right there and I'll go see what I can find out," she said.

Enid's imagination, already working on overload, conjured up the very worst. The reason they hadn't talked to her in the first place, the reason they were waiting for just one person to tell her, was because it was bad news, they were going to tell her her baby daughter had AIDS. She just knew it. After everything else, this would be the coup de grace, Joe's final post script. She paced back and forth, crying. She was at home. Her father sat in a chair across the dining room from her, helpless to do anything but, like Enid, wait it out.

The receptionist was gone three minutes. It was amazing how long three minutes could take when you're waiting for life-and-death news.

Finally, she was back.

"The results of the test are negative," she said. "Your daughter does not have HIV."

The phone sagged out of Enid's hands. She looked at her dad.

"She's OK," she said, barely above a whisper, and then she said it louder, "She's OK!" And she and her father cried in each other's arms.

□□□

Partisan politics being what they are, it wasn't always fun and games in the workplace, either. Nineteen ninety-five would go down in history as a very good year for Republicans. Not only had the Grand Old Party taken over both the House and Senate, but the Democrat in the White House was having to deflect an abnormal number of legal attacks. If it wasn't a sexual harassment lawsuit it was further questions about his involvement in the Whitewater investment case. Bill Clinton, and his party, had seen calmer years. But however inadvertent, Enid had given the Democrats a little relief. The Waldholtz scandal gave the opposition something to fire back at. It wasn't Newt Gingrich, but at least it was one of his troops.

Pat Schroeder, the Colorado Democrat who had first led the cries for Enid's resignation, also took the lead in the make-life-miserable-for-Enid cause, rallying with some Democratic congresswomen whom Enid referred to collectively, and without affection, as the "savage sisterhood." Enid tried to steer clear of the sisterhood. If she saw them coming, she walked the other way. But sometimes it was impossible. Sometimes, her job required that she speak to them.

The first time that happened was a week or so after the press conference, just a couple of days prior to the holiday recess. The issue on the floor of the House that day was welfare. Enid was involved with an amendmentl designed to streamline the interstate collection of child support payments. When it came time for her to address the assembled members of Congress she rose from her seat on the right side of the aisle–Republicans sit on the right, Democrats on the left, hence the phrase "both sides of the aisle"–and spoke from the microphone at the leadership table.

As she started, the hissing began. Hissing that grew in intensity as she continued. Suddenly, the United States House of Representatives sounded as if it was full of snakes.

The sisters were in full voice.

"The house is not in order," said a voice from the chair, and only then did the hissing subside. Enid cleared her throat. This was her first time in front of a full session of congress since Joe left. She delivered her speech, kept it short, turned, thanked the speaker, and, amid total silence, her head down, she moved up the aisle to return to her seat. As she did so, the chamber of the House suddenly filled with the sound of applause. Enid lifted her head and looked toward the sound. It was coming from the left side of the aisle, the Democrat's side, where she saw one lone congressman, Charlie Rangel from New York, clapping from his seat. He nodded at Enid, and continued clapping. A black man and a Democrat from Harlem was showing his support for his colleague, a white woman and a Republican from Salt Lake City, his applause communicating the clear message that he felt her courage, and her pain. Enid managed a thin but grateful smile. Charlie Rangel–a man whose vote always had and always would cancel out Enid Greene's–had given her an early Christmas gift.

□□□

If stability and some semblance of normalcy didn't return all at once to the life of Enid Greene Waldholtz, they didn't stage a total boycott either. Slowly the storm center moved on, revealing humanity in its wake. Others, even those who didn't agree with her reasoning for clinging to her seat, took Charlie Rangel's lead and did their best at showing compassion. It wasn't easy; it's always hard to know what to say to the dispossessed. Some made a fuss over little Elizabeth Waldholtz whenever she made an appearance on Capitol Hill. Others indicated their sympathy with short, passing gestures. Even the most stoical gave it their best shot. Once, Enid found herself standing on the House floor during a vote with the House majority leader, Dick Armey. Armey, a Texan through and through, quite obviously didn't know just what to say. For a moment he said nothing, just put his arm around her shoulder. Finally, he said, "Well, it's like my first wife used to say, 'Time wounds all heels.'"

It all helped. Every tiny, almost imperceptible bit. From within Congress and without. After the press conference Enid received bags of mail from all areas of the country, the majority of it supportive. Many of the letters were from people who had been betrayed sometime in their lives by someone they'd trusted and loved. Some of the letter writers detailed stories that were eerily similar to Enid's. One woman, writing from Nevada, said, "Your experience and mine were exactly the same, except I had a Rolls Royce." There were a lot of good people in the world who understood and cared.

Jim and Sue Parkinson brought two of their children, Brooke and Matt, to Washington and spent Christmas of 1995 with Enid and Morfar. Nobody bothered with a tree. Somehow it didn't seem right to move one into the House That Joe Leased. But Sue brought presents for everyone and family was there and Christmas was passable.

The hard parts were always at the start of a new phase. It had been that way after the press conference, and it was that way after Christmas. Enid had driven Jim, Sue and the kids to the airport in Ladonna's Pathfinder and was driving back to Georgetown. Her father, whose presence–almost omnipresence–the past two months had been the most valuable, would be leaving in a week. The nanny was gone. The rented furniture had all been sent back to the store. About the only thing left in the townhouse was the lease, which had another year to run. Basically, Enid realized, she and Elizabeth would be ringing in 1996 without a table to sit at.

The old familiar thought of suicide returned. Enid was alone in the car, approaching the top of a hill in Georgetown, with a solid brick wall on the other side. She drove this route often. She knew the wall was strong and thick. *All I'd have to do is gun it and in a few seconds it would all be over!* she thought. But it was Ladonna's car. She took her foot off the gas and slowed to a stop before turning left–and moving on down the road.

□□□

Although she never officially became a "target" of the federal grand jury's investigation looking into the finances of both her campaign and her joint banking accounts with Joe, the process itself cast a formidable disruptive influence on Enid's life. And not just on her, Enid came to realize, but on her reputation. Polls commissioned in Salt Lake City by the *Deseret News* and conducted by Dan Jones–the pollster Enid trusted–revealed an uphill battle, to put it kindly, for re-election. She trailed every Democratic challenger they polled her against, and by a wide margin.

She'd been around long enough to gauge the wind, and this wind said that unless something changed dramatically to alter the public mood, she was practically guaranteed of losing in November.

After sizing up the dire prospects, Enid announced on Tuesday, March 5th, thirteen days before the filing deadline, that she would not seek re-election.

"The facts will prove that, while I made some terrible mistakes of misplaced trust, for which I take responsibility, I am absolutely innocent of any intentional wrongdoing," Enid wrote in the official resignation announcement released by her office. "I have worked to resolve these questions as quickly as possible and have cooperated fully with the law enforcement authorities. I had hoped that the Department of Justice would have resolved these issues by now, but my attorneys have told me that they have been told by the government attorneys in Washington that they are going to take time to resolve this matter. Thus, for these reasons and for the sake of my family, friends and supporters, as well as our community, I will not be a candidate for Congress in 1996."

□□□

Not long after Enid voluntarily announced she would be bowing out, Joe was involuntarily bowing in–to jail.

He finally talked to someone who did something about his alibis, excuses, and lame explanations: a judge. Namely, the Honorable Robert A. Kelly, presiding over the court of common pleas in Allegheny County, Pennsylvania, Orphans' Court division, where Joe and his lawyer appeared to answer a charge of contempt for Joe's repeated failures to produce an accounting of the more than $600,000–his family suspected the actual amount was probably closer to a million–Joe's grandmother had given him dating back to 1986.

Over a period of nearly five months that extended back to the time of his disappearance, Joe had been ordered by the Pittsburgh court to produce such an accounting–so that Joe's father and his cousin, the guardians of the estate of Rebecca Levenson, could see where the money was. Over that same period of time, Joe had stiffed them at every turn. Using the same modus operandi that had always worked before, he concocted any number of stories to explain why the accounting hadn't taken place. He blamed the constant delays on banks, airlines, couriers, and, of course, the old standby: Federal Express. At one point he sent his father and his father's attorney to the Pittsburgh airport to pick up a package allegedly containing details of the mysterious hundreds of thousands, but they came up empty-handed at the airport. And this was when Joe was living in his old bedroom in his father's house.

The act was alive and well, and playing again in Pittsburgh.

Finally, Dr. Harvey Waldholtz and Steven Slesinger had enough. Each armed with an attorney, they brought Joe and his attorney in front of Judge Kelly on March 28th, 1996, to answer the contempt charges. Joe had continually ignored a court's commands and the court wanted to know why.

At the hearing, Joe was required to take the witness stand. He agreed to tell the truth, the whole truth, and nothing but the truth, so help him God.

Thus the stage was set, finally, for the public unveiling of Joseph Phillip Waldholtz, a man for whom the truth wasn't just illusive, but also ever-changing.

Amid questioning by his own attorney, Lester Nauhaus, the following exchange regarding the accounting of his grandmother's money took place:

Mr. Nauhaus: *"Mr. Waldholtz, you understand that you are under oath and statements made under oath to this court are punishable in the criminal code of Pennsylvania. Does the first and final account exist?"*

Mr. Waldholtz: *"Yes."*

Mr. Nauhaus: *"And where is it, sir?"*

Mr. Waldholtz: *"It is at 1671 34th Street, Northwest, in Washington, D.C."*

Mr. Nauhaus: *"Can you assure this court that within a week the first and final report will be in Allegheny County and be prepared in such a manner for filing with this court?"*

Mr. Waldholtz: *"Yes."*

The hearing then moved on to cross examinations by the attorneys for the guardians, Mr. William Stang and Mr. Bruce S. Gelman, both of whom questioned Joe concerning details as to the whereabouts of his grandmother's accounting and why he hadn't brought that accounting to the court as directed. What resulted was a documentary of Joe's verbal footwork, a court reporter's notarized account of his tactics and strategy–all of it designed to cloud, contort, and confuse. With a judge in a robe looking on, Joe finally performed his song and dance for the record. The performance, as recorded in the official court transcript, follows:

Q. (From Mr. Stang): *Who right now is residing at the–what is it–1671 what street?*

A. (From Mr. Waldholtz): *34th Street.*

Q: *Who resides there presently?*

A: *My wife, my daughter and another couple, I believe, but I am not positive of that.*

Q: *When is the last time you have been there?*

A: *Early November.*

Q: *Isn't it true that your wife has told you that she will not allow you to come into any of your marital residences?*

A: *No. That is where I am to visit the baby in an agreement that we came to two weeks ago. It is best for Elizabeth that I visit the baby in an environment she is familiar with.*

Q: *Do you know if your wife has removed any of your papers from that location?*

A: *I don't.*

Q: *So it is possible that the papers aren't there?*

A: *No, it was mail and mail she can't do anything with.*

Q: *I'm sorry. I can't hear you.*

A: *It was mail and mail they haven't done anything with, they have assured me of that.*

Q: *Have you asked her to forward your mail?*

A: *I made many requests and they did not do that.*

Q: *You know why they didn't do that?*

A: *I don't.*

Q: *Mr. Waldholtz, this accounting that, if I understand you correctly, you were speaking softly, you said accounting was prepared; is that right?*

A: *Yes.*

Q: *Who prepared this accounting?*

A: *Financial institutions that the money was at.*

Q: *Well, who is that?*

A: *There were several. It was PNC. It was Merrill Lynch. It was Bank of New York and I believe Bank of America.*

Q: *So you actually discussed this accounting with people at those institutions in order to get them to help you prepare this accounting?*

A: *Right.*

Q: *And is it typed?*

A: *Typed.*

Q: *Did a lawyer assist you in preparing this accounting?*

A: *I was advised.*

Q: *Can you tell me, this account, this lawyer, who was it that was advising you?*

A: *It was a friend. My friends have been put through so much I would prefer that that remain private.*

Q: *I would like to know who it was and I would like to know whether or not you believe he has kept a copy in his office?*

A: *No. there were no copies made.*

Q: *A lawyer prepared the accounting and didn't keep a copy?*

A: *The lawyer did not prepare it. I asked for advice on what I–what records I needed to get.*

Q: *So, then, you collected the records?*

A: *Well, the institutions collected the records.*

Q: *Then they forwarded them to you?*

A: *Right.*

Q: *And the records–where were you living when they were forwarded to you? How did you obtain them?*

A: *That was during–they came to the residence after I had left.*

Q: *And you haven't been back since?*

A: *No.*

Q: *How do you know they came?*

A: *They were mailed and before the housekeeper was terminated she mentioned that I had mail from these places. They haven't done anything with my mail. They have thrown it in a box as it has come.*

Q: *You think the housekeeper opened your mail?*

A: *No.*

Q: *So you don't really know what is in the mail; do you?*

A: *The records that were requested for the accounting.*

Q: *That you haven't seen yet?*

A: *Right, but it was exactly what the court–I mean, it was what the court asked for.*

Mr. Stang: *Nothing further, Judge.*

Judge Kelly: *Mr. Gelman.*

Mr. Gelman: *Yes, Your Honor.*

Q: (From Mr. Gelman): *Mr. Waldholtz, how long have you been in Pittsburgh?*

A: *Since late November, early December, sometime in there. I am not clear.*

Q: *You have been here at least three months; is that right?*

A: *Right.*

Q: *How many times have you taken trips back to Washington, D.C.?*

A: *I believe–well, there were several.*

Q: *At least two?*

A: *Yeah.*

Q: *And you took those trips back to D.C. after you already knew the court orders that were entered in this case requiring you to turn over all assets and make an accounting; isn't that right?*

A: *Right.*

Q: *Why when you went back to D.C. didn't you collect these papers that you say are there to bring back to present to the court?*

A: *I tried to.*

Q: *And why weren't you successful?*

A: *Because that was when there were some severe difficulties going on with my wife and myself and they preferred I not come to the house. And I was told they would be sent. I was told personal items would be sent and they weren't.*

Q: *How do you know–what has changed in the situation between you and your wife or any of that situation which would now all of a sudden allow you in the house to go through your documents and bring those documents back to Pittsburgh?*

A: *We reached an agreement on visitation and Enid and I decided that it would be best for visitation to be held somewhere where Elizabeth was familiar. They also said the personal items that they had from my office and from the house and mail, you know, that that would be there and that I could take it back.*

Q: *Um, did you have a key to the residence in Washington?*

A: *Yes.*

Q: *When you were down in Washington why didn't you just go in the place and get your stuff out and get the documents?*

A: *They changed the alarm code.*

Q: *Who were the people, the names of the people at PNC that you dealt with that sent you this information?*

A: *I–I–I can't recall.*

Q: *What were the names of the people at Merrill Lynch that you spoke with and said they would send the information?*

A: *That was in October–November. I can get them. I mean, after the last five months I can certainly get you the names of the people, get the court the names of the people.*

Q: *Okay. And you wouldn't know, then, the name of the per-*

son from Bank of America that allegedly sent stuff to your house in Washington?

A: *Not off the top of my head with what has gone on, no.*

Q: *When did you contact these people to get the information for the accounting; before or after November 1st?*

A: *That period of time is very, very hazy in my mind because there were so many difficulties going on, but it was around then. I don't recall what specific day.*

Q: *Isn't it after you finally got ordered by the court to make an accounting and produce assets that you allegedly contacted these people to get the information?*

A: *No. I think it was before because my dad and I talked about the need for that.*

Q: *No, in this case, Mr. Waldholtz, isn't it true that you have had not only myself but your father, Harvey Waldholtz, running around Pittsburgh on several goose chases when you said documents are coming in from out of town and then no documents were ever produced?*

A: *That was not done by me.*

Q: *You didn't tell me and your father that documents were coming in at the airport and for us to go out there and they would be waiting there when we get there and there was nothing there; you didn't have anything to do with that?*

A: *I was told by people who worked for us that the documentation was sent. I didn't realize at the time what was going on.*

Q: *When you say people working for us said they sent it, who is the people that were working for you and who is us?*

A: *Enid and me.*

Q: *Okay.*

A: *Well, I guess working for her but —*

Q: *What is the name?*

A: *People who were doing political work for us I had no idea at the time were isolating me and not doing some things that they said they had done, and I think the results of the last five months, you know, bear that out.*

Q: *Um, isn't it true that when you–you have your car here in Pittsburgh, right?*

A: *Uh-huh.*

Q: *And you had to go down to Washington to get it?*

A: *I was not able to.*

Q: *Somebody drove it back up here. Isn't it true that most of your possessions and mail and personal effects were in the trunk of your car?*

A: *No. The only thing they sent up was clothing. I'm sorry, clothing and things like deodorant and things like that.*

Q: *Instead of your going down to get this material haven't you ever asked them to send it to you?*

A: *Yes.*

Q: *Have you ever asked them to send it to your father's attorney or to the other co-guardian?*

A: *No, I just said send my stuff up.*

Q: *So you don't know whether any information is there or not; do you?*

A: *Information is there.*

Q: *How do you know?*

A: *Because when the mail came in before the housekeeper was terminated she told me so.*

Q: *She told you what?*

A: *I asked her did mail come for me from this place or that place and she said yes.*

Q: *What places?*

A: *Those institutions.*

Q: *From PNC?*

A: *And Merrill Lynch and Bank of America and Bank of New York.*

Q: *What about First Security Bank?*

A: *What about First Security?*

Q: *Did you ever have any information sent from First Security Bank?*

A: *Well, that is involved in the Federal case but not–no, I haven't.*

Q: *Didn't you have an account at First Security Bank?*

A: *Yes.*

Q: *And did you write checks out to your grandmother from that account?*

A: *I don't recall.*

Q: *Are there any accounts existing today which have your grandmother's money in it?*

A: *Yeah, yes.*

Q: *Where are they and what bank is it in?*

A: *The four that I have mentioned to you.*

Q: *PNC, Merrill Lynch, Bank of New York and Bank of America all have accounts?*

A: *I'm sorry. The PNC does not. PNC does not.*

Q: *Okay. So you are saying Merrill Lynch, Bank of New York and Bank of America all currently have accounts currently holding money which belongs to Rebecca Levenson?*

A: *Right.*

Q: *And whose names are those accounts in?*

A: *Hers.*

Q: *Whose?*

A: *Rebecca Levenson's.*

Mr. Gelman: *I don't think I have anything else, Your Honor.*

When the attorneys rested, Judge Kelly leaned back in his chair, attempting to assimilate everything he'd just heard. It wasn't easy. It had been quite a twisted path Mr. Waldholtz had taken them on, long on deflections and half-answers and short on anything substantive. It was vintage Joe. His "A" act. His best stuff. If Kate Watson or Kaylin Loveland or Ladonna Lee or Aaron Edens or Steve Taggart or Roger Dean or Keith Davis or any of dozens of others who had heard his ramblings and blame-transferring in Utah and in Washington, D.C. the past four years had been present, they would have stood up en masse and said, *That's it! That's what he does!"*

As for the judge, he stayed seated and, after a moment, spoke. As the record shows:

Judge Kelly: *You can have a seat, Mr. Waldholtz.*

The court is prepared to make the following findings of facts and conclusions:

This court entered an order on November 2, 1995 directing Mr. Waldholtz to file an accounting in the matter of Rebecca Levenson at No. 1290 of 1995, further was directed to turn over all assets connected with or concerning the estate of Rebecca Levenson.

On March 1 Mr. Waldholtz was directed to comply with the order of November 2, 1995 and was informed that a hearing would be held on March 28, 1996. He was advised in that order that the failure to file an accounting without adequate explanation may result in incarceration.

In the testimony which I have heard here there is no adequate explanation for the failure to file the account. If Mr. Waldholtz did not have certain information he could have gone to secondary sources such as the institutions themselves and had duplicates mailed to his residence here in Pittsburgh.

Further, he indicates by his own testimony that his wife has not prevented him from receiving the original records and, in fact, says an account does exist and has been produced in Washington, D.C.

The court will take notice that Washington, D.C. is a mere five hours by car away. Certainly Mr. Waldholtz if he would have left this time yesterday would have been back in plenty of time to produce the account. He has failed to do so or give adequate explanation . . .

In any event, I find Mr. Waldholtz in contempt of this court and will direct that he be remanded to the custody of the Allegheny County Sheriff until he complies with the directives of the order of November 2nd . . .

I am handing you the keys to the jailhouse, and if you comply and file the accounting and turn over the assets as directed by the order of November 2nd you will be immediately released from jail. do you understand that?

Mr. Waldholtz: *The only thing I would like to say . . .*

Judge Kelly: *No. I asked you if you understood that. I didn't ask you if you had anything you wanted to say.*

Mr. Waldholtz: *I think so.*

Judge Kelly: *Therefore, you will be in the county jail until those two items are produced.*

Ironically, while he was being investigated by a federal grand jury for embezzlement, wire fraud, bank fraud, false statements, securities fraud, and a grand total of 858 violations of the Federal Election Campaign Act, the reason Joe Waldholtz was finally going to jail was because he exasperated a judge.

Joe was stuck behind bars and he knew it. He could come up with all the excuses in the world, blame every messenger service and fax machine that ever existed, he could continue to buy the whole thing he'd ever truly been able to afford–time. But what would that gain him now? What did he want with jail time?

It took him less than twenty-four hours to come clean.

The next day in the same courtroom in front of the same judge, Lester Nauhaus addressed the Honorable Robert A. Kelly with this revelation:

Mr. Nauhaus: *I have an affidavit signed by Joseph P. Waldholtz which says as follows: "Before me, the undersigned notary public, personally appeared Joseph P. Waldholtz who, being duly sworn, deposes and says at the present time and at all times from January 1993 to the present time he has not been in possession of any funds or assets belonging to, either directly or indirectly, Rebecca Levenson.*

Judge Kelly: *Then yesterday he perjured himself.*

Mr. Nauhaus: *I don't know that, sir.*

Judge Kelly: *Didn't he yesterday say that his grandmother's money was in Merrill Lynch and several banks?*

Mr. Nauhaus: *I don't remember.*

Judge Kelly: *That was my recollection.*

Mr. Nauhaus: *Well, my recollection is that he said that the documents that he needed were in those particular accounts. The simple truth of the matter is there's no money, period.*

Judge Kelly: *Okay. Show the money is unaccounted for and whatever paper trail he should produce that he has.*

Mr. Nauhaus: *There is none. That's what I'm trying to . . .*

Judge Kelly: *Yesterday he said, "Judge, if you give me a couple more days, I'm willing to go down to Washington, D.C., to see my daughter this weekend, and I'll bring this abundance of mail and everything back."*

Mr. Nauhaus: *Well, I can't do that.*

Judge Kelly: *Was he lying to me yesterday?*

And although Lester Nauhaus continued to do his best to do his job as an advocate for his client, the bottom line was, yes, Joe Waldholtz had lied to the judge the day before. But the judge shouldn't take it personally. He always lied. He lied to everyone.

All the court hearing in Pittsburgh accomplished, besides sending Joe to jail, was establish what Joe's father and cousin had no doubt suspected all along. The money Gram Levenson gave Joe was gone. History. Out the door at the very latest by early 1992. The exact amount she'd given him was unknown, and given that the 87-year-old woman had been declared mentally incompetent by her doctors as of August of 1993, would never be known. But it was at least $600,000, and probably a lot more than that, that his Gram's favorite grandson went out and spent–on himself. As Joe had finally confessed to the court, from January of 1993 on, there was no money, period.

By that time he had moved on to Utah.

CHAPTER XIII

Enid Greene sat at her desk in the Cannon Building, surrounded by quiet. The reporter from the newspaper back home, satisfied with his story, had packed up his tape recorder and left. The staff wasn't around. Fifine, the woman who ran the special "fifth floor express" elevator down the hall, wasn't around. The building was practically deserted. The television sets, normally tuned to C-span, were dark. It was a weekday but the House wasn't in session, and wouldn't be for another few weeks. Outside it was already dark and it was only a little after six. The fall had come so fast, it seemed. Well, at least in some ways.

She signed some color photographs of a school group that had toured the Capitol in late summer. That finished, her desk was clear. She looked around her office. It hadn't changed much in the nearly two years since she took it over. On the credenza behind her was the same framed black and white photograph of her parents she placed there her first day in office, Forrest and Gerda, circa 1955, Forrest looking businesslike, Gerda looking good. To the left of that was the color photo signed by Rush Limbaugh that had been taken at the Heritage Foundation in Baltimore during freshman orientation.

On the walls the framed copies of the *Deseret News* and *Salt Lake Tribune* still hung where they had been nailed the day she moved in, proclaiming her victory for Utah's second district congressional seat. Next to them was the poster from Elizabeth's surprise baby shower, signed by all the House members who had attended.

Enid realized, sadly, that the few mementoes on the walls were from her first few months in office. She had hardly hung a single new thing for more than twelve months. A year had gone by and the office had not changed–except for the art. That was gone.

She looked at the calendar. It was almost mid-November. A year had come and gone since Jim and Joe went to the airport and Joe did his vanishing act. The national elections had been held just last Tuesday. Merrill Cook, of all people, a man who at various times had run for school board member, mayor, county commissioner, governor (twice), and Congressman and who, coming in, was 0 for six, lifetime, in elections, won the seat Enid was vacating. The race turned out to be no contest. The Democrats barely countered with a Sierra Clubber who wanted to save the forests and the whales. The guy got forty-two percent of the vote. Cook, who spent nearly $900,000 of his own money and a million dollars overall, got fifty-five percent, up thirty-seven points from his third place showing behind Shepherd and Waldholtz in '94.

In the race for President, Bill Clinton clobbered Bob Dole, winning forty-nine percent of the vote to Dole's forty-one. But the Republicans did manage to hang on to their majorities in both the House and the Senate. The Republicans hadn't retained a majority in the House of Representatives since 1926, so they had that to cheer about. The seventy-three members of the Republican freshman class of '94 had a lot to do with holding onto the House. Seventy-one of them ran for re-election and of that number, sixty were successful. Only two didn't seek another term, Wes Cooley of Oregon and Enid Greene of Utah.

Elizabeth was fourteen and a half months old now. Enid had taken her to the office on Halloween, dressed as a pink piglet, complete with a curly tail. Elizabeth couldn't quite walk yet, but she was getting her teeth, and if you listened closely you could hear her say "mama" and "Barney." And she liked M&M's. Already. Time flies when you're growing up. There's no better gauge to document that time really is moving along than watching an infant change right before your eyes. The spring and summer had been good to Elizabeth; and, as she watched her daughter grow, for her mother as well. Maybe not the best she'd ever known, but, still, life had settled down a little after March, once Enid announced she would not seek re-election. Not that Joe had gone away, of course, or stopped being Joe.

□□□

Maybe in the movies, Joe Waldholtz would have been castigated as a villain and treated as a pariah by a public appalled that he would steal from his own senile grandmother–an unmistakable conclusion after his Pittsburgh court appearance in April. But this wasn't the movies, this was real life, and the story caused barely a stir. The man who was front page news when he disappeared was barely yesterday's news when he got exposed.

Nor was there much reaction from the federal prosecutors working on Joe's "other" case in Washington. It didn't require a huge imagination to think that the same man who swindled his grandmother right in front of her unsuspecting son–and Joe's own father–could be capable of hatching a similar plot to swindle his father-in-law right in front of his unsuspecting daughter–and Joe's own wife. The moving parts were interchangeable. Rebecca Levenson and Harvey Waldholtz became Dunford Forrest Greene and Enid Greene Waldholtz. The only constant was Joe. But the feds showed no imagination whatever after Joe was jailed in paralleling Joe's M.O. from Pittsburgh to Utah. Undeterred from its course, the U.S. Attorneys office in Washington moved on relentlessly with its grand jury investigation of the Congresswomen from Utah, regardless of what was going on in Pennsylvania.

Countless witnesses were questioned in Washington, many of them flown (some more than once) back and forth from Utah at taxpayer expense. A lot of money was still disappearing because of Joe Waldholtz, and, as always, none of it was his.

The tally continued, of course, to include D. Forrest Greene's money. As long as the federal investigation continued, he and his daughter kept their team of high-priced accountants, consultants and lawyers on the case and at the ready. And Enid certainly didn't have the funds to pay for their services herself.

The public did stir, but hardly derisively, when Joe was indicted by the federal grand jury on May 2nd, 1996, on twenty seven counts of bank fraud. The indictment alleged that he was involved in a check kiting scheme involving thirty-four separate checks that totaled nearly $3 million dollars. Joe responded with a plea of "not guilty" on Friday, May 10th, at which time he also took the opportunity to wish his wife and daughter a happy Mother's Day.

"It's not exactly how I would have expected your first Mother's Day to be," Joe said, directing a statement that received coast-to-coast media play to his daughter Elizabeth, "but I hope you and Enid have a wonderful day."

To Enid he added: "The next time I'm in Washington, I hope you allow me the same luxury you have–and that's to spend time with our daughter."

Joe was still working the media.

He maintained his innocence for three weeks. But on the last day of May he decided he was guilty after all. In a plea agreement with the U.S. Attorney, he pled guilty to one count of bank fraud, one count of making a false statement on a campaign report, one count of submitting a false report to the Federal Election Commission, and one count of filing a fraudulent tax return. He also agreed to pay a fine, in conjunction with the bank fraud, of $14,910. In return for the feds dropping the rest of the charges against him, he agreed to cooperate fully with the prosecutors in a further investigation of the finances, both personal and having to do with the congressional campaigns, of Joe and Enid Waldholtz.

As the lead prosecutors on the case, Assistant U.S. Attorneys William Lawler and Craig Iscoe stood on the steps outside the

United States Courthouse in Washington, D.C. to announce the culmination of their "deal." They looked especially smug on Wednesday, June 5th, satisfied that they had made a terrific bargain in dropping the vast majority of the charges against Joe in exchange for his "inside information." The government prosecutors had thrown their saddle on a convicted liar and felon–convinced he would lead them to implicating his wife.

□□□

It was truly amazing where all bluff and no substance could still get you. Joe kept working his *schtick*, and his *schtick* kept working. Just like in the good old days, he continued to play the media, and public perception, paradoxically getting even more voice–and favorable reaction–the longer his rap sheet grew. When he talked, the media tuned in, no matter what he might say. The "Mother's Day Appeal" was just one example. When he stood on the courthouse steps on June 5th, the day of his arraignment, he was duly quoted as he said, with tears in his eyes, "Most importantly, always, always, tell the truth. Particularly to the people you love. Thank you." This, from the same man who had just moments before bought years off his jail term by lying to the authorities about his cache of "additional information."

Left to his own recognizance and required periodic check-ins to the FBI before sentencing, which wasn't scheduled until the fall, an unchecked Joe undauntedly carried on. He was cleared to visit Elizabeth at the Georgetown townhouse in May, and he turned their "reunion" into a media event, alerting various television stations and newspapers in advance of the "big day." He arrived early for the court-approved supervised afternoon visit, and after parking his car he got out and walked across the street to where Charles Sherrill of Salt Lake City's KSL Television was waiting in his car. Joe greeted Sherrill as if he were a long-lost Army buddy. They talked for a few minutes and then Joe, checking to make sure the cameras were rolling, walked to the door. Dale Bowen answered the knock. A college student at nearby American University, Dale, his wife, Corinne, and their baby daughter,

Sydney, had moved into the townhouse in January. In exchange for Corinne's nanny services–and their dining room table–they got rent from Enid.

Joe had never met Dale before, but after the introduction at the front entrance Joe closed the door behind them, let out a huge sigh and, with a great amount of annoyance, said conspiratorially, "Can you believe Charles Sherrill had the nerve to come out here on the first day I get to see my daughter? The media just won't leave me alone!"

Dale, who had just watched the entire scene between Joe and the television reporter from the upstairs kitchen window, could only stare in amazement at the fat man standing in front of him. He had watched Joe initiate the interaction with Sherrill. He had watched Joe make sure the cameras were on when he went to the door. Dale had known Joe Waldholtz what, all of thirty seconds, and already Joe had lied to him.

It took maybe another five minutes before he lied again. He told Dale he needed to use the phone. Dale showed him where the phone was–Joe's movements during visitation were restricted to the townhouse's bottom floor family room, where his big screen TV still stood, a kind of silent testament to his greatest scam–but refused to give him Enid's unlisted number.

As it turned out, Joe merely called his own answering machine in Pittsburgh, where he had caller I.D. Upon his return, all he had to do was check his messages to find out Enid's unlisted number–his quest in asking for the phone in the first place. He began calling the townhouse immediately, and the number had to be changed again. Much to Dale Bowen's chagrin. In looking for a part-time job, just that week he had papered D.C. with his resume, listing a phone number that was now obsolete. In subsequent visits by Joe, Dale himself made sure the downstairs telephone was unplugged and taken upstairs.

Joe's visits to see his daughter tended to be equal parts disruptive and erratic. He wouldn't show when he said he would and he would show when he'd given no advance notice, as was legally required. Invariably he would complain to the media, who would air his gripes.

In general, he'd just gone on being Joe, living in his own world, insulated by whatever it was that allowed him to get up every morning and do it all again.

Every now and then he would slip up and expose his real self. On one occasion he managed to send chills down the spine of not just a newspaper reporter, but a political reporter, and that's not easy. But Joe pulled it off. It was in Washington, on the eve of his guilty plea. The reporter, political columnist Dennis Roddy of the *Pittsburgh Post-Gazette*, managed to track Joe down at his hotel, the Park Hyatt. Joe had checked in under an assumed name but Roddy, ever the enterprising journalist, was not only able to ferret out the hotel, but the exact location of Joe's room. The reporter checked into another room in the hotel and, hoping for an interview that would give him material for a column in the next morning's *Post-Gazette*, he eaves-dropped outside Joe's room. From inside the room he heard a number of voices. Wishing to talk to Joe alone, Roddy went back to his room and waited. Later, he came back and knocked on the door, but got no answer. Still later, he tried again, and still no answer. To add to his frustration, the hotel switchboard told him the guest in that room had asked that his phone be shut off for the night.

With his writing deadline quickly approaching, Roddy got inventive. He stuck a small wad of paper in a crack in the door. If he came back later and the paper wasn't there, it would mean the door had been opened and Joe–who he suspected was away from the room–had returned. Sure enough, a few minutes later, when the reporter checked again, the paper was gone. He pounded on the door until Joe answered.

"I thought you were trying to dodge me," he said to Joe as he made his way into the hotel room. Roddy was a veteran reporter, known for his savvy and for a very entertaining writing style. Over the years, Joe, being a Pittsburgh boy, had given him plenty of good material. Roddy had followed Joe's rather meteoric rise as a player in Pennsylvania politics, and now he was following his meteoric fall.

Probably because it was late, and they were in a strange hotel room in Washington, Joe relaxed and adopted a conspiratorial tone with the reporter. He told Roddy that the men he'd heard talking in his room earlier were from a P.R. firm he'd hired. They were coaching him on how to handle his statement the next day–the one he planned to give on the steps of the courthouse the next morning after he pled guilty. The plan, Joe explained, was to deliver a very emotional, heartfelt speech that would appeal to everyone's sympathy. He planned to apologize to just about everyone–including Enid's campaign opponent Karen Shepherd, although not to his wife or his newest enemy, her attorney.

The emotional high point, he told Roddy, would come at the end, when he talked about his baby daughter Elizabeth.

"Here's the part where I'll cry," he said, and then Joe began to read that part of the rehearsed statement. Right on cue, he began to cry.

The next morning on the courthouse steps, Roddy watched as Joe, in exactly the same place in his script, exactly as he'd practiced, as his P.R. guys stood off to the side–cried again.

Convicted felon or not, Joe continued to live in his own world, play by his own rules, and hold onto his own fantasies. Occasionally he would call people from "the old days," choosing those he felt might not hang up on him. He telephoned Kate Watson, Enid's administrative assistant, at home late one night during the summer. "Hi Kate," he began, and proceeded to talk as if they'd just left the office maybe an hour ago. He talked about politics, throwing in a few snide asides about the Clintons, and finally said, "Kate, the reason I called is I know you'll be looking for a job soon and I want you to know that I'll be happy to write a letter of recommendation to anyone you wish. I'm happy to help. I want to help."

Kate Watson, a woman not often at a loss for words, was rendered speechless. So the man who had, in effect, cost her her job–who had cost all of them their jobs–and who was on his way to jail, was offering his support?

□□□

Through it all, Joe was transformed during the summer of '96 into a folk hero. If G. Gordon Liddy could become a talk show host, D.B. Cooper could have night clubs named after him, and Butch Cassidy could be played by Paul Newman, then Joseph P. Waldholtz could at least have people hound him for his autograph. Joe hadn't gone in and held up a bank with a mask, a sack, and a gun; he'd done it with a fountain pen. He hadn't gone down to the welfare office and ripped off little old retired people's social security checks; he'd sweet-talked a couple of millionaires out of their millions. He sure didn't walk like a bad guy, or talk like a bad guy. To the man on the street, it wasn't that easy not to confuse him with Robin Hood.

In Pittsburgh and Salt Lake City both, total strangers would stop Joe for an autograph or ask to have their picture taken with him. He stayed back East, mostly, but when he finally returned to Utah in early August for a divorce hearing he made a grand entrance. The *Salt Lake Tribune* ran two color photos of Joe, one on the front page and another on the front of the local section. Both shots were flattering, with Joe bathed in bright light and looking relaxed and content–in sharp contrast to the one color photograph the newspaper used of Enid, her face in a scowl and the background dark. The front page headline said, "From Bliss To Hiss" and the B-1 headline read, "Joe Comes Back to Town."

The article, written by reporter Laurie Sullivan Maddox, reflected the giddy atmosphere surrounding Joe's return:

". . . He breezed into town early Thursday, stunning everyone but the lawyers and a handful of others who were warned that the Waldholtz whirlwind was about to touch ground.

"Tension was thick at the law offices of Rep. Enid Greene's attorneys where the once-happy political couple met face-to-face for the first time since he bolted out of her life and into national headlines in November.

"Greene could be seen gesturing inside the conference room, at times rearing out of her seat and leaning across the table to point an accusatory finger at Joe.

"'She was just gesturing what she wanted for lunch,' Joe said afterward . . .

" . . . Autograph seekers sought him out at the airport. He was recognized right away at Beans & Brews where he and Skordas stopped for coffee. From there, Joe was chauffeured downtown by his lawyer in a red Rodeo sporting an Anderson-for-Congress bumper sticker.

"'It's OK,' Waldholtz assured Skordas, a backer of the Democratic candidate for Greene's congressional seat. 'Republicans always hire Democrats when they're in trouble.'"

And so the public perception went–Joe, the man with the one-liners; Enid, the woman scorned.

□□□

Only one man ever packed much of a wallop with Joe, that being Chuck Roistacher. If Joe could bamboozle or at least side-track everyone else, Enid's $310-an-hour attorney was always another story. Iscoe and Lawler didn't scare him. Roistacher did.

Joe did what he could to try and discredit the lawyer from Washington, a man he derisively called "Ratstacker" to anyone who would listen. He intimated that "Ratstacker" and Enid were having an affair; he suggested that "Ratstacker" was in on the "conspiracy" with the Greene family; he called him "The Greene family's hired assassin." But he could neither flap the attorney nor get him off his trail. If Chuck Roistacher was going to be there, Joe stayed away. On Joe's first visit to Salt Lake City he had showed up at the last minute unannounced–except to his attorney and a few well-chosen people in the media–and successfully avoided a showdown with Roistacher, who was still two thousand miles across the country in Washington. But it was a short-lived victory. For a second hearing scheduled the next week, this time Roistacher used the press himself, announcing that not only was he coming to Salt Lake, but he'd be bringing several boxes of documents with him so he could educate the divorce judge about the case.

Roistacher showed, Joe didn't–and the judge finalized the

divorce agreement, granting Enid virtually all of the marital assets and full custody of Elizabeth. All Joe got was a $20,000 "credit" from the marital assets–a credit that was immediately applied to the $3,987,426 Joe had been ordered by another Utah court to pay back to D. Forrest Greene, who had filed suit on his own behalf. In essence, then, all Joe "owned" after the divorce settlement was a total indebtedness of $3,967,426.

Roistacher stayed in Salt Lake for four days, just to make sure everything was a done deal. No one asked him for his autograph.

□□□

With the exception of the meeting in the lawyer's office in Salt Lake City in August, Enid and Joe did not cross paths. Whenever Joe came to the Georgetown house for his visits with Elizabeth, Enid either made a point of being out of the house or confining her movements to the upper floors, where Joe was not allowed (security officers were on the premises during his visits). He tried to call her several times, but she would not take his calls.

The dwindling days of her Congressional term, if anything, made Enid drive even harder than before. She made virtually every vote and every Rules Committee meeting. In August she went to the Republican National Convention in San Diego. For a lame duck, she didn't act like one. By and large, she was determined to go on. She went to her twenty-year high school class reunion in Salt Lake City for the simple reason she didn't want people saying she dodged it.

She caught her share of grief. A Salt Lake acting group put together a play that was a parody of her ordeal. It played to sellout crowd throughout the summer; the toughest ticket in town. But others continued to be kind. She'd never forget the day just after her divorce was final and she walked into the members-only ladies lounge in the Capitol, more a shrine than a restroom that occupies a space where President John Quincy Adams died. On one entire wall of the lounge are photographs, in alphabetical order, of every woman who is currently serving in the United

States House of Representatives. When Enid walked in, the first thing she noticed was that she wasn't with the W's any longer. She was now among the G's–Enid Greene from Utah.

It hadn't been easy, adjusting each photograph below "Greene" so hers could be inserted in its new position. More than half the wall had to be changed. But it had been done, and quickly. Somebody, somewhere, knew that it mattered.

□□□

Just as Enid–and Joe–moved on, so did the others whose lives had been affected, and changed, by the swath cut by the Waldholtz Family Trust.

Chuck Roistacher continued his law practice, moving on to other cases even as he kept Enid's case "open"; in the summer he and Susan found the time to travel to San Diego, where their son had passed the California bar and learned how to surf. Jim Parkinson also continued his law practice, winning for one client an $839,500 jury verdict against Wal-Mart. Ladonna Lee and Eddie Mahe helped Jon Fox retain his Congressional seat in Pennsylvania (by less than a hundred votes) and helped Congressman Sonny Bono win reelection in California; away from politics, the consultant gurus helped South Korea win the bid to co-host the 2002 soccer World Cup with Japan, South Korea's longtime nemesis and the country that, going in, had been considered a sure thing to host the Cup alone. Forensics accountant Fred Miller, ever the white-collar master sleuth, helped the federal government solve a $4 billion dollar fraud case against McDonnell Douglas Aircraft, an investigation that saved the taxpayers $250 million.

As for Forrest and Gerda Greene, Mormor and Morfar returned as best they could to what could be called normal life on Penrose Drive in Salt Lake City. Whenever Enid traveled back to Utah she would stay "back home" and Elizabeth would be watched over by her grandparents. The little girl particularly took to Morfar, their bond dating back to the many days and nights they spent together in Georgetown. Gerda continued to shine her husband's shoes, clean her own sinks, and pester her husband about buying her a new station wagon, which by the end of the year he still hadn't done. Forrest would constantly rail at the bills that kept poring in from the attorneys and accountants in Washington, just as he would rail at those who dared question his daughter's good name. On one occasion, during a luncheon meeting of the downtown Salt Lake Rotary Club, he stood up when a speaker, not knowing her father was in the audience, began to talk disparagingly of Congresswoman Greene. "She was conned!" shouted the normally reserved Forrest Greene. "She was conned!" In the early fall, Forrest began to experience problems with his heart skipping. His doctor told him to reduce the stress in his life.

□□□

It wasn't until late September that the Joe Waldholtz express ran out of track.

His own government finally let him have it. Acting on tips from Joe's family and friends in Pittsburgh, the FBI discovered that during the summer, while he was living at home awaiting sentencing, he had forged prescriptions for drugs, stolen checks, written bad checks, stolen credit cards (including his own lawyer's), and used heroin.

Not for one minute had Joe stopped being Joe.

He finally landed in a Washington, D.C. jail on Friday, September 26th, when the government officially requested that he be incarcerated for violating the terms of his release pending sentencing.

Represented by a court-appointed attorney from the public defender's office (his previous lawyers had withdrawn due to the fact Joe had stolen their credit cards), Joe requested that he be sent to a hospital in Pittsburgh for drug treatment. But U.S. District Judge Norma Holloway Johnson denied his request, remanding him instead to the Washington jail. "This court believes there is but one thing I can do," said Judge Johnson. "And that is to take you into custody to make sure you will not commit any additional crimes."

Finally, Joe was out of advocates. Even his own father didn't attend the Washington hearings. Harvey Waldholtz told the federal authorities that he no longer wanted his son in his house and changed the locks to all the doors.

Just as Enid Greene Waldholtz had done eleven months earlier.

Harvey and Joe's stepmother, Marilyn, had taken Joe into their Pittsburgh home and, for a time, believed his stories that his former wife was behind many of his problems, financial and otherwise. In return for their loyalty and kindness, Joe stole checks from Marilyn's purse, which he forged and cashed; wrote $24,600 worth of worthless checks from his own checking account to Harvey and Marilyn; stole Harvey's Discover card and charged $1,446 in purchases; and stole a prescription pad from his father's office, and used his father's physician number to write prescriptions for himself for Vicodin pain-killers.

According to the official record, Joe also used a female friend's American Express card for approximately $550 of unapproved charges, and later stole the same friend's Mastercard from her purse and used it for another $193 in purchases. All this, in addition to fraudulently using the credit cards of his Washington-based attorneys.

When pressed by the FBI, Joe, who had bruise marks on his thighs consistent with needle punctures, not only admitted to daily heroin use "for several weeks" but also to an addiction to prescription drugs dating back "to the early 1980's."

In the wake of these news revelations of "the real Joe," Dennis Roddy, the *Pittsburgh Post-Gazette* political writer, brought his Pittsburgh readers a particularly penetrating and succinct take on the walking contradiction named Joe Waldholtz:

Wrote Roddy:

"Once redeemed and by his own words a new man, Joe Waldholtz, Republican, bon vivant, raconteur and fraud, is on the crest of yet another pinnacle: He soon will be the federal prison inmate with the worst credit rating.

"No one, not John Gotti, not Al Capone, not even the Honor-

able Daniel Rostenkowski, D-Leavenworth, can approach Waldholtz's virtuosity with a credit card, his energetic imagination with a checkbook, his capacity to transform someone else's signature into a gourmet meal and a size 60 suit. Before us stands the greatest redistributor of wealth since Karl Marx became dust. If he takes up murder, expect all of Maryland to vanish in a week. I am in awe.

"Three months ago, Waldholtz was the criminal success story of the decade. He pleaded to a mere four counts after single-handedly bankrupting two families, defrauding his grandmother, shoplifting a congressional election and demolishing the career of his ex-wife, the Honorable Enid Greene, R-Utah.

"In return for leniency, he would testify against Enid at the grand jury exploring the fraud and deceit by which she was relieved of the burdens of anonymity, and her father was unburdened of several million dollars. She knew, he told anyone in hearing range. Enid knew all about the counterfeit donors scribbled onto her campaign reports. She knew, she knew, she knew, and Joe, converted from a lying fraud into an honest one, would tell all.

"Joe Waldholtz was the 300-pound man who had skated across the most watery part of the ice and miraculously survived the crossing. Who among us could have expected him to attempt a recrossing on a pogo stick?"

Although Joe's '96 summer rampage of drugs, lies and stolen money paled to his rampages in '94 and '95, this rampage not only opened the eyes of the media, but it also opened the eyes of the feds, who were compelled, finally, to yell uncle. At long last, the prosecutors clued into the fact that the convicted liar they'd teamed up with didn't have what they thought he had.

He constantly hinted that "Enid had to know what was going on" and "he'd fallen on the sword for her" and "it was agreed I would be the fall guy," but for all his subtle innuendoes in the press, for all his undertones to the prosecutors suggesting sinister behavior, beyond showing the U.S. Attorneys his two thousand dollar suits, his twenty thousand dollar wristwatches, the receipts from a $1.7 million congressional campaign, and everything else he'd blown everyone else's money on, the only additional information he had for them was the same message he'd had for his own family, for the Greene family, and for all others unlucky enough to have crossed his path: you've been had.

After not looking for almost a full calendar year at the preponderance of evidence that showed Joe to be a full-time con man, thief and liar–choosing instead to cling to their conspiracy theories that somehow Enid was involved in a plot that wound up imploding her life–their case was reduced to yet another example of Joe's ability to betray.

"We wanted to listen to find out what he could tell us. But these additional developments make it very hard to find anything that Joe Waldholtz says pertaining to the investigation to be entirely credible," said assistant U.S. Attorney Craig Iscoe on the day of Joe's hearing. Iscoe spoke from the same courthouse steps where less than three months earlier he'd triumphantly talked of Joe's "cooperation"–and where Joe delivered his emotional pitch about always telling the truth.

It wasn't exactly full vindication for Enid and her father, who had found out firsthand that "justice delayed is justice denied." But, still, in the end, there was a kind of symmetry to the whole sordid caper that the man Chuck Roistacher maintained from the start was a "stone-cold pathological liar" even swindled the feds.

□□□

By the first of November, the government officially closed its investigation of Enid's and Joe's finances. Prosecutor Iscoe sent a "declination" letter to Roistacher, stating that the government would decline to delve any further into the matter. Enid Greene's name was officially clear, as was her father's. That night, Roistacher reserved a private room at the Capitol Grille on Pennsylvania Avenue and threw a celebration dinner for Team Enid. The dinner was on him.

Just a few days later, Joe was escorted from his cell at the D.C. jail to the federal courthouse, where he was formally sentenced to federal prison. As she had over Joe's previous court appearance, Judge Norma Johnson presided. Before sentencing, the judge allowed Joe to speak. For the first time, he apologized publicly to his wife and her family.

"This past year has been a nightmare for so many people–my family, my friends, my former wife, and her family," Joe said. "I would like to express my deepest regret and sorrow for my actions. My behavior was deplorable. And I alone am responsible. I did commit crimes against the United States. It is my responsibility, and my responsibility alone. These actions go against everything that I was taught and everything that I thought I believed in.

"I became active in politics because I revere this nation. To have violated its laws and hurt the people I love, in addition to causing a scandal for the 104th Congress that I cared so much about, is something that will haunt me the rest of the days of my life . . .

. . . I want to pay whatever debt to society is appropriate in the opinion of this court. In the days that follow, I look forward to having the chance to earn back the opportunities and responsibilities that have always gone hand-in-hand with citizenship in a free society. Having failed to be responsible, I know that I must suffer the consequences of my actions. I accept that honestly and wholeheartedly. Only by doing so can I begin the painful, but rewarding, process of rehabilitation. Thank you."

Judge Johnson was largely unmoved by Joe's speech. "I'm pleased to hear what you had to say," she told Joe, "But despite your guilty pleas, you continued, even until this minute, to shift the blame for your actions . . . I'm simply not convinced by your self-serving statements that you were corrupted by politics, or even that you revere the Constitution. Anyone who reveres the Constitution would certainly, I think, be willing to obey the laws of the country."

Taking into account the criminal activity Joe engaged in during the summer, Judge Johnson adjusted upward the allowable federal sentencing guidelines and gave Joseph Phillip Waldholtz thirty-seven months in the U.S. Bureau of Prisons, to be followed by five years probation. The defendant was also ordered to pay $10,920 in restitution to the Internal Revenue Service.

A. J. Kramer, Joe's federally appointed attorney, asked that Joe be remanded to one of the federal government's intensive confinement prisons, commonly called "boot camps." These boot camps are designed for young, first-time offenders and are intended to rehabilitate with intensive hard work and discipline (the sentencing limit is thirty months and the hard-time limit is six months). Instead, Judge Johnson, noting that she did not believe the "boot camp to be appropriate," recommended that Joe be incarcerated in Allenwood, a prison where the mainstream population is comprised chiefly of white-collar criminals. Birds of a feather. Allenwood is located in Pennsylvania, where Joe's family would be in better position to visit.

Enid was there, in the audience, as Joe was sentenced. "For closure," she said. She cried when the judge summed up her reprimand to Joe by saying, "Perhaps the person who shall suffer most because of your criminal conduct is your infant daughter. You certainly have not taken a step to consider how your crimes and misdeeds shall forever stain her."

The date of the sentencing was Nov. 7, 1996–four days shy of one calendar year since the day Joe gave Jim Parkinson the slip at National Airport, and nine days shy of six calendar years since the evening in Newport Beach, California, when he emerged from the limo and first laid eyes on Enid Greene.

□□□

. . . Her work finished, Congresswoman Enid Greene stood up from her congressional issue desk and walked over to her congressional issue coat rack. She reached for her coat, a light wool jacket. She looked around the office again. The clock above the door ticked away as usual, but the red lights on the top–the ones that warned you that a vote was about to take place on the floor–were unlit and would stay unlit until the 105th Congress was sworn in, two months hence. This would be someone else's office by then, and those lights would summon some new freshman who got a crummy draw for an office.

Enid paused as she stood at the office door, letting the aloneness settle around her, then she put on her coat and made her way through the outer office, the office where Kennedy started out. She locked the entry door, turned out the lights, and walked away, the echoes from her footsteps the only sounds remaining in the hall.

EPILOGUE

As most psychologists and all country songs will tell you, the only good part about emotional trauma–often the only good part–is that it diminishes with time. Although scars will remain, a broken heart can, and usually is, mended and healed.

Less pervious to time, however, are the questions that linger following an abandonment or a betrayal; questions that attempt to make some sense of it all. Not "Why me" as much as "Why" period.

As her heart slowly made its way back to recovery, the question that haunted Enid Greene above all the rest was this: *How much of it was sick, and how much of it was evil?*

After Joe left she never returned to their master bedroom in the Georgetown townhouse. Her father slept there during his stay in Washington, and when Dale and Corinne Bowen moved in, that's where they stayed. But Enid avoided that room. Too many memories. Too many reminders. Too much pain. When the nanny left, she moved into the guest bedroom, next door to the nursery. Prior to that, she slept in the living room, on the couch.

But even with the change of bedroom venue, and the passage of time, that same question persistently kept her awake at night, staring at the ceiling as the thought kept recycling over and over in her mind: *How much of it was sick, and how much of it was evil?*

Only she and she alone would ever know the incredible depths of Joe's deceit; a knowledge that stalked her especially in her quietest moments. He had been so charming to her, so enchanting, so convincing . . . for so long. He had listened to her, helped her, encouraged her, even chastised her. He had made her feel like the most special woman in the world. A coach, mentor, lover and No. 1 supporter, all in one. Joe Waldholtz really *was* too good to be true.

She found she could square the fact that something in Joe's makeup made him crave security and attention well beyond what could be considered normal and healthy. That she could understand. Some people had to win, some people had to be right, some people had to be wealthy. Whatever the cost. Joe just *had* to be a rich guy. What she could not square was why, after he'd been exposed–undeniably exposed–had he continued the charade? Why did he continue to lie and hurt? Why did he drag her and her family into the mire? Why would he say even one word against her father, a man kind enough to *loan him four million dollars!* Why did he say he was going to "turn yellow and sing like a canary" when there was nothing to sing about–other than his own behavior? What could possess a human being to behave in such an unconscionable manner?

There might have been days when she wasn't everything he wanted her to be, but she knew for a fact that in all the time she'd known him, she never wished him a bad day or bad fortune. She stood up for him when he was beleaguered. She supported his needs. She looked out for him. She sympathized with him. She held his hand through thick and thin. When he wanted to protect his mother, she understood. When he needed money from her father, she swallowed her pride and joined in the asking. Even when he disappeared, she feared for his life.

But the feeling wasn't mutual. It was never mutual.

In her mind's eye, Enid knew she would never be able to eradicate the image of Joe, the minute after they'd become husband and wife, leaning toward her and whispering, "The five million dollars, it's all yours Enid!" Nor would she be able to dismiss the image of Joe in the hospital, on the verge of back surgery, assuring her the trustees would take care of her after he died. Trustees that DID NOT EXIST.

How much was sick, how much was evil?

She wound up asking these questions so often and to enough people that finally, while she got no concrete answers, she did get directions to where she might find some help. Several of her friends referred her to the same book, entitled *The Mask of Sanity*, written by Hervey Cleckley, M.D., a psychiatrist also noted for co-authoring *The Three Faces of Eve,* a non-fiction study of schizophrenia, or multiple personalities.

Intrigued by the number of recommendations, Enid looked for a copy of *The Mask of Sanity* only to discover that it had gone out of print. It was first published in 1941 and then revised in 1982; by the summer of 1996 it was not readily available at commercial bookstores.

Fortunately, the Congresswoman's office in the Cannon Building in Washington, D.C. sat next door to the Library of Congress, where all books published in the United States of America are collected. Out of print or not.

One phone call and she had the book.

The Mask of Sanity's title page states that it is a book that *"illumines people who on the surface appear graced with the most winning human virtues, yet who embody the darkest drives and desires . . . Arrogant, shameless, immoral, impulsive, antisocial, superficial, alert, self-assured, boastful, callous, remorseless, charming, irresponsible–this is the poisonous mix of traits that make up the psychopathic personality. For everyone who must deal with such human beings . . . and whose lives are grievously affected by them, The Mask of Sanity is essential to understanding their mystery, their power, their menace."*

Enid's questions had led her to a book about psychopaths.

As a read, *The Mask of Sanity* is ponderous at best, written in just the kind of language you would expect from a professor of psychiatry. And yet it has become, if not a classic in the mainstream sense, very much a classic in its genre. As Dr. Cleckley, at the time an emeritus professor of psychiatry at the Medical College of Georgia, acknowledged in the Preface of his updated 1982 version, *"Apparently many psychiatrists, and many other physi-*

cians, have over the years advised relatives of psychopaths to read The Mask of Sanity. The response of these relatives has given me deep satisfaction and has helped me to feel that efforts to pursue this study are not in vain.

"Even now, forty-one years after the first edition of this book was published, I often receive several letters a week from wives, parents, brothers, or other kinsmen of psychopaths. Most of these letters help me to feel that this book has at least enabled many people to see more clearly and realistically the nature of the problem with which they have had to deal blindly and in a strange and almost unique confusion."

Those words–*in a strange and almost unique confusion*– stopped Enid Greene cold. She knew just such a confusion. She had been living it. Could it be possible she was not alone?

She turned to Chapter Six, where Dr. Cleckley listed a profile of "the psychopath":

"Let us . . . attempt to say what the psychopath is in terms of his actions and his apparent intentions," writes Dr. Cleckley, *"so that we may recognize him readily and distinguish him from others. We shall list the characteristic points:*

1. Superficial charm and good "intelligence."

2. Absence of delusions and other signs of irrational thinking.

3. Absence of "nervousness" or psychoneurotic manifestations.

4. Unreliability.

5. Untruthfulness and insincerity.

6. Lack of remorse and shame.

7. Inadequately motivated antisocial behavior.

8. Poor judgment and failure to learn by experience.

9. Pathologic egocentricity and incapacity for love.

10. General poverty in major affective reactions.

11. Specific loss of insight.

12. Unresponsiveness in general interpersonal relations.

13. Fantastic and uninviting behavior with drink and sometimes without.

14. Suicide rarely carried out.

15. Sex life impersonal, trivial, and poorly integrated.
16. Failure to follow any life plan."

Enid read on as the chapter went into more detail on these "psychopathic traits":

* *Easy to talk with . . . there is nothing at all odd or queer about him.*

* *He does not hear voices. Genuine delusions cannot be demonstrated.*

* *He is likely to be judged a man of warm human responses, capable of full devotion and loyalty.*

* *The psychopath is nearly always free from minor reactions popularly regarded as "neurotic."*

* *It will soon be found that on many occasions he shows no sense of responsibility whatsoever.*

* *The psychopath shows a remarkable disregard for truth.*

* *Usually he denies emphatically all responsibility and directly accuses others as responsible, but often he will go through an idle ritual of saying that much of his trouble is his own fault. When the latter course is adopted, subsequent events indicate that it is empty of sincerity.*

* *Not only is the psychopath undependable, but also in more active ways he cheats, deserts, annoys, brawls, fails, and lies without any apparent compunction.*

* *He will commit theft, forgery, adultery, fraud, and other deeds for astonishingly small stakes and under much greater risks of being discovered than will the ordinary scoundrel. He will, in fact, commit such deeds in the absence of any apparent goal at all.*

* *Despite his excellent rational powers, the psychopath continues to show the most execrable judgment about attaining what one might presume to be his ends. He throws away excellent opportunities to make money, to achieve a rapprochement with his wife . . . or to gain other ends that he has sometimes spent considerable effort toward gaining.*

* *Deep probing will always reveal a self-centeredness that is apparently unmodifiable and all but complete.*

* *Psychopaths are sometimes skillful in pretending a love for women or simulating parental devotion to their children.*

* *The psychopath seldom shows anything that, if the chief facts were known, would pass even in the eyes of lay observers as object love. His absolute indifference to the financial, social, emotional, physical, and other hardships that he brings upon those for whom he professes love confirms the appraisal . . . of his true attitude."*

* *Although it is true that he sometimes becomes excited and shouts as if in rage or seems to exult in enthusiasm and again weeps in what appears to be bitter tears or speaks eloquent and mournful words about his misfortunes or his follies, the conviction dawns on those who observe him carefully that here we deal with a readiness of expression rather than a strength of feeling.*

* *Psychopaths are often witty and sometimes give a superficial impression of that far different and very serious thing, humor. Humor, however, in what may be its full, true sense, they never have.*

* *In a special sense, the psychopath lacks insight to a degree seldom, if ever, found in any but the most seriously disturbed psychotic patients . . . he has absolutely no capacity to see himself as others see him.*

* *We often find him attentive in small courtesies and favors, perhaps even habitually generous or quasi-generous when the cost is not decisive.*

* *Since suicidal threats, like promises and well-formulated plans to adopt a new course, are so frequently offered by these patients, there is good reason to keep in mind the fact that they are nearly always empty. Many bogus attempts are made, sometimes with remarkable cleverness, premeditation, and histrionics.*

* *The psychopath's sex life invariably shows peculiarities. In psychopaths there are varying degrees of susceptibility or inclination to immature or deviated sex practices.*

* *The psychopath does not maintain an effort toward any far goal at all.*

** The criminal usually spares himself as much as possible and harms others. The psychopath, though he heedlessly causes sorrow and trouble for others, usually puts himself also in a position that would be shameful and most uncomfortable for the ordinary man or for the typical criminal.*

Enid shivered.

It all fit. Right down the checklist.

She knew who Dr. Cleckley was writing about.

He was writing about Joe.

Enid's thoughts turned to Elizabeth's first birthday. The day she turned one, on August 31st, 1996, the doorbell rang. It was Federal Express. Enid opened the large package and recognized at once the signature of the sender. There was a wide assortment of toys, story books and stuffed animals, and there were multiple cards to go with them. The first card was humorous, and the sentiment grew from card to card. This was Joe, vintage Joe. He knew full well when Elizabeth's birthday was, he could have sent all this two days before by regular postage, but he ignored the expense and used Federal Express. He could have sent one toy to a one-year-old, but he sent many. He could have dispensed with all the cards, since Elizabeth, after all, couldn't even read.

Enid had seen this act before, seen it and lived it, and she wondered, for herself and for Elizabeth, *would it ever end?*

She carried *The Mask of Sanity* to her bookshelf, reading two more paragraphs written by the esteemed doctor:

"There is, we must conclude, no evidence to indicate that psychiatry has yet found a therapy that cures or profoundly changes the psychopath.

And finally:

"If we cannot agree that the psychopath has anything like a psychosis or even a mental disorder, can we not all agree that some means is urgently needed of dealing more realistically with whatever it is that may be the matter with him? If some practical

means of controlling the psychopath can be devised, perhaps eventually we may find this disorder to be not altogether beyond our practice."

Was there hope for Joe? Enid honestly did not know. Was there hope for her?

She looked at Elizabeth, and then she closed the book.

AUTHOR'S AFTERWORD

The foregoing is the product of a yearlong exploration that wound through Salt Lake City, Pittsburgh, and Washington, D.C., with repeated stops at the Chesapeake Bagel Shop on Capitol Hill, a stone's throw from the Supreme Court.

No names were changed to protect the innocent, the guilty, or anyone in between.

No names, or agendas, were added for anyone's gratuitous benefit.

And neither Enid Greene, nor any of the other characters herein, exercised any editorial control over the content.

From the start, the sole objective of my expedition was to as accurately and impartially as possible tell the story of what happened, when it happened, and to what extent the different participants were involved.

To keep this objective in focus, side trips into campaign slush, and other box canyons where snow tires are advised, were kept to a bare minimum. This story does not purport to detail or take sides in any peripheral disputes, political and otherwise.

Neither, for that matter, does it purport to psycho-analyze those characters, who, as detailed within these pages, combined to create the atmosphere that enabled a fraud of astonishing proportions to occur. This tells what they did, not why.

What happened, happened.

The story I uncovered is the story I told.

Lee Benson